PLAY THIS BOOK LOUD

CRUX
THE GEORGIA SERIES IN LITERARY NONFICTION

PLAY THIS BOOK LOUD

NOISY ESSAYS

JOE BONOMO

The University of Georgia Press *Athens*

Published by the University of Georgia Press
Athens, Georgia 30602
www.ugapress.org

Designed by Erin Kirk
Set in Miller Roman
Printed and bound by Sheridan Books

The paper in this book meets the guidelines for permanence and durability of the Committee on Production Guidelines for Book Longevity of the Council on Library Resources.

Most University of Georgia Press titles are available from popular e-book vendors.

Printed in the United States of America
29 28 27 26 25 P 5 4 3 2 1

EU Authorized Representative
Easy Access System Europe—Mustamäe tee 50,
10621 Tallinn, Estonia, gpsr.requests@easproject.com

Library of Congress Control Number: 2024950349
ISBN: 9780820373805 (paperback)
ISBN: 9780820373812 (epub)
ISBN: 9780820373829 (PDF)

FOR AMY

THE REAL QUESTION IS WHAT TO LIVE FOR. AND I CAN'T ANSWER IT. EXCEPT ANOTHER ONE OF YOUR RECORDS. AND ANOTHER CHANCE FOR ME TO WRITE.

Contents

Touch Me, Baby

I missed the tangibility of records and shows during the COVID pandemic, the lives of previous owners pressed into the grooves of used records, the shoulder-to-shoulder humanity at a packed venue. I wrote this during the first spring of the lockdown, when shuttered record stores and music clubs, online shows, and virtual merch tables were as close to the old normal as we'd get.

Reckless Records, Wicker Park, Chicago. I'm sitting on the floor, wrist deep in a crate of 45s. Folks walk past, chatting; I overhear one couple rehashing an odd dinner party from the other night, three kids exclaiming over finding a record that one of their dads likes. They move past, knees at my eyeline, sometimes pausing and standing inches away, rifling through a bin of LPs, in a tableau that's very difficult to imagine now.

As I write, vast swaths of the country are under stay-at-home orders due to the COVID pandemic. Social distancing has become the surreal norm. Streets and grocery stores in my small town are quiet, semifilled. My local record store, Green Tangerine, closed a few weeks ago. The last time I'd visited, a couple of days before the coronavirus fears and a new way of living settled on us, the employee at the register offered the use of a hand sanitizer and disposable plastic gloves moments after I'd entered. "My boss says we have to," she explained from the opposite end of the store.

Weeks earlier, I'd been engaged in a favorite pastime at a few record stores in Chicagoland and up in Rockford, regular joints that I hit every couple of months as new crops of used 45s and LPs arrive. What the last couple of weeks have illustrated to me in stark clarity is the *thinginess* of crate diving and how badly I miss the pursuit, the presence of hands that have held these records before me—from the original owner to the scores of others who may have owned them, played them, loved them, lost them, to the record store proprietors themselves. (Somehow, it had never occurred to me how rough a time a germaphobe must have in a used record store or thrift shop.) I'm prohibited now from leisurely flipping through a box of 45s or a bin of LPs at my favorite stores or somewhere out on the road, looking for that long-sought B-side or rare mono pressing, alert to the surprises that any motley assortment of vinyl might deliver me on a lucky day. I might come upon a record I hadn't seen in decades, say, or a picture sleeve unique to a U.K. release, maybe a dare purchase of a beat-up, scratched single, or a record issued on that subsidiary label that I think was based in Memphis (I think) or which design or mod colors on the label I just really dig. I deeply miss this poor man's treasure hunting, where fifty cents might land me a seven-inch that I'll cherish forever. I find myself pausing in the middle of the afternoon, sniffing the air for the musty scent of thrift shops, eyeing my boxes of records unhappily, wishing I could toss in a few more records to keep the party going.

I must say here that in the relative ease of my isolation—which is far less taxing compared with others' suffering and losses—I feel silly acknowledging that this is what I miss so deeply. Yet the kinds of physical nearness that we're urged to avoid now are manifest in used record stores and shows, in bookstores and thrift shops, places where people gather, sometimes closely, to hold what others once held, in a kind of continuum of acquiring and of letting go, objects passed along, home to home. I miss the communal aspect of record shopping, the overheard, often illuminating conversations between a customer and the owner, the joking banter, the friendly side-eye appraisals of a neighbor's purchases, stray comments about a song being played in the store that might lead to a murmured conversation among customers about the first time they saw that band. (From a couple bins down: "Oh, I was at that show, too!") Fingerprints, scuffs, pen marks, dust, smudges. The proof of people living, or having lived: these are what I love about vinyl, the virtual conversations taking place among scratchy, sleeveless 45s in a cardboard box on a floor, the ghosts of chatty, previous owners through which I sift, a gathering of folk.

Recently I found "Big Bird," a brilliant Eddie Floyd single from 1968 and an all-time favorite, in a cramped box in a cramped store in Rockford. Cost me a couple of bucks. It looked worn as hell but, like an old house or used paperback or dirt road, and that's what drew me to it. Nothing a Spin Clean couldn't help, anyway, which did in fact brighten the highs and deepen the lows of this beauty, written by Floyd with Booker T. Jones, who produced it for Stax Records. Those pops and clicks in the opening: the sound the ground makes under your feet on the approach to your grandma's or your new girlfriend's; that creak in the front door of the beach house you stayed in that summer when you were . . . That handwritten number "4" on the pale blue label? I have no idea, but I could come up with five imagined storylines to explain it. A previous owner had inked the initials "MB" on the label of a recently scored copy of Love's galloping "7 and 7 Is" 45, from 1966; the song's so intense that I guess "MB" was spooked, and let it go. Or maybe "MB's" mom did the honors, without asking.

Shuffling through a box of old 45s is like letting fistfuls of soil sift through your fingers. Organic matter, minerals, microbes all seem present on vinyl and worn labels, the grooves veritable garden rows. Heft, ballast, stuff in my hands. For what it's worth, I've never found such tactile sense memories among my CDs (which have been boxed away in the dark of our basement for some time), even the first ones I bought in the late 1980s. For several decades I'd dropped loads of money on CDs, had bought into the overwhelming argument that 1s and 0s paved the virtual road to the future, there's no looking back. Sure, the shelf of old mixtapes I made swapping with friends and wooing my girlfriend tells lots of stories, as does a stack of chipped compact disc cases or the obscure handwriting on a CD-R discovered randomly in a Salvation

Army, but plastic only bends so far before it snaps. Fingerprints on a CD case, the robot-like error when a damaged disc plays: these lack the depth and the *sponginess* of vinyl and of album covers and 45 sleeves, softened with the years and the touch of hands—strangers' and my own.

This is in no small way generational, of course. I still listen to, and discover, a lot of music via Spotify and YouTube. Streaming is too pleasurable, fun, easy, the lure of millions of songs at one's fingers too hard to resist. (And why should I? There are countless revelations there.) And yet as has been well documented, sales of vinyl have been improving for years. "The vinyl boom is not going bust anytime soon," *Variety* reported in July 2023. In the first half of that year, "vinyl LP sales were up 21.7% from the same period the year before, a robust vote of confidence for the format that has dominated album sales in recent years." Twenty twenty-two marked "the 17th consecutive year that vinyl saw a rise, so it was perhaps inevitable that 2023 would keep the streak going."

My continual anecdotal evidence for this is certainly persuasive. Many of my students are buying vinyl beyond gestures in hipster irony—the numbers of twentysomethings now equal those of their older, graying counterparts at the stores where I shop—and the DJ culture never turned its back on the 45 and the twelve-inch. Yet the golden age of vinyl, it seems, is finished. Some personal history from another century: Christmas mornings with LP-shaped gifts under the tree; the epic, many-colored sweep of the Columbia Record Club inventory. I can still conjure the smell of the insides of my favorite record stores when I was growing up, from Kemp Mill Records and Backstreet Records in Wheaton, Maryland, to Yesterday and Today in Rockville to Record and Tape Exchange in College Park. . . .

During these weeks of restrictions, I've been required to teach remotely, as have, at once, hundreds of thousands of teachers around the world. I've long resisted online teaching, yet I've learned that, as substitutes go, a Zoom essay-writing workshop is decent enough. Though it's novel to see students lounging on their beds at home or hanging in their basements during class, occasionally startled by a wandering, yipping dog or a very young sibling who asks to be held, the pixel experience can't replicate the intimacies and physical presence of a classroom, where back-and-forth conversing, surprises, arguments, flirting, and side-glances, not to mention the politics of bookbag buttons and patches, create dimensional, warm, dynamic learning experiences.

Last week during class I was alerting my students to some revamped deadlines when I noticed that R. in the top left window of rowed students appeared frozen in place, her head tilted to her left and angled upward. I asked if her screen had locked up. *Yeah*, she replied unhappily in a disembodied voice. *Bad connection.* As I'd spoken, she'd turned to gaze at the calendar on her wall and her laptop froze, fixing her in a pose at once local and universal: looking longingly, or was it despairingly, at time.

The last hand I shook before the lockdown turned out to have been my student K's, at the start of a class in early March when I congratulated him on his internship to Japan, which was, of course, subsequently cancelled.

I've got *things* on my mind.

During the summer of 1987, I worked for Telesec, a temporary employment agency that staffed Maryland, Virginia, and Washington, D.C., libraries with part-time workers. The work was often tedious. My initial job site was the first of many austere and wholly foreign tax libraries I was to wander into over the next couple of summers: I'd be the anonymous young temp toiling in a sterile cubicle alphabetizing Library of Congress book order forms, or organizing a more efficient system of routing periodicals to the partners and junior partners, or setting to the task of refiling the multiplying government dockets received each Monday morning from Capitol Hill. Mandy, my pleasant placement director, was consistently good to me during those summers. The money was fine, and for a summer gig, working in air-conditioned offices, where I was allowed some measure of anonymity and independence, and could work with my Walkman on, the job was ideal. For a couple of months, I "headed" a team of motley temps at the Museum of Natural History's staff library hired expressly to merge that mammoth institution's entire Library of Congress and Dewey catalogs. The work was about as exciting as it sounds—what I mostly recall are endless hours in musty stacks, dozens of overweighted book carts, and lonely lunches sitting along the Mall in whatever shade I could find.

One rather remarkable incident occurred on that job. I held with my ungloved hands the first copy of *National Geographic Magazine*, although I probably wasn't supposed to; memory blurs, and looking back I wonder if I'd daringly followed one or two of my more courageous (reckless) colleagues into the rarefied stacks where the issue was located. My fingers trembled as I held the magazine—which was published on September 22, 1888—and history, somehow *the history* of history, became a tangible presence, the deliverance of a past century to me. As I look back, I recognize that I held that issue nearly one hundred years after it had been published; to me, that afternoon, it had felt a thousand years old. The pages were thick and heavy, mysterious, as if the past had deepened into the fabric of the pages much as personality can deepen into character, and character into wisdom. A relic from a different age, and more real to my touch than the doorknobs, lunch sandwiches, and desks around me. Every generation bemoans, or takes note of, the speed of its present versus the languor of its past, yet things are radically faster now than at any point in human history. Of course, the older one gets, the further into the past the past vanishes; though hardly news, that still rankles. I was in my early twenties when I held that *National Geographic Magazine*: my childhood had ended the month before, it seemed; adolescence began just a week later; I didn't have a whole lot of perspective yet. But I sensed the gravity of distance before I could adequately essay it. History was a physical thing, humming in my hands.

One modest year of playing snare drum in the school band and several years of piano lessons notwithstanding, I'm not a musician. My tactile pleasures from music issue not in the feel of pics, strings, or drumsticks but only from records and the sonic waves roaring from backlines and from bodies pressed against up against me at shows.

"When I sing, I feel like when you're first in love. It's more than sex. It's that point two people can get to they call love, when you really touch someone for the first time, but it's gigantic, multiplied by the whole audience. I feel chills." That's Janis Joplin. When I was younger, and single (or cheating), I'd flirt with women at shows, nearness, eye glances, shoulder-to-shoulder, sweat. Now, a crowded show to me is no less thrillingly physical, shoulder-to-shoulder, toe-crunching, beer-flying animation under lights and perspiration. Such fleshly proximity—the cramming of bodies into a small room—is hard to imagine as I write this, as social distancing and bans on large gatherings of crowds having rendered shows impossible.

In addition to the staggering losses of the revenue that musicians and venue owners rely on—and in this age of streaming music, only pennies of which make it into the coffers of labels and the threadbare pockets of musicians, touring has become a reliable if grueling money-making reality—there's a concomitant loss of physical intimacies, of strangers pressed together in low-lit clubs in the bliss of amplified music, colliding and, grinning, shaking it off. I'm grateful for the musicians and bands that are getting it together and hosting virtual shows from their living rooms or otherwise empty venues, but, like teaching online, the energy that's transmitted back and forth is of a lesser wattage, dimmed, if still cherished.

In March 2020, I caught Reigning Sound at Sleeping Village on the west side of Chicago, a club with a smallish stage and crowd area. The band's original lineup of Greg Cartwright, Greg Roberson, Alex Greene, and Jeremy Scott made a brief swing through the Midwest, showing few signs of rust. "We haven't done this together in seventeen years!" bass player Scott proclaimed, looking fondly at his bandmates; such was the warmth of the gig, pulsating yet loose, urgent and restrained. The guys have decades' worth of long nights among them, yet they played with ferocity and precision, save one or two fuckups and good-natured responses, the desperate ballads and stomping four-on-the-floor rave-ups charting the wide interval that these wonderful players roam in their music. Grins, laughter, shut-eyed bliss—Reigning Sound ran the gamut of responses to the songs that they played, vibing on the packed club. After the show, they warmly received well-wishers, a few of whom were bearing drinks, congregating on the floor in the front of the stage in the kind of relaxed, back-slapping, album-signing post-show familiarity between band and fans that's now gone, leaving us longing and surprised. Already that show feels as if it occurred a year ago. The warm, chatty camaraderie at a merch table gives the impression of a long-lost communal rite, now, of a prohibited religious gathering.

Here's legendary bluesman Buddy Guy from his autobiography *When I Left Home* (cowritten with David Ritz), on the lure of plugging in:

> I cottoned to the electricity because it was something I could turn up. Volume did a lot for me. If I couldn't play better than the guitarists around me, at least I could play louder. I could also play wilder. When I heard the buzzin' and the fuzz tones distorting the amps, that didn't bother me none. I figured fuzz tones and distortion added to the excitement of the sound. Didn't mind jammin' notes together in a way that wasn't proper. Notes crashing into each other was another way to get attention. I learned how to ride high on electricity.

He says succinctly: "The blues electricity got into the people."

Guy arrived in Chicago in 1957, via Louisiana, and was stunned by the din and excitement in blues joints like the 708 Club, on East 47th Street. "Lord, have mercy—those barrooms in Chicago are loud," he writes. "The folk are happy and excited to be off work, and they wanna talk and tell stories at the top of their lungs. They got energy to release. So if you a musician and wanna be heard, you gotta pump up and project. Baby, you got to shout. That shouting is a thrilling thing to behold. If you went into a Chicago barroom, say, in 1958, you'd be thrilled out of your mind. The electrical music would throw you back on your heels." Recognizing that he might have to outplay and outperform other local guitarists, the fiery breath of competition on his neck, Guy made the calculated decision—motivated by native joy and urgency—to show off, and to dismantle the divide between stage and audience, a time-honored, usually nervy, always thrilling rock and roll gesture that's very dear to my heart.

Guy recalls one snowy night—there were three-foot drifts along the sidewalk and street—when he hooked up his 150-foot guitar cord and started playing from inside a car parked outside the bar. "The crowd was screaming long before they ever saw me," he writes. Unlike other local guitarists, Guy never sat down when he played.

> I never started playing inside the club. No matter how cold or hot the evening, I'd come marching in, my guitar screaming. I might march into the men's room and play from there. Hell, I might march in the ladies' room and play from there. I'd jump off the bandstand and sit at some pretty woman's table if she was alone. I'd leap up on the bar and play flat on my back. I'd pick the thing with my teeth. I'd put it between my legs and stroke it all sexy. I'd wave it around the room like it was a flag. I'd do any goddamn thing to get them to like me.

I would've loved to have been in a club—or the men's room—and witnessed Buddy Guy Enter Playing Guitar. Boundaries erased. Let's grab another beer.

At the height of the lockdown, Greg Cartwright was asked in *New Noise* if streaming concerts were in the works. He didn't think so. "I think it's an interesting concept for a way to move forward," he said. "It doesn't interest me. Maybe my mind will change after time, and especially if this goes on a lot longer than I hope it will. Then, it might be part of the new reality." Yep. Three months after Reigning Sound played Sleeping Village, they climbed up on a stage in an empty club, the B-Side in Memphis, and played a rousing set.

I didn't have to wait in line for a beer, though, like many others, I wish I'd been there. The show was streamed via GonerTV, and I watched from home. As when I'd caught them in Chicago, the band was warm and loose and clearly enjoying themselves, and like the bunch of old buds they are they looked back fondly and bemusedly as they revived the very songs that scored their shared past. “Hey Greg,” the always good-natured nostalgist Scott remarked to Cartwright between numbers, “do you know that in August it will have been twenty years since we recorded our debut album?” Cartwright smiled and muttered something about how some folks have had to suffer him for even longer than that. Good jokes, great songs.

The set was divided among the band’s first four albums, with a few covers thrown in, notably the 1960s-era Memphis band Tommy Burk and the Counts’ “Change Your Mind” and a wistful version of Hoagy Carmichael’s “Memphis in June.” Head down, eyes closed, and committed to his material, Cartwright was all business (when he wasn’t tuning up; he’d needed to borrow Goner Records co-owner Zac Ives’s guitar, and the strings’ heavier-weight gauge caused him some troubles). Scott, Roberson, and Greene confidently muscled the songs and/or held them gently aloft, depending on the mood those songs created. There was very little vibing off of the crowd—because there wasn’t a crowd, apart from the venue’s staff and maybe a few friends. (One or two “Happy Birthdays” were offered from the stage.) “Wow, a studio audience!” Cartwright crowed at one point, peering between songs into the venue’s barely peopled dark. “I never get to say that. The best kind of audience, too, a captive one.” Grins all around.

Rob Sheffield wrote a terrific piece for *Rolling Stone* about his live-show withdrawals in this pandemic era, a suffering that I share. Recounting both the joys and the tedium of going to shows, he recognizes that the gulf between the two experiences is what gives shows their dimension, and often their surprises. He wrote,

> I go through my phone scrounging for karaoke photos I meant to delete, though now I’m glad I didn’t—proof I have friends who don’t run in terror when I’m on my sixth “Shallow” of the night. Was it just a couple months ago in late February when I got up to karaoke “People Who Died”? And everyone danced and nobody felt a single pang of fear? Did this all really happen? I chew on these memories like a crust of prison bread. They nourish me. They also torment me. I think of all

> the crappiest bands I've seen live, and picture myself crawling through broken glass to hear them tune up. I think of the lamest bands I've walked out on, even worse than the ones I hear in my sleep.

He added, "Even more than the great shows, I find myself missing the mediocre ones. The nights when you drop by on a whim, run into friends, enjoy the music in the most transitory way, then walk home, stop for a slice on the way, maybe forget the band the next day. What a luxury."

Live streams have done no small part in helping soothe things. And I'm thankful for the bands and artists who can manage to put on events like these, singing into empty studios or venues or their own cramped living rooms, eager to help the many listening and watching to sing along, to dance and move again, to elate in favorite songs and onstage fuckups and the odd new arrangement of a classic tune. If their Venmo account bulges as the evening progresses, more power to them. During the Reigning Sound streaming show, the silence between songs was odd to listen to—I clapped at home, watching in my music room/office—and I'm sure even more odd for the band. I was grateful for every song. The advantages of watching a streaming show (I'm home already, there's all the beer I want in the fridge a few steps away) are finally outweighed by the losses (the intimacy of a crowd of friends and strangers, the excitement of a dark club, the decibels in my chest) but the contest was a friendly one; I enjoyed having a favorite band playing for me in the comfort of my own home, and I really wished I could've been there plugging my ears against the din.

There was no merch table. There were far fewer bodies in the room and hugs and slaps on the back. After the show, as the DJ played Merle Spears's "I Want to Know," the camera lingered on the stage as Greene stood and wrapped a bandana around his face; across the room, Scott opted for a more conventional mask, and the two stepped off of the stage into the dark into the new reality.

The owners of music venues and of shuttered record stores risk losing their businesses, and I fervently hope that the lockdown ends for good before too many *For Sale* signs hang in windows.

The patrons and customers are losing, too: I gaze at dozens of cancelled listings at my favorite clubs, at images of empty floors and stages, and my heart aches. As this pandemic rises and crests, I remind myself on my best days that the global lockdown is temporary. Yet I'm skeptical of the wisdom of exploring my feelings about an event as it's occurring and as it's shifting daily. I admire artists who can turn out work for official occasions, but I've always been shy of that gesture. Thoughts, observations, and attitudes marinate over time, *in* time, deepen and change molecules and their relative values like ingredients in a complex soup, or a painting that's given dimension across its many drafts. Perspective and widened contexts give writing its depth and value.

And yet. I'm reacting today. To dark rock and roll clubs. To empty basements or backyards where lo-fi folk-punk shows sprout like weeds. To shuttered record stores, where I sat on my butt with a flimsy cardboard box of scratchy 45s on my lap, decades of songs and stories, the apparitions of hundreds of previous owners, their presences virtually visible on the vinyl surfaces and ink-tagged labels, while around me others walked, clueless to the sweet nearness we'd soon give up.

Home

John D. Loudermilk wrote "Tobacco Road" about a particular place in a particular time, and yet the song refuses to stay in one place.

In 1950, 73,368 people lived in Durham, North Carolina, seventy thousand more than who'd lived and toiled there in the 1880s when W. Duke & Sons and W. T. Blackwell & Co. Tobacco manufacturers began business, securing the area's economic future. The 1920s through the 40s brought the establishment of religious and secular schools and colleges, including Trinity College, later renamed Duke University, and the North Carolina College for Negroes, which would add a law school. Churches, arts organizations, newspapers, and medical schools prospered, and desegregation lawsuits reigned under the widening shadow of racism and within shafts of light brought by a vital and active civil rights movement. Despite antitrust lawsuits initiated by the federal government, the tobacco industry flourished, defining central North Carolina identity and spurring economic and cultural growth, but at a cost, exploiting the poor and working class who assured its manufacturing.

John D. Loudermilk was born and raised in Durham. In the early 1950s he was a teenager in need of some pocket change, so he delivered telegrams and money orders along an alley known locally as Marvin's Alley, sometimes called Morven's Alley—now it's Morven Place—on the east side of town. "Along that road were a lot of real tough, seedy-type people," Loudermilk recalled, "and your folks would have just died if they thought you ever went down there." Such "tobacco roads"—named for the massive industry that begat them—proliferated in the early and midcentury south. "There were a bunch of [them]," Loudermilk noted. "Anytime you had the tobacco industry in a town down south you had a tobacco road, because that's where the people lived who were the workers in that industry. They just developed that way." It was thought that because the tobacco, cotton, and other industry mills virtually owned the street and the meager houses on it, Marvin's Alley was mostly shielded from the police; truth or not, the street became notorious for its gambling and prostitution, for the drunks splayed out on front porches as the sun rose. "Run-down, Victorian, white clapboard houses," Loudermilk remembers. "Workers."

Loudermilk rode his bicycle to Marvin's Alley with a flashlight and a fistful of orders to deliver: muddy road, no cars, seven or eight houses, each darker than the next. "But each porch lamp had a light in it of different colors," he remembered. "I didn't know what that meant. So I knock on the door of the first house, and the lights come on inside. And it was full of people. Quiet. Because they were not supposed to be so free with their Saturday nights." Loudermilk would peer through the front doorway at the suddenly illuminated folks inside who, propped up on the couch, would quietly smile and nod back at him. "And when the guy was through with the business at the front door, I left, and he'd turn the lights off. And I went to the next house. That was Tobacco Road."

A decade later, the imagery of the dark, mysterious alley and the people who lived there haunted Loudermilk and the words of the song he'd write and record. That kid born in a lump—some will sing "bunk," or "trunk"—whose parents vanish, who's left to live or die alone, who hates Tobacco Road, enacts the great dream: he leaves town and, blessed by the Lord, earns lots of money, comes back, bulldozes that lousy road, and rebuilds it, proud, at long last, of the name. But there's a paradox in the chorus made graphic by a change in melody and mood, a nagging conflict that makes the song real: the place will always be home, no matter how bleak and despised, as it's the only life he knew. Can a song solve that puzzle, make something joyful of it?

Raised in the Baptist church, Loudermilk didn't know the world and the people of Marvin's Alley. He wasn't writing autobiography. "My mother didn't die in childbirth," he made clear. "My daddy didn't get drunk. I never saw him drink a drop. He smoked cigarettes and died as a result of it. I never heard a dirty joke or a curse word from my father." The angry man in "Tobacco Road" lives in that space between Loudermilk's upbringing and the zones he crossed into Marvin's Alley, between home and fantasy, real life and fiction. Loudermilk already knew the power of the imagination, of an interior life engaged with the world outside. "Dad, he was very, very quiet. I'd come home at night after work and he and mother would be sitting in the dark having watched the sunset go down. And I said, 'What are y'all doing in here?' He said, 'You'll know someday.'"

Loudermilk died on September 21, 2016, at the age of eighty-two; nearly every obituary referenced "Tobacco Road" in the first paragraph, if not the headline. Like most writers chiefly identified with one song, Loudermilk's career accomplishments tend to be flattened. Born into musical bloodlines (his cousins were Ira and Charlie Loudermilk, the peerless and influential Louvin Brothers), he learned the guitar early. When he was a boy, his father, a carpenter whose hands helped build local tobacco and hosiery factories, made a ukulele out of a cigar box for him; his mother, a missionary, taught him how to play it. He made appearances on regional radio and television stations and, while in college, wrote a poem that he set to music. At the television studio where Loudermilk worked as a set painter and house musician, the country singer George Hamilton IV happened to hear him singing. He recorded and released "A Rose and a Baby Ruth" on the Colonial label in 1956. It reached number six on *Billboard* Pop.

Inspired, Loudermilk dropped out of college and moved to Nashville, where Chet Atkins introduced him to Boudleaux and Felice Bryant, two professional songwriters who, Loudermilk noted, weren't pursuing a recording career of their own. Fifty years later, Loudermilk described that meeting as "a revelation and a revolution." He joined the Acuff-Rose publishing company, and soon the songs came tumbling out of him: they included "Sittin' in the Balcony," a hit for Eddie Cochran; "Amigo's Guitar," a hit for Kitty Wells; "Waterloo," a hit for Stonewall Jackson; "Bad News," a hit for Johnny Cash; "I Wanna Live," a hit for Glen Campbell; "Sad Movies (Make Me Cry)" and "Paper Tiger," hits for Sue Thompson; "Talk Back Trembling Lips," a country hit for Ernest Ashworth and a pop hit for Johnny Tillotson; "Then You Can Tell Me Goodbye," a hit for the Casinos; "Ebony Eyes," a hit for the Everly Brothers; "Abilene," another hit for George Hamilton IV, his biggest; "This Little Bird," a hit for Marianne Faithfull; and "Indian Reservation," a hit for Paul Revere and the Raiders.

Over a ten-year span, Loudermilk released a half dozen albums and over twenty singles under his own name, and, earlier in his career, under the name Johnny Dee, sometimes with the Blue Notes, but scored only one Top 40 song, "Language of Love," in 1961. His songwriting reputation would grow to sterling proportions—the run of charting singles illustrates it; his induction to the Nashville Songwriters Hall of Fame in 1976 confirmed it—but he would never earn with his own recordings the kind of commercial successes his songs gave others. Columbia released "Tobacco Road," Loudermilk's tenth single, in early 1960. It sniffed the charts and retreated. A year earlier, he'd discussed his songwriting with the *Tennessean*: "I'm looking for the most different thing I can find. Everybody's writing 'I love you truly.' You've got to find something new. I talk to drunks at the bus station, browse through kiddie books at the public library, [and] get phrases from college kids and our babysitter. You've got to be looking all the time."

Loudermilk never stopped seeing those shadows along Marvin's Alley, the briefly lit faces in dark homes. The song's swampy, recognizable opening melody issues from Loudermilk's acoustic guitar; the essential, ominous emphases in the verses—*one*, two, three, *four*—are less menacing here than they'll be in others' versions of the song, but there's a disquieting, tense hush surrounding them. It's cinematic: something has happened here, or will soon. Ageless with reverb, Loudermilk's singing voice is plain but emotive, assured, and in touch with the tensions the song describes. Born in a *lump*? What does that mean? A small scrap, an afterthought, a cousin to the "great unnumbered multitude of souls that come and go," as Kate Chopin wrote in her novella about love and lust and childbirth in the Victorian south sixty years earlier? Momma dies, daddy's wasted, a child is left to die in the middle of a road. In the signature, end-of-verse two-bar reckoning of time and place—*tobacco road-whoa-whoa-whoa*—the external setting moves to an interior space that the singer can't ever really escape, both liberation and trap. And we're only thirty seconds into the song.

The remaining three verses flesh out the story. The singer grew up in this shack, with few clothes and necessities, and has grown to hate the place—*loathe* is the word that Loudermilk chooses; you don't hear that word in pop songs too often these days. Who's the "you," the only one who understands? The Lord? A girl? The listener spinning the 45 in a rec room or bedroom? There's an implicit invitation to witness the journey of redemption and renewal that follows: success, rebranding, the inability to shake the past. The chorus tells this old-as-dirt story, and in Loudermilk's original, the tone lightens, becomes kinder, as though the singer's made some sort of bemused peace with his past: the bass walks now, laying down a groove of ease into which the drummer and piano player are relieved to settle. But two words, "loathe" and "home," gnaw at this ease. The bothersome, nagging four-one emphases in the verses soon come back to haunt, for good, until—and as—the song's bittersweet end.

"An interesting tale of back-shack existence," opined *Billboard* in a January 25, 1960, review of the song. "The tune has a minor flavor employing a repetitive figure. Loudermilk wrote the tune and handles it with conviction."

Sincerity wasn't enough to put "Tobacco Road" on the charts. Loudermilk pressed on, rerecording the song for his second album, *12 Sides of John D. Loudermilk*, released on RCA in 1962, and ultimately turning his attention to writing and recording other songs. But "Tobacco Road" wouldn't lay low. Loudermilk had unwittingly located a pulse. He wrote his song about homes that he'd only glimpsed, and imagined someone leaving one of those homes in bitterness and returning in triumph, only to find that triumph made uneasy. Loudermilk's argument—we flee home, and remain there—is so universal in its absurd logic that men and women of differing backgrounds can enter the song and make it their own.

A decade after "Tobacco Road," *Billboard* ran an advertisement for Loudermilk's latest album, *Volume 1: Elloree*, proclaiming that "John Loudermilk, the author of 'Tobacco Road,' 'Abilene,' and countless other modern standards is his own best interpreter." History has proven that claim suspect. Soon after its release, "Tobacco Road" was picked up by other artists who sensed something between commercial potential and timelessness in the song. In 1961, Johnny Duncan & His Blue Grass Boys recorded a spare, twangy version as a B-side; Frank Ifield issued a version, also a B-side, in the United Kingdom. In 1962, Bobby Brinkley ("With Orchestra and Chorus") recorded a somewhat melodramatic, brassy take, again for a flip side, and the Bluegrass Gentlemen issued an acoustic honky-tonk version on their self-titled album, complete with close harmonies on the chorus.

The following year, "Tobacco Road" would receive its most accomplished interpretation yet. Born and raised in the south Chicago projects, Lou Rawls grew up singing in the Greater Mount Olive Baptist Church and later in several gospel groups, both in Chicago and Los Angeles, including the Chosen Gospel Singers and the Pilgrim Travelers. Following a stint in the army, and a near-fatal car crash, in 1962, Rawls, with his rich baritone, signed with Capital Records, where he was paired with jazz pianist and arranger Onzy Matthews and turned his attention to recording secular music.

Backed by a big band, Rawls cut "Tobacco Road" as the title track for his third album. He wastes no time with an introduction, singing "I was born in a dump" impatiently as his band begins to play. His voice is stern, admonishing—*listen to this*. Utter silence greets the title phrase; he's got his audience. A harmonica joins in the second verse, answering his lines as the band settles in and Rawls sings about home and the stubborn ways it defines us, his voice too finding its home in the gorgeous lower register of his range. Now you listen to this and you hear Lou Rawls—the voice from the records, from movies and television, from the malt liquor and beer ads—in 1963 you heard only the voice, absent of later celebrity, a man on a road in his head looking ahead, looking back. Stuck.

A minute in, the band grows more confident and supportive: a saxophone enters in the left, a drum fill allows in some blaring horns, and before we know it, Rawls has drifted away, the horn player is soloing, and the band has taken over the song, expanding it. This is what can happen in a cover version: musicians approach from whatever angle their gifts and enthusiasm and biases give them, and the words, key, and melody of the original must adapt or collapse. Written by a young Southern white man having peered down a dark alley where he doesn't belong, played in a quiet folk arrangement, "Tobacco Road," a few years later, becomes a big band swing number sung in southern California by a midwestern Black man steeped in the gospel tradition.

I've often wondered if writers can cover literature in the way musicians cover songs. A band can get up on stage and cover a song by a well-known artist, or an obscure one, sometimes slavishly respectfully, sometimes turning it over and reinventing. Bands and musicians release entire albums devoted to other artists' material—there's a cottage industry of cover and tribute albums. We think nothing of a singer turning another's song inside-out, paying respect to influence and history. Some cover songs are ironic jokes, some are overly earnest. (Let's forget about tribute bands for now.) Occasionally a writer will read another writer's work at her own reading, or at a benefit or tribute to another writer. But that's not covering the work as a musician does. We don't think of a band playing another's song as much as we think of the band interpreting that song, assuming it. Where is this tradition in literature? Where's the poet who covers Wallace Stevens? The fiction writer who covers Colson Whitehead? The essayist who covers M. F. K. Fisher?

I'm not thinking here of a self-conscious homage, or of an imitation written as an exercise or to shed a writer's block. I can go in front of a crowd and read a piece by, say, Lester Bangs, or, more intriguingly, by James Baldwin or Nancy Mairs or Roxane Gay—but how would I cover it, where would my interpretation come in? How would I filter the essay's style and content and place in history through my own? I can mimic it, cop a certain voice or tic of style, but could I really deconstruct, rebuild, or newly, wholly inhabit the piece the way, say, the Byrds did with Dylan, the way the Beatles did with Little Richard, the way the Ramones did with Chris Montez? [Insert your own favorite transformative cover version here.] Or for that matter, the way Roy Lichenstein and Andy Warhol co-opted popular, mass-produced imagery and made it their own? Perhaps if I collaged three or more essays by different writers à la Richard Hamilton. Lyric essays. The messes that David Shields curates. Maybe.

A song is covered for any number of commercial, audience-pleasing, or personal-stake reasons. A singer might announce, onstage or in front of his bedroom mirror, "This song matters to me because . . ." Sometimes a musician covers a song to learn something technical inside of the playing, in the odd chord or tricky time changes. Sometimes a musician covers a song she's loved since she was a child and first heard on the radio or in her dad's record or CD collection; sometimes a musician covers a song dictated by his manager or record label. A song has an opening: you climb in. Or a song casts a silhouette: sometimes you step inside of it and you're home.

They came together in Surrey, England, in 1962, their name inspired by an Everly Brothers song. The Nashville Teens were a brawny outfit, muscling their way through American R&B and blues, forging a reputation for magnificent live shows, one of which was seen by Mickie Most, a studio producer associated with Columbia Records in the United Kingdom. Most produced "Tobacco Road," the Teens' debut single, and it was a major success, hitting number six in the U.K. Singles Chart and fourteen in the

Billboard Hot 100 in the heady summer of 1964. Art Sharp, one of the Nashville Teens' two lead singers (the other was Ray Phillips), worked in a record store in Woking, and among the American imports he'd discovered there was *12 Sides of John D. Loudermilk*, which included the rerecorded "Tobacco Road." Sharp brought the song to his band, who loved the earthy Americana in the lyrics and mood. The Teens' version was my introduction to the song, as it was for millions of others.

The recording gives the impression of a marauding group of juvees. The Teens stomp their way through it, the original's somber and reflective tone replaced with amperage and assault. Drummer Barrie Jenkins and bassist Pete Harris need their collective weight to hold down John Allen's guitar line in the song's excitable opening; snarling, the guitar threatens to break loose. The noisy approach originates in the band's considerable native energy. (They had been tested: Jenkins, Harris, and Allen famously backed Jerry Lee Lewis at the Star-Club in Hamburg, West Germany, in April 1964, and they'd needed every ounce of their strength and stamina to keep up with the Killer.) The Teens seem to find particular glee in the song's destroy-the-place-with-dynamite-and-a-crane scene, a laddish taste for annihilation.

By the time Most entered the studio with the Nashville Teens, he'd produced hit records for the lightweight Herman's Hermits ("I'm into Something Good") and also the rough-and-tumble Animals ("House of the Rising Sun"), so the Teens' arrangement didn't trouble him; it sounds like he just turned up the faders and said to the lads, *Let it rip!* The four-one emphases are hammered down, the land beneath Marvin's Alley withstanding the territory-staking shocks as if the Teens want to pulverize the song's paradoxes to dust beneath their feet. Fighting for the rare spaces offered by the band, and competing at the mic, Sharp and Phillips sing the cinematic "I was born in a bunk" against the more abstract "lump," and harmonize on the title phrase and verses. Rollicking, the chorus seems to have gotten loose and made it to the local pub, where John Hawken's barrelhouse-piano sixteenth notes and boogie woogie runs send things into a different, gladder direction, the darkness of the verses giving way to boozy joy—anything, I guess, to ignore the conflicts in the song, which, naturally, return. Loudermilk may have plugged his ears against the noise that the Teens made, but he understood it.

There are many different ways to tell the same tale. Three thousand five hundred miles away in the Bronx, New York, five kids who call themselves the Trenchcoats were kicking up some noise of their own. After the lineup shuffling and identity crises common to young bands, the guys changed their name to Bloos Magoos—a yoking together of their beloved blues and of Moo Goo Gai Pan, the latter routinely consumed by the band's manager, who suggested the name change. They later revised their name to the more conventional Blues Magoos. After releasing a single ("The People Had No Faces") that went nowhere, the band signed to Mercury in 1966 and cut their debut, *Psychedelic Lollipop*, with producers Bob Wyn and Art Polhemus. We grin at the title a half century later, but the album was among the first to use the word "psychedelic," an early, visionary pivot from Top 100 ethos toward the hallucinogenic culture just on the horizon. Mercury released two singles from *Psychedelic Lollipop*, "We Ain't Nothing Yet," which charted in early 1967, and "Tobacco Road." By the mid- and late 1960s, Loudermilk's song was on its way to becoming a standard of sorts, a minimally difficult song for kids in bands to love, turn up loud, and learn, and Blues Magoos stepped into that tradition. At nearly five minutes, their visit to the alley is an extended one, by mid-1960s AM radio standards, anyway. Six years later, the song would close the third side of Lenny Kaye's wildly influential compilation *Nuggets*, securing the ear-ringing version as a staple of American psychedelic garage rock and roll.

Here's a good yarn. A young director needs a band to score a controlled building implosion in Staten Island for a silent sixteen-millimeter art film. Blues Magoos, through some friends of friends they know in the West Village, where they were the resident band at Night Owl Club, are hipped to the gig. They decamp to the site, dig the chaotic scene, and return home to write and record a two-minute avant-garde instrumental of atmospheric amp feedback and tape echo. "Peppy" Thielhelm and Mike Esposito's slashing guitar chords and anxious riffs, Ralph Scala's stabbed organ notes, and Geoff Daking's menacing drumming create a soundscape that conjures toppling buildings, smoky ash, rubble, air-raid sirens, noxious fumes, and a lone witness laughing and whooping it up on the sidelines just beyond the warning tape. You need a hard hat to listen to it. But the film project falls through—the director's trust fund dried up—and Blue Magoos are left with an instrumental piece without a home. Straggling along in the Village the next week, one of the band members starts humming "Tobacco Road" and, in an instant of clarity, the guys know where to use that instrumental, the perfect musical translation of returning home with dynamite and a crane, *blow you up start all over again*. They might have to convince the skeptical suits at Mercury, but . . .

None of this true, of course, save for the Night Owl Club, where Blues Magoos did often play, with exotic lava lamps next to them onstage. I spin this yarn as a way to make sense of the middle two-and-a-half minutes of "Tobacco Road." Virtual audio vérité, the fantastic passage is of its era, the band pushing the limits of a three-minute pop song, deconstructing something that, though only six years old, likely felt passé in form; the rave-up double-time also suggests that there were plenty of Yardbirds records lying around their rehearsal room. Whatever its origin, the middle takes "Tobacco Road" to a new sonic place, far removed from Loudermilk's stately, folky original. The band finds its way back to the song's original riff by the end, but, at that point, after we've ducked and braved the maelstrom in the middle, we're solidly in the rowdy second half of the 1960s, which, come to think of it, may have begun during one of Esposito's detonations on this record. Scala's Farfisa organ is back to its noble and cheery frat-rock obligations by the end, but the road under our feet feels different now. In a little more than half a decade, Loudermilk's song has popped up on sonic maps in cities large and small, sped up, slowed down, quieted, shrieked, strummed, garlanded with brass, pummeled with amps, played in cramped garages and mammoth studios, stretched beyond recognition.

A cover song suggests as much about the era it's performed in as about the men and women who play it. *Look around you, the song says to the singer, what have you got?* The end of the 1960s felt a century removed from the opening of the decade, and yet "Tobacco Road" remained in the rehearsals and set lists of musicians and bands. Among others, Jefferson Airplane recorded a version, for *Takes Off* in 1966; Brother Jack McDuff issued a jazz-arranged instrumental, also in 1966; Spooky Tooth covered it on *It's All About* in 1968; David Allen Coe released a version as a single in 1969; and in 1970 Eric Burdon and War, on *Declares "War,"* rolled out the horizon of Loudermilk's tale to nearly fourteen minutes.

Detroit natives Rare Earth issued their second album, *Get Ready*, in the fall of 1969. The band was known to loudly indulge the era's propensity for jamming, weed- and acid-enhanced improvisations aimed at expanding a pop song as one's consciousness expanded; simultaneously, albums grew suite-stuffed, their two, sometimes four, sides emboldened with conceptual and aesthetic possibilities as endless as the skies above open-air festivals. Bubblegum stuck to the ribs of Top 40, to be sure, and tiny regional labels saw to it that the pop and R&B 45 would never die, yet songs on albums were growing longer, sensual journeys of amplification and tactile sound textures that favored virtuosity of ensemble and soloist playing.

Infamous for their twenty-one-minute-long version of the Temptations' "Get Ready," Rare Earth reign in things a bit down at Marvin's Alley. At over seven minutes, their "Tobacco Road" is to my ears less about the song than about the band, Loudermilk's original now a vast stage where players swap solos as their way into and out of the song. Things start dramatically, the opening riff played slowly, vividly etched with percussive strikes and Kenny James's organ wandering curiously up and down the road. Peter Hoorelbeke's vocal is characteristically robust as he takes center stage, and as Rod Richards's snaking guitar leads replace the organ, Hoorelbeke demurs, allowing Richards's playing to dominate. The full band arrives in the chorus, which, before concluding, makes room for saxophonist Gil Bridges, followed by room for James. More solos compete with the verses as the song comes to a close, the finish extended in the era's fashionable way, the chords prolonged until their shelf life expires. The second verse didn't arrive until nearly four minutes into the song. Loudermilk would've delivered his money orders and nervously scampered home twice already.

The immensely gifted, multi-instrumentalist Edgar Winter recorded "Tobacco Road" for his debut *Entrance*, in 1970. He enters the alley scatting, reaching deep into his adolescence in Beaumont, Texas, where he and his brothers were exposed to jazz and blues as well as rock and roll, his controlled miasmas and occasional, startling Bobby Marchan–meets–Little Richard screeching foregrounding his presence in the song, which is otherwise performed conventionally. Winters's remarkable, virtuosic vocal performance is, finally, more about itself than about the unraveling of words and story. The following year, backed by his rocking band White Trash, he released a popular live version on *Roadwork*, devoting the entire third side to a seventeen-minute blues workout overflowing with competing sax and guitar solos. I feel stiff-armed from versions like Rare Earth's and Winters's, as if I must pay homage to the musicians' considerable on-display talents before I can hear the song's complexities. This is my problem, of course, not yours. You've got your collection, I've got mine.

I'm equally curious about Bobbie Gentry's version. Gentry was aloft on the mammoth success of "Ode to Billie Joe" when she returned to Hollywood with producer Kelly Gordon to record her second album. Released in March 1968, *The Delta Sweete* didn't match the commercial success of *Ode to Billie Joe*—it topped out at 132 on *Billboard*—and it's a sadly underrated Americana original, an imaginative collection of linked songs about the tensions of Southern life near the close of a tumultuous decade, the bulk of it written by the Mississippi-bred Gentry. "Tobacco Road" opens the second side in an evocative wash of widescreen orchestral strings and brass; soon a waltz emerges, then a scratchy, dirty fuzz guitar announces the song's riff, a harmonica and an acoustic guitar sweeten things, and we settle into the signature 4/4 beat. The echo of that strange waltz is still on her mind as Gentry sings, familiarly close-miked and dryly recorded, her wonderful voice low in register, a woman assuming the naturalistic doom of Loudermilk's song. The waltz returns in the fourth bar of the verse, sticking around until the chorus, an odd push-pull between time signatures and between moods.

The Delta Sweete's liner notes promised a concept of sorts, narrative songs concerning "the dust, the fragrance, the molasses, grits and grit, the love, sorrow, and the humor of the Delta country . . . the people, young and old, bad and good, from Monday to Sunday." Jimmie Haskel and Shorty Rogers were tasked with arranging and cohering these songs. Haskel had worked with Gordon on Gentry's debut, but Rogers was a new addition. Primarily a jazz trumpeter and producer/arranger, by the 1960s he had moved into pop production, including records for, among others, Bobby Darin, the Walker Brothers, and the Monkees. For *The Delta Sweete*, Haskel and Rogers seem to have had in mind a kind of pop-rococo storyscape, a yoking together of genteel and melancholy steamboat-era strings and brass with earthy, bedrock rural balladry, blues, and soul—a fascinating and illuminating blend of styles that's echoed on the album's memorable cover, where Gentry's preoccupied countenance is superimposed over an image of a dilapidated backwoods shack.

I appreciate this instinct for bold arranging, and it works for much of the album, especially on "Oklahoma River Bottom Band," "Parchman Farm," and "Sermon," and on the hushed songs in the second half. But I'm unsure about "Tobacco Road." The song starts by saying: Let's dreamily waltz around, over, and through our past, our woeful upbringing, with a faraway smile on our faces. The adamant 4/4 in tension with the graceful 3/4 evokes the desire to leave a gloomy home against that romanticized home inevitably calling you back. Or is it the other way around? Haskel's and Rogers's hybrid confuses things; though intriguing and ambitious, their somewhat fussy arrangement remains, to my ears, theoretical. (Writer Holly George-Warren describes Gentry's version as "humid," and, though she's being complimentary, to me that's an apt way of describing a song that's warm but fails to catch fire in the studio.) The chorus plays it safe, swinging gently in variety-show manner, and I'm always afraid that the Gothic waltz is going to return, and it always does. Gentry's greatest instrument is her voice. Her arrangers get in the way here.

Forty years later, on an album suffused with rural and religious imagery, the Seattle-based hip hop duo Common Market—DJ Sabzi (Saba Mohajerjasbi) and MC RA Scion (Ryan Abeo)—released a "Tobacco Road" that isn't Loudermilk's, and yet is. Scion was born and raised in Louisville, Kentucky, but the Southern references in "Tobacco Road" are mostly abstracted, universalized, impressionistic, with Loudermilk present in Common Market's song as a ghostly template. On top of a minimal, midpaced groove that samples a loop of the sunny piano lick from Cat Stevens's "Child for a Day," Scion narrates a story about death and grief, both personal and regional, about work and success, about leaving but never truly leaving. "I will forever call it home," he says. "And I feel it whenever I call home." Nostalgia implies a return—it's really the inability to return to a home that calls to us though we've paradoxically defined it by its absence. "There is no harvest without work," Scion said later when asked to explain. "It means that sacrifice is necessary for prosperity. It means that these experiences are seasonal and cyclical. It means there is pain in life and hope in death. It means it's okay to run away from home, but it's unforgiveable to never look back."

If there are an infinite number of ways to define home, there are also an infinite number of ways to return to it. The same month that Bobbie Gentry released her version of "Tobacco Road," Junior Wells is sitting with his band—guitarists Buddy Guy and Walter Williams on lead and rhythm, respectively, Tom Crawford on bass, Levi Warren on drums, Douglas Fagan on sax—at a recording studio in Chicago, observed by producer Samuel Charters. Wells had lived in Chicago for two decades already, but you wonder about the storehouse of imagery he must've carried with him from Memphis, Tennessee, where he was born and grew up. He'd been a South Sider since the age of twelve—in addition to the harmonica licks he learned at the feet of Little Junior Parker, he must've brought north with him intuitions that become sobering realities. In the studio, he's cocky. He's thirty-three. He's played with Muddy Waters. He's got a story to tell. "It's gonna kill you, right here," he says at one point.

Loudermilk glanced from the threshold; Junior invites you inside. Here's the story: he was born in the city, raised in the country, with no money, nothing but a cotton sack on his shoulder. The song's pace is grippingly slow. Fagan's cheery riff and Guy's eighth-note lines say it's okay, and for a while it is. But in the second verse, Wells starts telling the story that he really wants to tell, or needs to tell, and it, too, is as old as the dirt out front: you lifted me up, you threw me down, you stole my money and my clothes, and if I see you again I'm gonna bust your nose. We're inside Wells's version of the song, now, and things have become pretty intimate. His harmonica picks up the story for the next sixteen bars, and when he returns to sing, the story hasn't changed much. If anything, he's more pissed off, but helpless, the song's signature *road-whoa-woah-woah* replaced by a far more personal and plaintive cry: *I don't know-whoa-whoa-whoa.* What to do or where to go? In the last verse, she promises that she'll leave, and she does, and he begs her to return to come see him on Tobacco Road. But here's the dilemma, which Wells understands enough to utter, though it sounds like he hopes the song will end before he has to: "You don't know like I know, and I don't know like you know." As the song fades, you can practically see him waving goodbye to her from the front door, still railing about where his money went. In Wells's story, the singer doesn't leave Tobacco Road. Someone else does. She might've lived in one of those barely lit homes in Loudermilk's version. There are a lot of stories to tell there.

Is It Me? or Withering Sadness, Self-pity, Loneliness, Abandonment, Spiritual Desperation, the Loss of Romance, of Love, and of Childhood, as Well as the More Obvious Rage and Frustration

Listening to the Who's *Quadrophenia*, I draw some common threads (mod pun intended) between a kid banging around in London in the midsixties and a kid with my name banging around Washington, D.C., twenty years later. Jimmy was a figment of Pete Townshend's imagination. In many ways, I was a figment of my own, as well.

In his memoir *Who I Am*, Pete Townshend recalled a pivotal episode from the early 1970s. During intense rehearsals for an Eric Clapton comeback show at The Rainbow that Townshend had taken on himself to organize, he'd become dependent on amyl nitrate. With the concert and the drug abuse behind him, he suffered a wicked comedown at his riverside home in London, where he felt "cold, depressed, tragic, lost and hopeless." He wrote, "On a dark, wet, winter weekend in the jerry-built cottage at Cleeve, with the river flooding part of the lawns, the wind howling through the badly made doors and windows, my memory pulled me back to a single night when I was 19 years old." Riding in on waves of druggy exhaustion and emotional distress, vivid and powerful, this reminiscence was of a few fleeting hours spent under a pier in Brighton on the southern coast of England in 1964 with his art school friend, "the pretty, strawberry-blonde Liz Reid. We had been together for a riotous night at the Aquarium Ballroom after [the Who's] gig on the night of a mod-rocker street battle on the seafront." Dodging the drizzling rain under the dark pier, they'd come across "a group of mod boys in their anoraks. They were giggling as the tide came in, getting their feet wet. We sat with them for a while. We were all coming down from taking purple hearts, the fashionable uppers of the period."

Remembering all of this a decade later, with his family asleep upstairs, Townshend experienced a

> sense of falling and vertigo came flooding back with the flooding river outside—I felt that same sense of depression and hopelessness. But I also felt again the remembered romantic warmth of nodding off on the milk-train home in the early hours, with Liz by my side. For a short time we had both felt like Mods. There was something wonderful in all that. We also fell in love, and yet I didn't go on another date with Liz, never again. The moment with her was frozen, exalted and would always be special.

Under the spell of that memory, Townshend wrote the story that would appear in the inner jacket of the Who's 1973 album *Quadrophenia*, a teenager's rambling complaint about vexed family life, love, identity, paranoia, drugs, fitting in, not fitting in, belief, betrayal, frustrating glimpses of an authentic self—the highs and lows of a typical adolescent's week. That the Who's album originated in a few hours of teenage transcendence says all you need to know.

Quadrophenia tells the story of Jimmy, a young mod in London besotted with male fashion, rock and roll, rhythm and blues, Vespa GS scooters, dancing on speed at all-night parties, and the paradox of striving to be an individual in a community of like-minded, and like-dressed, people. The sprawling and ambitious album contains some of the most powerful songs Townshend's written and some of the most stirring studio performances from the Who, yet when it was released, it was greeted in many quarters as a frustrating failure. The primary complaint from American audiences generally unfamiliar with the very British ethos of mods and rockers, yet from many native Englanders also, was that the album's story was unclear, that Jimmy's transformation from a snotty, self-absorbed teen to an adult searching for love and transcendence was unearned.

As *Quadrophenia* opens, Jimmy's on the brink of suicide, sitting alone in a downpour on a rock jutting out of the dark waters off the coast of southern England. Over the course of the double album we learn what drove him here—he fights with his parents, sees an unhelpful psychiatrist and a hypocritical priest for counsel, crushes on a girl who likes him but who sleeps with his best friend, and craves amphetamines and his fellow mod mates with whom he forms a rambunctious, laddish community. They dress smartly, ride scooters to dance parties and occasionally on weekends to the beach on the prowl for leather-jacketed rockers to mess with. Jimmy loves the Who and had at one point strongly identified with the band, but has come to view them bitterly as out of touch with youth and the idealism of rock and roll, a band that has exploited the mods for subject matter. He detests his dead-end job as a garbage collector and fails to identify with the politics of his older, subjugated coworkers, whom he sees withering into irrelevancy under the unbending and unsympathetic British class system. Exasperated by his recklessness and irresponsibility, Jimmy's parents kick him out of their home, shortly after which he wrecks his beloved scooter; jobless, friendless, demoralized, emotionally and physically exhausted, doubting his own worth, he swallows a fistful of uppers and takes a commuter train to Brighton, where a few weeks earlier he'd danced, fought, and fucked his way through a kicks-filled weekend. Coming down from the pills alongside the majesty and vast anonymity of the sea, he feels restored and he glimpses his true self. Yet he soon runs into Ace Face, a top-of-the-food-chain mod whom Jimmy had fan-boy worshipped during an earlier weekend, but who's now a harried, faceless, dull bellboy at a posh hotel, suffering the indignities of a blue-collar job. Distressed and feeling deceived yet again, Jimmy pinches a bottle of gin and briefly stokes his crude and violent side, then steals a small motorboat and rides out to the rock. Having set the boat adrift, there he sits, distraught but contemplative, psychically drained yet ripe for transformation—and the album ends where it begins.

"Jimmy is on his rock, the tide comes in and rages around him. He has made a mistake. He has run to the ocean for help, in his drug-addled comedown he expects to hear a benign and guiding voice, but all that happens is that he gets wet. It rains, not the divine love he prayed for, but freezing rain from the clouds above. He has lost everything that meant anything to him, and now he is cold and wet." This is Townshend in "Two Stormy Summers," a lengthy essay he wrote for the 2011 "Director's Cut" *Quadrophenia* box set, an essential purchase for anyone who wants a fuller look at one of the great works of musical narrative art of the 1970s. "Jimmy is loved nonetheless. We love him. We will always love him. In fact, it seems to me we love him far more than the phantom God he cried out to at the end of his very bad day."

In addition to clarifying the story, Townshend revealingly asks a series of rhetorical questions that he's long heard his detractors pose: "Why would I deliberately avoid a story that made sense? Why would I purposely create characters for my stories who are shadows? Why don't I obey the easy-to-learn rules of plot construction?"

His answers go a long way toward explaining the kind of narrative he hoped to create for the album, a story pulled between cause and effect and abstract sensations. "I feel my first audience back in the mod days commissioned me to say what they felt disinclined or unable to say for whatever reason," he explained. "For my first Who recording, I wrote some lyrics—'I Can't Explain'—and our fans found themselves in those lyrics, they each came and told me their own story. They asked me how I could have known how they felt and what they had experienced. How could I have explained what they could not explain, that they could not explain anything at all? This discovery was an accident." He adds, "People who liked my songs were able to put themselves inside them and find their own stories. And so rock music differs from all other art and entertainment forms, I think. Usually, the conventional writer, composer or dramatist has a story to tell. A rock composer has to create a tangible and useful hole to be filled. The listener jumps into the music and it is only then that the real story begins. Too much information, too much detail, too much plot, makes this leap impossible."

Townshend's been explaining, correcting, and elaborating on *Quadrophenia* since the day it was released. Inspired yet ultimately burdened by the ambitious story, he then characteristically added layer upon layer to the original idea, ultimately expanding the album's goals to tell not only Jimmy's story but the Who's as well. By the early 1970s, with the band's career-making *Tommy* and its massively popular follow-up *Who's Next* behind him, Townshend felt pressured to create an album that would provide his band with new touring material and also make sense of their place in rock history. After abandoning a couple of plans, he committed to the idea of presenting the character of Jimmy as an unusual quadrophenic, the four sides of his personality reflecting each member of the Who, who were given "themes" on the album. These four motifs blend affectingly as melody, yet I was never very interested in this aspect of *Quadrophenia*, and neither was the band, I don't think; it clearly mattered to Townshend, who felt that the Who had earned enough history that their story, which is part of the history of rock music, was as interesting and important as the fictional Jimmy's.

Another knot in the process was Townshend's desire to record the album in quadrophonic sound, which he'd hoped would aurally dramatize Jimmy's split-four-ways personality, an ill-fated decision that was muddied by the haphazard manner in which the band's studio was being assembled while they were recording, and by the still-evolving quadrophonic recording technology. (Quadrophonic records never took off commercially.) Finally, he and the band simply ran out of time, with their label eager for the album and a tour looming at the end of the year.

Townshend also faced the practical limits of the album's length. Even at two discs, he didn't have enough time and space to tell Jimmy's story as dimensionally as he'd hoped to. Discarded along the way, gathered in impressive bulk on the 2011 box set, were demos that more fully developed Jimmy's childhood and adolescence, his relationship with his parents, with his music and with girls, and with other characters on the album, including a tangential storyline involving Ace Face and Jimmy's father. *Quadrophenia*'s seventeen songs by necessity leap across plot points, settling for impressionistic, sometimes vague evocations of Jimmy's real-world problems, joining story points with atmospheric touches such as news and music radio broadcasts and, most suggestively, recorded sounds from train stations and of stormy weather, shore birds, and crashing ocean waves.

I love the album for all this. What some listeners characterize as hazy or incomplete has always felt to me very much like adolescence itself, filtered through memory: shards, impressions, melody translating the untranslatable, words and sense and logic paling in the glare of hormonal vibrations and irrationality, the natural world and the city speaking urgent languages all their own. The story of one's adolescence, choked with romantic notions, wordless dreams far more exciting than tedious daily life, is difficult to tell with a clear beginning-middle-end. And I think Townshend knew that. He acknowledges that in the song "I'm One" he was trying to capture "a mood that most people can identify with, a transition in adolescence when anxiety and confidence vie for supremacy in our minds and hearts and we can feel fractured." A touching, four-note leitmotif rises to the surface several times throughout *Quadrophenia*, a question Jimmy asks that's central to his problems: "Is it me, for a moment?" That the answer to that question is *Yes* doesn't mean that its fleetingness isn't maddening. Try charting that on Freytag's Triangle.

Nonetheless, for decades Townshend has felt obligated to defend his album's perceived shortcomings, to explain, as he writes in "Two Stormy Summers," how *Quadrophenia* taught him that "the 'story' in rock music is not the same as the plot-driven stories we are used to in movies, novels and TV series, and must never try to obey the same rules." His most appealing justification for the album's sparse storyline, beyond the limitations imposed by the album's length, is that Jimmy worked best as a symbol, stripped of the kind of time- and place-stamped details that situate a character in a specific context. *Quadrophenia* isn't "a conventional narrative but a kind of distorted dream-view of two or three days in the life of Jimmy the Mod," he explains, adding, "It was only later, as the Who went into powerdrive in the recording studio in the early summer of 1973, that it became clear that in order for Jimmy to function as someone with whom the listener would identify, even inhabit, he had to be conveyed and carried by the music, not the story or the characters in it. Jimmy had to belong to the listener, not to the story." As Townshend composed more and more songs about Jimmy and as Jimmy's life began to take shape, the character "became less of a boy in his own right and more of an emblem, a cipher for the universal Mod."

Townshend's hope? "That everyone who sits to listen to the album finds themselves in it, and finds their own story."

Ten years ago in the *Guardian*, James Wood wrote about poring over his older brother's copy of *Quadrophenia* when he was thirteen, losing himself—as did I, with *my* older brother's copy—in the remarkable forty-four-page book of lyrics and grainy black-and-white photos that came with the album. "*Quadrophenia* was immediately alluring as a narrative, before I had heard a minute's music," Wood wrote. Ethan Russell's photographs, taken over the course of two weeks at the beach in Brighton, and in Goring, Cornwall, and the Battersea area near where the Who were recording, cast Terry Kennett, a local kid who Townshend discovered in a pub, in the role of Jimmy. The shots narrate dour postwar London life: Jimmy rides his scooter and walks down solitary roads and lanes, argues with his parents in a cramped kitchen, endures dreary breakfasts, hangs with his mates in tiny diners and dance halls, lugs trash, and plays juvenile delinquent in grimy streets throwing stones at buildings and vans.

Most effective are the photos taken in Brighton following Jimmy's escape, prefaced by a memorable shot of a wild-eyed, besuited Jimmy slouched on the commuter train between two impervious and oblivious bowler-hatted gents reading the newspapers. In the song "Bell Boy," Jimmy marvels that the beach is a place where genuine solitude might be found, and Russell's photos capture Jimmy's sense of personal isolation and subsequent identification with the starkly immense shore and the dark, roaring ocean. In the final fifteen photos, Russell dramatizes Jimmy's last hours at Brighton—dejected in a café, walking alone on an empty boardwalk and beach and sleeping under any shelter he can find, stealing the boat and sailing out into the sea. These images—bleak, monochrome, dense—evoke but don't fully narrate, let alone explain, the album's plot, but provide a wonderful photo-essay accompaniment to Townshend's impressionistic story.

As they were for Wood, the songs and photos were my way into Jimmy's profound alienation and aloneness. Over the decades I've listened to this record countless times, bobbing on its dark waves in an ecstatic yet abstractly melancholy identification with Jimmy and his self-doubt and uncertainties, allowing myself to slip into his silhouette, an emblem of youthful disenchantment. (My solitary walks took place in the 1980s along blocks of abandoned buildings and storefronts in and near Washington, D.C.'s old Downtown, not along the shore, but the gestures felt kindred.) Townshend remarked in *Melody Maker* in 1973 that at the album's close Jimmy's "lost the hang-up of past fears and anxieties into compartments. He's not saying anymore that he's got to be tough and a winner, or a dare devil, to earn other people's respect. He's just realized the emptiness of those labels stuck on what is just a spiritual desperation which everybody has. In this kid's case, he's just going through a speedy maturing process." He added that, on the rock, Jimmy's been "stripped of all excuses . . . the feeling of him being on his knees, but being stronger crying in the rain than he ever was drinking gin, knocking back pills, and kicking rockers, and whatever it was he thought was the meaning of life." As a teenager listening to the album in the family rec room, loudly on the stereo or more intimately with headphones, I aligned myself with Jimmy's hard-earned lessons. And I still do.

A more explicitly visual adaptation of these lessons arrived with director Franc Roddam's *Quadrophenia*, released in 1979, starring Phil Daniels as Jimmy. Roddam's film, produced with the Who's' endorsement, tidies up much of Townshend's narrative, making explicit Jimmy's ill-fated relationship with his girl Steph (Leslie Ash), his betrayal by her and his mates, his dislocation from ordinary working-class life, and his belief in the wonderful but idealized promises of Brighton. The beach fights between mods and rockers, briefly alluded to in the album in a couple of songs and via a fictionalized news report, become the film's central action, given an ambitious wide-screen treatment—they're immense, rowdy, choreographed battles—and though the final shot of Jimmy's riderless scooter plummeting off the cliff edge into the water makes it symbolically clear that he's cut ties with the demanding mod lifestyle, Jimmy's fate at the end remains uncertain. I loved the movie and the soundtrack. Nearly drowning in his parka, Daniels and his bug-eyed, desperate portrayal felt viscerally true, especially his growing alienation from his surroundings and his fraught crush on Steph. I longed for his clothes, his style sense, his loose-limbed recklessness on the streets and on the dance floors—boyish unruliness I'd never allow myself to fully explore and that I envied in others.

Like Townshend and long-ago Liz and those giggling boys in Brighton, I wanted to feel like a mod. In my teen years and early twenties in suburban Washington, D.C., I hesitantly self-identified as one. But I was an outsider. I loved the source-brew of 1960s rhythm and blues and rock and roll that bands such as the Who, the Kinks, the Small Faces, and the Creation drew from, and I worshipfully listened to Secret Affair and, especially, to the Jam, and bought up as many mod 45s and compilations as I could afford. I affixed arrows and targets and pictures of blokes on scooters and blocks of bright neon-colored paper and mod designs on my bedroom wall.

On the occasional weekend, my high school buddies David, Steve, and I headed down to the long-gone bar The Company in Georgetown, in D.C. (As David reminded me recently, they never carded there.) Local singer-songwriter Dennis Jay would DJ, having set up a couple of rickety tables near the back on top of which he'd stack numerous boxes of old 45s next to a turntable. I went to The Company less for the scene than for the music. Jay was an older guy, quiet and unassuming, with a shy smile, a slight physique, and thinning hair, but he exuded timeless cool, in part because of his encyclopedic knowledge of rock and roll and rhythm and blues. The place was a quasi-mod hangout on these nights—it may have been advertised as such, promising hours of sixties R&B, northern soul, and modbeat jams—and in the dark I'd secretly admire the sharper-dressed guys, those who genuinely leaned into the period look and style, removing their parkas after having alighted from scooters parked out front on M Street. I'd wear a skinny tie and thrift shop sport jacket, trying my best but staying put in the shadows.

I was sartorially challenged. My poorly pegged jeans, thrift shop suits, and ties mildly compensated for my lack of more genuine (and expensive) mod gear such as a parka, Ben Sherman shirts, Italian shoes, and three-button suits, let alone a Vespa. There was a tiny mod revival scene in Washington, D.C., in the early and mid-1980s. I knew that I'd never be able to compete with members of the bands who played in the scene or the fans who attended their shows. Similarly to Jimmy, I instinctively rebelled against the requirements to conform, even as I belittled myself, home after nights at a club or bar or facing the mirror during low points, for not trying harder to fit in, for not being reverent enough, eyeing the kid next to me in class whose pea coat was the perfect color or that one whose tab-collar shirt fit just so. I was too—what, self-conscious? skeptical?—to wear my jeans wet straight out of the washer and to let them dry on me ensuring a snug fit as I'd seen Jimmy do in *Quadrophenia*, or perhaps I read about it somewhere. I lived at home and didn't want to have to explain to my mom why I walked around dripping wet. I felt embarrassed enough asking her to haul out her sewing machine to narrow the ankle width on my jeans.

One summer, my brother Phil returned from Croydon, England, where he'd been visiting his girlfriend's family, and he presented me with a sky-blue, high-collar dress shirt with white polka-dots that he'd bought at a trendy Carnaby Street boutique in London. No one else in Maryland or D.C. had one that I'd seen, and I wore it with pride on weekend nights. At Poseurs, another Georgetown bar where my friends and I would head to drink and dance, I was approached by Neal Augenstein, the singer of the D.C.-area mod revival group Modest Proposal, a band I'd gone to see and whose

45 I'd soon play on my radio show at WMUC. Tall and commanding, handsome, supremely well-dressed in mod style, Augenstein looked a bit like the minor character John in *Quadrophenia*, and was revered by the small but active mod revival community. On the dance floor Neal openly envied my Carnaby Street shirt, and told me so. His public affirmation was childishly pleasing to me, and that was the closest I'd ever get to acceptance in a scene I didn't work hard enough to blend into.

I wore target buttons and put duct tape arrows on the back of my jean jacket. When I was supposed to have been studying John Donne for lit class, I instead obsessed over Colin MacInnes's 1959 novel *Absolute Beginners*, which I read because many in the U.K. and U.S. mod scenes spoke of it as holy writ, and because Paul Weller had written a song for the Jam with that title. I named my college radio show "Innocent Startings" in tribute to MacInnes's book and a community I pretended to care about more than I did. When I finally visited London in July 1988, the mod revival was long gone. I walked along Carnaby Street pining for a girl back at school who didn't care about me, bought a striped shirt and V-neck sweater, and thought about Weller, who was then mired in the sad, final days of the Style Council, a ghost commercially. On July 4, I took in a show at the legendary Marquee Club on Wardour Street—the Rolling Stones, the Yardbirds, Led Zeppelin, the Who, Hendrix, Pink Floyd, and countless others had played there at its early incarnation on Oxford Street, and mod revival bands such as Purple Hearts and the Chords tore up the joint's later Wardour Street location—and who was playing but Soul Asylum, an American band from the Midwest. Figured.

Sometime in the mid-1980s a few buddies and I went to see a midnight screening of *Quadrophenia* on campus. During the scene when Ace Face, played by Sting, stumbles oafishly at his job as a bellboy at a posh hotel, several in the theater crowd around me began shouting, "Sell out! Sell out!" I joined in, screwing up my face in mock outrage, yelling half-heartedly with them, but I felt stupid, adopting a pose in which I didn't believe; I didn't care if the Face needed to get a real job, if he had to act like a grown-up.

That seemed inevitable to me. The pressure I felt to align myself with that crowd reminded me of a shameful incident when I was a kid, about ten or eleven years old, when I shouted an epithet at a family out for a stroll on Bucknell Drive, behind my house. I'd been dared, and dared myself to keep up with my friend Mike, who was older and cooler. The curse felt hollow in my chest—something I couldn't name, but what I now call sorrow—and I felt foolish, an imposter. I immediately felt red-faced and regretful.

The final song on *Quadrophenia* is the album's best-known track. Townshend wrote the lyrics to "Love Reign o'er Me" to describe "the most extreme and miserable pathos of the soul ridiculed and abandoned by everyone and everything." Roger Daltrey's at his most dramatically expressive (or most melodramatically over-the-top, if you're not a fan; to writer Rick Moody, "the big production number" feels "cloying") especially in the yearning chorus when Jimmy's on the rock. A full-throated Daltrey beseeches the rain for love and answers. Townshend writes, "I learned that such an iconic Daltrey bellow can symbolically carry withering sadness, self-pity, loneliness, abandonment, spiritual desperation, the loss of romance, of love and of childhood as well as the more obvious rage and frustration," adding, "The angst of those teenage years, in which all of us feel misunderstood, is easy to make fun of but it is real and brings my hero, Jimmy, to consider suicide." *Easy to make fun of but real.* I love that phrase, which could be the title of anyone's teenage memoirs.

I recently braved the terrain of boxes in our basement storage room and unearthed "One Little Sheep Goes Askew," a short story I wrote in high school for my AP English class. On the cover sheet I'd carefully drawn in pencil a moody silhouette of my fictional counterpart, a mod boy clad in a parka with up-and-down arrows sewn onto the back. He's Pete Blyfield, an introspective high school student who spends his weekends bowling at a low-rent joint and running out on the tab, and his weeknights dreaming and scribbling poetry in his bedroom. Feeling trapped in the tacky suburbs, Pete pines for London and stylish scenes, for the smartly dressed boys and girls who traipse up and down Kings Road and Carnaby Street. He deplores his fellow students, whom he views as passionless and unstylish clods.

One day, Pete walks into a classroom, and his life alters. A new transfer student has landed at school, Dave Cooper, an aloof New Yorker, "dressed in pseudo-Beatle boots, complete with shiny, pointy toes, a pair of jet-black pegged trousers (pleated, of course), a black-and-white-spotted button-down shirt, and—draped casually over the young boy's slender frame—was the hippest, best-tailored, narrowest-lapelled 1964 suit jacket a silently awestruck Pete Blyfield ever laid eyes on. A one-inch bright red tie, razor-clean, close-cropped hair, and a pin that said 'The Jam' completed this glimpsing picture." Pete stands transfixed in the doorway, "staring at Him. A few in the class snickered. Little did they know, though, that Pete was not regarding Him as a screwed-up loser."[1]

It soon becomes clear to Pete that in Dave he's met a soulmate, someone with whom he's intensely connected, and for the next several weeks, he and Dave bond in head-lifting rapture. Pete learns that Dave's father was in the military, and so he's lived in many places, including London, a fact that, for the Anglophile Pete, elevates Dave to mythic proportions. The two dub themselves "Stylists" and spend long afternoons in secondhand thrift shops or rummaging through record stores. They meet like-minded guys and girls at D.C. clubs and spend hours together in their bedrooms and at Tastee Diner in Bethesda reading and writing poems, eventually self-printing them in 'zines and distributing them at clubs and record stores and tying them in thick stacks onto benches in D.C. parks.

Pete begins to notices some upsetting changes at school: "A jacket here. A narrow tie there. Prepubescent trousers with 'Stylist' labels. Stores selling out of black loafers. . . . It seemed to hit [Pete] all in one morning. He remembers feeling doom and frantically

1 Yes, I used capital personal pronouns when referring to Dave. Forgive me and I'll spare you excerpts from my two other mod-related short stories from this era, "The Buildings of 12th Street Circle" and "Shake and Shout!"

searching the halls for Dave. He could not find him. He searched with a passion never before recorded and ended in a weeping frustration in the bathroom. He couldn't find Him. He wept." The kicker: "Soon everyone was writing poetry at Tastee Diner." The final unraveling comes brutally swiftly as Pete learns that the military has moved Dave Cooper's family to Idaho. Bereft, Blyfield stands "stripped of soul and meaning" near a busy street. "Before walking into the street he remembers saying 'It's not we who learn, but the system.' Or was that Dave Cooper who said that? Or Paul Weller? Or Eric? Or Chuck? Or . . . Oh, it will be the catch phrase of the nation soon. Credit won't matter."

I laughed out loud reading this story again for the first time in decades, and cringed at the melodrama. Blyfield is a poor man's version of Jimmy, and a corny stand-in for myself. Yet I have affection for the seventeen-year-old me who believed so earnestly that a stylish mise-en-scène and well-dressed figures on the stage might quench a deep thirst for experience and wisdom, might, in fact, be the solution. I also still dig Pete's fierce if narrow-minded desire to step out of the norms and live life as an outsider, even as he cultivated like-minded souls in the mod community, a brave and single-minded impulse that I'd have been too scared to fully commit to myself. And though the line that Pete mutters to himself as he enters the street is obscure to me now, I still like the cynicism in the final sentence. Writing this feverish fantasy, I was living on the surface, as teenagers do, putting far too much faith in style over substance, believing in clichés before I recognized their banality, trusting that passion—that is, Passion—will be the answer to any and all thorny questions that life poses. Poor Pete Blyfield. He has some hard lessons coming his way.

"Intriguing portrait of alienation and condescension," my teacher Mr. Trick wrote at the top of the story. Still attached is the peer-review sheet that two of my poor classmates were obliged to fill out. In answer to the question "Does the story show us anything or give us something to think about?," they left the space blank. Hilarious! And apt. I certainly *felt* as if I were pursuing Grand Ideas and Themes when I wrote the story, but I was a kid who hadn't yet learned the distinctions between sentiment and sentimentality, between substance and sensation. Though the story's embarrassing and melodramatic, it's no less true because of that. It was me, for a moment.

The Who are infamous among fans and detractors alike for having never recorded a conventional love song (that's the reputation, anyway, and though Townshend's said as much himself, the claim's exaggerated; listen to the transcendent "Sunrise" from *The Who Sell Out*, among others). It's likely true that as many of Townshend's love songs were directed to Meher Baba, his lifelong spiritual master, as to women. The fact is, his tunes rarely take a point of view other than a young man's, and *Quadrophenia* is no exception. "I'm only interested in rites of passage stories," he declared. He wanted everyone to find their story in Jimmy's, but that's a big ask.

"How to recognize a story?" Sylvia Plath asked herself in her journals when she was planning to write a novel. "There is so much experience but the real outcome tyrannizes over it." The events in Plath's *The Bell Jar* occur in the mid-1950s, but the novel appeared around the time fictitious Jimmy was enduring his long days and nights of London alienation. (Plath published the novel in 1963 under the pseudonym Victoria Lucas.) Esther Greenwood's descent into unhappiness bears a striking resemblance to Jimmy's, yet the boundaries of her experiences are far narrower. Esther struggles to fit in with the other girls with whom she's spending a summer in Manhattan on a fashion magazine internship. She behaves as decorously as she's expected to, wears the right clothes in the proper style, is careful with boys, but recognizes that she yearns for something beyond the proper and provincially domestic, low-ceilinged fate she's been dealt. She wants to write a novel, but stalls. In the second half of the book, she returns to her family home in Massachusetts and drifts into depression, ultimately enduring electroshock therapy and a stay in an asylum, all the while struggling to discover her authentic self and admitting to growing suicidal ideation. As Jimmy did, during a particularly difficult day at the beach Esther swims out toward a rock in the ocean, intent on drowning once she's exhausted herself. She can't bring herself to die—her body resists the impulse—and at the novel's end she feels more assured and confident mentally, closer to her "old self" than she has been in weeks.

The differences between the two characters are stark. At his breaking point, Jimmy escapes to the beach, where he wanders aimlessly, pilled-up and drunk, taking long solitary walks along the shore into evening and sleeping wherever he can find shelter. For a while, these gestures sustain him; in fact, Jimmy's far happiest when by the sea. Perhaps *happy* isn't the right word—maybe *whole*. (Townshend has acknowledged that when writing *Quadrophenia* he drew heavily on Meher Baba's notion that the sea represents God's infinite love, and that humans are merely drops of water in that immense body.) The sense of mental cohesion that Jimmy gratefully receives in the salt air and crashing waves is fleeting, so strong is the battle among his selves, the desire to conform versus the need to be an individual.

Esther has fewer options. Though she goes solo occasionally in the novel—walking more than forty blocks to her all-girls hotel after an unfortunate late-night date, visiting the beach near her childhood home—those are the exceptions; as a female, her avenues toward freedom are more circumscribed, especially in the era in which she lived and suffered. "Being born a woman is my awful tragedy," Plath complained in her journals. "From the moment I was conceived I was doomed to sprout breasts and ovaries rather than penis and scrotum; to have my whole circle of action, thought and feeling rigidly circumscribed by my inescapable femininity." She bitterly adds,

> Yes, my consuming desire to mingle with road crews, sailors and soldiers, bar room regulars—to be a part of a scene, anonymous, listening, recording—all is spoiled by the fact that I am a girl, a female always in danger of assault and battery. My consuming interest in men and their lives is often misconstrued as a desire to seduce them, or as an invitation to intimacy. Yet, God, I want to talk to everybody I can as deeply as I can. I want to be able to sleep in an open field, to travel west, to walk freely at night.

And: to escape alone on a train without worry or fear, to walk in solitude by an ocean through the long night, to sleep unmolested on the sand until the sun lifts and with it some measure of peace.

I was fictionalizing myself in Pete Blyfield, not writing autobiography, yet I didn't make contact with much beyond the drama of teenage angst. I forgive my seventeen-year-old self's narrowness of emotional range and experience, but solipsism is hardly limited to one's teen years. Writer and editor Joseph Epstein notes that autobiography fails when the writer's experience "has no generalizing quality . . . isn't really about anything more than the [writer's] experience, merely, solely, wholly, and only." He adds that "true magic is entailed" to make the particular experience of the writer "part of universal experience."

How to transcend melodrama and banality when writing about adolescence? A challenge for my writing students is to recognize what in their experiences might be emblematic of the human experience, while at the same time embracing the sometimes crushing fact that their experiences, though they feel new, aren't particularly; add to that the argument that cliché is the death of art, and the order to write about adolescence becomes tall indeed. You can be an inventive storyteller and a master of detail and figurative language like Plath, who saw in Esther not only herself but countless women in her situation, or you can compose stirring songs like Townshend, who, it's important to remember, purposefully left out characterful touches that might have added unique personality traits to Jimmy in order to leave room for him to become more universal.

Working within a long tradition, both Plath and Townshend use fiction to explore their own lives. A year after *Quadrophenia* was released, Townshend was asked by Cameron Crowe in *Penthouse* if Jimmy was "a thinly disguised Pete Townshend." He answered that the character wasn't, but that he identified "very strongly with Jimmy in several ways," before clarifying that Jimmy was "a workshop figure. An invention." He couldn't identify fully with Jimmy's early years—"his romanticism, his neurosis, his craziness. I never went through a tormented childhood. When I was a kid, it was just me and the guitar and the belief that if I ever learned the secret of rock'n'roll I would own the world"—rather, he felt closest to Jimmy

> when he's reached the stage, late in the album, of being stuck on the Rock. He's surrendered himself to the inevitable, whatever that is, and has put all his problems behind him. Jimmy's not become any kind of saint or sage, he hasn't even found anything, much less himself. Basically, he isn't gonna be any different. He's just reached the point in his life where he's seriously contemplated suicide—as we all have—and the fact that he chose not to kill himself has left him with a fantastic emptiness. A need to be filled.

At the conclusion of *The Bell Jar*, Esther is alive, her mental health improving, and at the close of *Quadrophenia*, Jimmy is alive yet drained. That paradox—lost but found—adds dimension to well-worn teenage angst. In fact, paradox might be the way out of cliché when writing about childhood and adolescence. I was too naive to recognize that what Pete Blyfield desperately craved may in the end have brought him little but melancholy and uncertainty (his "anxiety and confidence" at war, leaving him ultimately "fractured," as Townshend puts it). Instead I use the lame deus ex machina of Cooper's move to Idaho to bring about Blyfield's end.

Paradox. Esther and Jimmy both fiercely want to belong to a like-minded group, yet both are fierce individualists. Both dress and behave the way their community's cultural standards require them to, and both rebel. Both long for the comforts and affirmation of the hive, imagining that their self-worth buzzes therein, but both natively resist the siren call of conformity even as they believe that they need it. Both glimpse their genuine selves only in isolation, and both reject the world the way the world is offered to them. Plath and Townshend strive for their characters' redemptions at the close of their works, but both Jimmy and Esther, in the infinite present tense of their stories' ends, are poised unsteadily, unable to solve the riddle.

Much Too Real to Ever Disappear

Funny, what gets in and stays there. Decades after the Jam released *Sound Affects*, the album's lean, righteous sound remains endlessly renewable.

October, 2018. A man-about-town sits on a stool onstage at the Royal Festival Hall. His hair is white-gray. On an acoustic guitar and with the accompaniment of the London Metropolitan Orchestra he's about to sing a rambunctious, high-spirited rock and roll song that he wrote when he was barely twenty-two years old. Four decades later, we're hearing a bit of melancholy. The arrangement's at half speed, the voice is shy of the higher notes. Youthful exuberance has been replaced with middle-aged wistfulness, or is it familiar pride wearing an unfamiliar jacket?

The Jam's run of charting singles preceding their fifth album *Sound Affects* equals any band's output in the punk/new wave era, or arguably in any era. From "'A' Bomb in Wardour Street" paired with a streak through the Kinks' "David Watts," a double A-side released in March 1978, through to "Start!," released in August 1980, Paul Weller documented, dramatized, and thrilled a young, mostly male audience who tuned in devotedly to his band's blend of hooks, power, political righteousness, and style. "Down in the Tube Station at Midnight" (October 1978), "Strange Town" (March 1979), "When You're Young" (August 1979), "The Eton Rifles" (October 1979), the March 1980 double A-side "Going Underground" and "Dreams of

Children": these are the tuneful roars of lads in pubs, on playing fields, and in streets in front of council blocks on the way to shitty jobs shadowed by low ceilings of expectations. Delivered by Weller (on guitar), Bruce Foxton (bass), and Rick Buckler (drums) with a powerful backline, dour faces, mod attire, and wry suburban humor, those singles—and the terrific albums that they appeared on or supported, *All Mod Cons* (1978) and *Setting Sons* (1979)—are very English and of the Thatcher era, yet timeless. *When you're young, you fall in love with anyone*, Weller sang in 1979, as someone sang somewhere in 1679.

"Art School." "All Around the World." "All Mod Cons." "The Place I Love." "When You're Young." "Saturday's Kids." Listening to the Jam often gives the impression that I'm playing catchup: somehow the tunes begin before I even drop the needle, and I'm left chasing the band, who's running after the song they created, or that's created them. The Jam reached a pinnacle with the fierce, scarily powerful "Going Underground," their first number one single in the United Kingdom and, to many, the Platonic ideal of the band's sound. The sonic equivalent of an epiphany—a loud one—the song gives voice to the disenfranchised, bitter outsider, the one who doesn't like what's on offer and who chooses instead to hang out below, away from the brass bands, the "braying sheep" on television, the politicians' "nuclear textbooks" and their "atomic crimes." My heart quickens reading the lyrics; accompanied by the band's full-on assault—the guitars sound as if they'd leap from Weller and Foxton's hands if the musicians didn't grip them tightly enough—the words fight to be heard, tumbling, gaspingly, from verse to verse, each line arriving like a sudden insight. There's a startling moment following the eight-bar, half-time bridge where Weller's Rickenbacker guitar slashes at the surface of the song, slicing it open and awakening the singer from his dreamy singsong take on the title phrase, impatient with anything in the face of toxic lethargy, groupthink, and lazy consumerism that isn't urgently, angrily expressed. The moment's one of the greatest in any Jam song. A slap in the face.

Weller felt that the mood and tone of "Going Underground" marked an end point of sorts for his band, and the single's other

A-side hinted at what was to come. When the Jam were touring the United States in February and March 1980 the Beatles' *Revolver* played on high rotation in the band's van; writing and recording "Dreams of Children" had led them back to that 1966 classic. A midpaced, backward tape-laden psychedelic lament, the song churns dreamy nostalgia made bitter by awakening to "a modern nightmare" of "tall dark buildings" and dirty streets, where children's dreams have little purchase. John Lennon's dark, guitar-rich, trippy *Revolver* tracks were the sonic tributaries leading to "Dreams of Children," and for the next Jam album Weller was curious to see where those currents might take him. (The Jam cancelled the remainder of the U.S. tour after learning of the success of "Going Underground," and in April, before sessions for *Sound Affects* began, Weller cut demos of "Rain" and "And Your Bird Can Sing.")

Meanwhile, Weller was reading quite a bit, and new influences were pouring in, two books in particular striking a chord. Geoffrey Ashe's 1975 cultural history *Camelot and the Vision of Albion* explored the Arthurian legend and the Middle Ages' grappling with Camelot, romance, and the loss of innocence. In 2010 Weller related to John Harris that he'd organized "a bit of a works beano" while working on *Sound Affects*, "a big coach trip with all the roadies and their wives and the band, and I managed to get them to go to Glastonbury for a few days. I really wanted to go and see where King Arthur and Guinevere were buried," he said, adding, "there was also that whole 'Blakean' thing, about how we'd lost our vision, and been blighted by science, and distracted by politicians, and we needed to get back to a much more natural, pure vision. It caught my imagination. I found it very inspiring."

In *Homage to Catalonia*, George Orwell, long a favorite of Weller's, recounted his experiences fighting fascist totalitarianism during the Spanish Civil War in the 1930s, a seminal era that would influence his political beliefs for a lifetime. "Orwell describes arriving in Barcelona for the first time and seeing his own vision of democratic socialism at work," Graham Willmott wrote in 2003, adding that while there Orwell took note of how "like-minded people traveled from the world with the same ideals as the writer himself. They could barely communicate with each other but all instinctively embraced this new socialist ideal and fought together to preserve it." Weller absorbed Orwell's political passions, his provocative ideals and purity of belief, his persuasive argument that artists should respond in their work politically, and felt an instinctive kinship with the writer.

An even greater inspiration awaited. The second episode of the television program *Something Else* aired in England on BBC2 on September 15, 1979, and, like the inaugural episode, was charmingly, earnestly youthful. This was by design: *Something Else* was produced to appeal to the young audience that BBC programming had largely ignored, or otherwise misunderstood wildly. The magazine-style show employed a young crew between the ages of sixteen and twenty, and featured appealingly self-conscious hosts, unposh regional accents, spirited debates, a nervy, artistic tone, and music. The Jam, wrapping up work on *Setting Sons*, bookended the second episode playing "When You're Young" and their forthcoming single "The Eton Rifles."

The performances were explosive and striking, the band getting off playing for the crowd of teenagers only feet away from the stage. Equally notable was the content of the episode itself. A segment following the Jam's performance introduces Ellen, a nineteen-year-old single mother of two struggling in a dismal council block (it's got "a bad name") in Salford, a mile from the city center of Manchester—she's also a member of the *Something Else* production team, lending authenticity to the show's interest in presenting genuine teenage lives. The cameras enter Ellen's cramped flat, with its grey view out of tiny windows onto grey expanse, and film her looking after her fussy children. In a voiceover, Ellen speaks plainly about the difficulties of paying rent, of struggling up and down the stairs with her pram, her kids in tow, the local youngsters unwilling to assist her. She matter-of-factly shares that over Christmas her flat was broken into, many of her possessions looted and destroyed. The tone of the segment is authentically grim yet moving in its clear-eyed detailing, all the more impressive given the producers' youthful, unvarnished point of view.

Man-on-the-street interviews with middle-aged Mancunians follow ("What do you think of teenagers?") as well as conversations with local politicians and police about legal drinking and teenagers' legal rights, a discussion between Tony Wilson, of the upstart Factory Records, and BBC Radio 1 DJ Paul Burnett about the difficulties getting punk rock records on the radio, and, threaded throughout, "punk poet" John Cooper Clarke reciting a list poem while riding up and down escalators in a shopping center (and later a men's room) trailed by besotted teenage fans. The Jam end the show by righteously storming through "When You're Young," Weller and Foxton harmonizing on the more bitter lines, the song sounding like nothing less than a tailor-made theme, a soundtrack to the often frustrated, always wide-eyed young kids whom we'd just watched.

Sitting in on the conversation with Wilson and Burnett was Stephen Morris, a quiet, twenty-two-year-old drummer whose band Joy Division Weller had been tuning into with keen interest. New sounds were abounding: earlier in the year Weller had gone to see Gang of Four, a politically minded band out of Leeds, and he dug their tough, terrific debut *Entertainment!*, released the same month that the *Something Else* episode aired. (Weller remembers seeing Gang of Four at The Nashville in West London in 1979; they did play there on February 24, though on that date the Jam were between gigs in Wiesbaden, Germany, and Paris, so it's possible that his memory's off.) He'd also been turned on by the London band Wire, whose tunes "Dot Dash" and "Ex-Lion Tamer" "were great," Weller enthused, "pop songs, but slightly jagged, and distorted. I really liked that."

Joy Division's two performances on *Something Else* are extraordinary. (The broadcast was their first and, sadly, last national television appearance; singer Ian Curtis killed himself eight months later.) Spiky, tightly wound, brittle, anxious, minimal: the hallmarks of Joy Division's arresting and wholly original sound were laid bare for the *Something Else* audience, wild-eyed Curtis singing atonally but urgently, dancing and flailing about like a restless marionette. Morris and bassist Peter Hook are locked in, translating a nervous tension agitated further by Bernard Sumner's busy guitar work. Both "Transmission" and "She's Lost Control" registered with Weller's growing sense of his own band's limits, and its possibilities, and he was enthralled with the nerviness of it all. (And pleased with the band's unaffectedness: "I remember being pleasantly surprised to find out [Joy Division] were very normal working-class lads," he said. "In my mind, I had an image of them being 'poncey art-school, studenty-type' people, and they were quite the opposite.") Weller watched, listened, bought the records of these new, exceptionally original bands. And he went to work.

Recording sessions for *Sound Affects* faced an early uphill climb. "I probably had about five or six songs written upfront," Weller remembered. "The rest were a real struggle to write. I had loads of ideas: very sort of abstract, vague ideas of what I wanted to do, and how I wanted it to sound, but nothing was actually written."

Following demo recordings in April ("just me and one of the roadies fucking about, really"), Weller convened Foxton and Buckler at the Townhouse Studio in London in mid-June, and sessions with producer Vic Coppersmith-Heaven began in earnest. The Jam had debuted two songs onstage: "But I'm Different Now" at the Pinkpop 1980 festival in Geleen, Netherlands, on May 26, and "Start!" at Victoria Hall in Hanley, England, on June 4. Beyond these, the band had little of substance to work with. "So we would jam," Weller recalls, "and out of that would come a riff" [see "Instrumental" and the backing track to "Scrape Away," both issued on the 2010 deluxe reissue of *Sound Affects*] "and then I would start to piece something together. It's very laborious and expensive, to do that in a studio. But that's the way that record was made." He added, "You're not really familiar with what you're doing, and you're just kind of following your nose, but sometimes good things come out of that. It introduces things you wouldn't normally do. You have certain techniques and ways of working, and it throws all of that stuff out the window. That can be a very good thing."

Across the summer and fall Weller laid melodies, evocative scraps of lyric, and vocals on top of the tracks, and songs slowly began to take shape. Sources indicate that recording for "Pretty Green" began on June 15, "Dream Time" on the sixteenth, "But I'm Different Now" on the seventeenth, and "Start!" on the nineteenth. On the twenty-first the band paused to head north and play the Loch Lomond Festival in Scotland, and then began rehearsals for their first visit to Japan, where they would play five well-received shows during the first week of July. On the way back home they stopped at Los Angeles for a July 11 appearance on the ABC-TV show *Fridays* (looking smart and ignoring jet lag, they played "Private Hell" from *Setting Sons* and "Start!"). On the 22nd they played the Civic Hall, in Guildford, England, on that day beginning sessions for "Monday." Nearly a month passed before recording of the group-written instrumental "Music for the Last Couple" commenced on August 27, and, as the boys consciously eyed a label-issued hard deadline, swift sessions occurred for "Boy About Town" (September 1), "Scrape Away" (September 30), "Set the House Ablaze" (October 2), "Man in the Corner Shop" (October 6), and "That's Entertainment" (October 22).

"Start!," backed with "Liza Radley" (recorded in April), was issued as a single on August 15. The eleven-track *Sound Affects* LP followed on November 28. On the inner sleeve the band poses in soft-focus in the country near a pond, staring into the middle distance as the rising sun pinks the sky. An excerpt from Percy Bysshe Shelley's 1819 poem "The Masque of Anarchy" runs on the back sleeve, with phrases such as "Rise like lions," "Shake your chains," and "Declare with measured words that ye / Are, as God has made ye, free," evoking the struggle between alienation and liberty Weller sings about inside. A fan had sent him the poem. "In those days, there was a lot of interaction with our fans: a lot of people used to send me stuff, and I'd send them stuff," Weller recalled. "I just thought it was amazing: it seemed to capture where my mind was at."

The cover art, based on a midcentury BBC sound affects album that Weller chanced upon in the studio, was an abstract storyboard of images. A taxi cab. A barking dog. An exclamation point.

A phone booth. City rooftops. A speeding train. An office building. A baby. A hearse. *POW!* An open window. A hi-fi. Scrawled graffiti: *From The Cradle To The Grave.* A face. An electricity pylon. A £ sign. Fish and chips. A jukebox. A police car. A cheering crowd.

Sound Affects has never left my head. When I listen, the music washes over me in sensations, in snatches of images and phrases, singsong/singalong melodies competing against slashing guitars. The Jam on *Sound Affects* sound different than the Jam of the first four albums and the singles. By the time of *Setting Sons*, their songs were becoming glossy and mammoth, stuffed and layered with overdubs. The songs here are leaner, punchier, stripped to bare arrangements that leave spaces in the music you can put your fist through. Before Weller encountered the work of Gang of Four, Wire, and Joy Division, the Jam's sound had been "very sort of tracked-up: loads of guitars," Weller reflects, adding, "Now, I wanted to get to the bare bones of the songs." Overdubs on *Sound Affects* are rare, a distant piano here, a tambourine and chirpy trumpets there, the occasional backward guitar; the essential soundscape is of three young men playing live in the studio, moving inside the songwriting process from yet-to-be-named lo-fi funky instrumentals to acerbic songs sweetened with harmonies and simple, childlike melodies. Foxton's bass is up-front and everything stays spare and wiry. Weller has confessed that he was obsessed with electricity pylons while writing *Sound Affects*, the images of which he couldn't shake. I sense them in these songs' direct impact, in the taut wires of the guitar strings, the amps buzzing, speakers humming, the surges of current in the studio.

The lyrics reflect a minimal aesthetic as well. On songs on earlier albums Weller sang in chewy mouthfuls, cramming as many syllables as he could into a line—the rush of words, ideas, and sensations evoking the urgency and exuberance of youth. On *Sound Affects* Weller pares back his excesses, trading stuffed lines for skeletal phrases and simple sentences that evoke the primary straightforwardness and unassuming line drawings of a children's book. Many earlier Jam songs were packed with details—place names and city landmarks and references to laddish gear—while others were cinematic story-songs or Ray Davies–styled character sketches. Here Weller defocuses the lens, and places, people, and things soften to universals. (Still, Weller's affection for Davies couldn't be denied; the band recorded versions of the Kinks' "Waterloo Sunset" and "Dead End Street" near the end of the sessions.) Not that I didn't puzzle over some of Weller's Anglicisms when I listened to the album as a teenager. *A fruit machine. Sticky black tarmac. Eating your tea. A hardened MP.* But mostly, with the exception of the diary-like "That's Entertainment," Weller ignores the daily urban/travelogue style for something more elemental, a kind of mod aphoristic. If *All Mod Cons* and *Setting Sons* are rich with British colors and particulars, *Sound Affects* offers a monochromatic world, all the more inviting for us to step into the silhouettes that Weller's sparse lyrics create and find that we fit there.

Songs group themselves together as I listen. "Pretty Green," "Dream Time," "Man in the Corner Shop," and "Music for the Last Couple" suggests one thread of a narrative, "Monday," "But I'm Different Now," and "Start!" another. "That's Entertainment" and "Boy About Town" feel like foils to "Scrape Away" and "Set the House Ablaze." The album gives the impression of being a soundtrack of a weekend: a kid in his early twenties strolling up streets and down streets, worn paperback copies of Shelley and Orwell under his arm, suffering existential crises in the supermarket watching people go crazy, enjoying pints in the pub on Friday night where he hears about a former mate devolving into fascism and hatred, on Saturday night where another's becoming twisted by cynicism, heading home drunk and writing all of these sense impressions down, struggling to see splendor in the daily dross, waking up hungover on Sunday and strolling past a church, thinking on the ironies of the class distinctions of those worshipping inside, dreading work on Monday, where he'll dream of boats and planes to spirit him away and pine for the girl whom he'll see there. He's different now, he'll show her . . .

Weller adorns both "Pretty Green" and "Man in the Corner Shop" with simple melodies, yet they feel like antilullabies. "Pretty

Green," the album's opening track, sets the template: simple, direct, unadorned, and danceable, the unassuming melody sweetening a morality tale about the free market. Weller's always been interested in class—few English songwriters in the late 1970s weren't—and many of his songs decry the inherent unfairness of capitalism while cranking the amps. "Pretty Green" puts it simply: *I've got a pocketful of cash and the slot machines, sandwich shops, and jukeboxes will empty it.* By the time Foxton sweetly sings the title phrase against the repeating verse, the song's turned dreadful: *you can't do nothing unless it's in the pocket.* Sweet dreams. I hear Joy Division/Gang of Four influences here, less in the grim lyrics than in Foxton's machine-like bass lines and Buckler's high-hat work, wound-up tension momentarily relieved by the burst of the chorus before the perpetual motion of the verse machines—the singer's gonna eat, and then search out more—reminds us of capitalism's pure hunger.

The incongruities of class are especially apparent in the mid-paced "Man in the Corner Shop." The simple, pleasant melody describes a shop owner, his customer, and the customer's boss, each measuring his worth against the other—envy, pride, and power competing. The shop owner's life is hard, yet it's nice to be his own boss. The customer, envious of the shop owner's freedom, will rue his own fate tomorrow at his stifling factory job, where his boss will haughtily smoke cigars he purchased from the shop owner, who, it turns out, is tired of struggling and dreams of owning his own factory: The End. The timelessness of this cycle of complacency and resentment is mocked in Weller's descending "la-la-la-la-las," honeyed in affect but bitterly pointed. The Jam loved their *la-la-la*s and their *fa-fa-fa*s—think "David Watts," "Saturday's Kids," "Going Underground"—yet on *Sound Affects* they sound less like drunken-lad pub or football chants or rallying street cries and more like prelanguage wordless expression, filling in the blanks of Weller's abstractly minimal lyrics, responses to the emotional content that the words evoke. Do the "la-la-la-la-las" here blissfully deny class warfare that's as old as dirt, or perversely sing along with the struggle? The song's bridge, one of the few passages on the album I still puzzle over, brings the three men together in church where they pray communally, equal under God's hand. Is this a calming insight, or irony? What do your ears tell you?

Swirl of backward guitar, ghostly percussion, a disembodied falsetto cry slowly ascends and slowly retreats as we're lulled to hypnotic rest . . . *POW!* The band comes crashing in with the opening verse of "Dream Time," a fraught cry against commercialism. The swingin' chorus buoys things, until we stop dancing and listen to the words. The singer's anxious and sweating, and he's taking stock of a nasty cityscape that he wishes to flee but that traps him. The usual balms—pretty girls and city lights—fail to distract from his paranoia or soften his nightmarish discovery that his love comes in frozen packs bought in a supermarket.

Weller claims that as he was writing *Sound Affects*, he was in thrall to Michael Jackson's *Off the Wall*, released in August 1979, a record that he asserted was as strong an influence as *Revolver*. A deep background influence, perhaps; any dancing to *Sound Affects* stems more from desperation than joy. I do hear Jackson in the surprising, thirty-five-bar middle of "Dream Time." The band interrupts itself, striking the same chord for a few bars as if distracted by a new, incoming idea, which Weller reduces to a simple premise: the word's tough, so you've got to respond in kind. He repeats the second phrase as his band gains steam, surer inside this new conceit, though they're playing a different song now. Then Weller leaps for a falsetto, singing variations of *tough with it* as a horn section arrives out of the blue and punches the phrase with gusto, and the nightmare turns into a dance floor. If this propulsive section grew from a studio jam, Weller was smart to surrender to it and see where it took the band. Buckler lands on a four-on-the-floor groove and the thing really *moves*, a pop-up night club to dance away all of your problems. To my ears it's among the most moving passages on the album, as Weller's falsetto surprises him into the complex joys of the moment. A sweaty, full-body groove against hate and despair, the passage points to the soul/R&B sound that the band would consciously adopt over the next two years. The

Jam infamously declined to smile in nearly all of their publicity photos, but it's tough to imagine that they're wearing scowls as they're laying this down.

Nothing less than the theme to a dreary job, the band-composed "Music for the Last Couple" is a postpunk version of the kind of music that played behind scenes of bustling factories in old Warner Brothers cartoons. The syncopated rhythms evoke pistons, cogs, and spinning gears, and a punch-in/punch-out, company man joviality; he's hard at work yet happy for the opportunity. That is until his inner voice, in a moment of yearning, rises to the surface of the smooth-gliding office works. This passes quickly, is dismissed, and it's head down and back to work.

The silver lining of a monotonous office job is that he might run into *her* there. "Monday," one of Weller's great love songs, arrives after the stern "Pretty Green," and its tender conjuring of a work romance softens things. "There were always romantic songs on Jam albums—a long line of them," Weller insisted in 2010. "But I like the twist in ["Monday"]—that Monday's probably the least romantic day you can think of." He adds, "It's very English; really suburban." Gorgeous in its lyric and melodic simplicity, especially in the soaring chorus, "Monday" is a dreamy reprieve from the album's gloom, and is strikingly vulnerable. In one of the more powerful discoveries on the album, Weller sings about never being ashamed of love again. That he sees her on Mondays, and not on the weekends, suggests that whatever romance he imagines might be in his head, but his gratitude for her redemptive presence in his life is raw and real.

"But I'm Different Now"— the other love song on *Sound Affects*—hearkens back to an earlier Jam sound. A strutting avowal given charge by Weller's raw guitar riff and Buckler's pace-quickening high-hat work, the song arrives and vanishes in under two minutes before the singer, or his girl, has much time to doubt its promises and apologies. In my high school English notebooks I scrawled the line about fun lasting for seconds and love for days, romantically indulging the cynicism and marveling at the way it's rescued by the heart-pumping stomp of the music. Foxton's ascending bass line in the chorus sounds like the heart when it's happy. And those "hay yay-yay-yay-yays" in the bridge—yet another moment where Weller surrenders to the wordless language of excitement.

There was apparently some grumbling among the executives at Polydor Records when the band insisted that "Start!" be the advance single, not "Pretty Green," the label's choice. In retrospect it's clear how sharp the band's instincts were: "Start!" is one of the Jam's outstanding singles, a metasong that's as infectiously joyous as it is slyly smart. Kicking off with the indelible bass riff from the Beatles' "Taxman" (another nod to *Revolver*), the song establishes its danceable argument. "The lyrics to that reflected what I was thinking sound-wise: to be very minimal, and make the point as quickly as possible, and get in and out," Weller says, adding, "I was very, very hung up on communication." He relished the power of the pop song "to communicate so much in such a very short space of time. I was really drawn to it."

Weller had written about alienation since the first Jam album ("Away from the Numbers") and it's an obsession threaded throughout his songs—listen to "Standards," "In the Crowd," "Strange Town," "Private Hell," and others. Yet this is the first song where a solution for the debilitating effects of isolation might be found in the song itself. Like so much great rock and roll, "Start!" is about rock and roll—the 45 single in particular, that two-minute window onto the human condition issuing weekly from the radio, each more mind-bending or hip-moving than the last. But "Start!" isn't about easy answers; he's singing, after all, to someone who feels as anxious as he does, someone for whom a cheerful night out at the club or evening alone with a stack of 45s might ease things, but who will likely wake up the next morning faced with the same old dilemmas. *What you give is what you get*, Weller wryly reminds us as two minutes end and the needle lifts.

Rock and roll might solve alienation for a couple of minutes. It can't be an antidote to racist indoctrination, but it can evoke its nastiness. Weller recalled that in England in the late 1970s "you used to see a lot of the audience getting hooked into that whole National Front thing: young kids, a bit like that film *This Is England* [a 2006 drama about early eighties U.K. skinheads, written and directed by Shane Meadows]. You'd see elements of it in the audience, or the kids you used to meet at sound-checks, who seemed susceptible to that sort of brainwashing." Weller wrote the confrontational "Set the House Ablaze" in response to this unwelcome development.

The singer's addressing a mate whom a mutual friend had seen in the pub. These days he's wearing the fascist uniform: leather belt, black boots. He looks macho, but "oh, what a bastard to get off," the singer laments as the lockstep, martial beat behind him leads inevitably to the explosive chorus, Weller's guitar slashing in anger at his mate's vile conversion. We never learn precisely *what* he says that's so incendiary, a bit of narrative brilliance on the part of Weller who evokes the foul things the lad's spewing with the image of the strutting, malevolent uniform. In another powerful move, Weller cuts the second verse short, as if he can't hold back the rising hopelessness in the song's chorus. In the twelve-bar middle, this reflection yields to a kind of futility—listen to the way Buckler's rolling drums mimic the singer's turmoil—as he's screaming and shouting in the very song in which he's admitting futility, the irony burned to a crisp like everything else in this ferocious song.

Wordless passages convey so much on *Sound Affects*: the menacing opening riff; the rigid, portentous four-in-the-bar beat; the whistling in the opening bars, and throughout, that evoke nasty, goose-stepping marches. In a troubled, thirty-five-bar passage that follows the second chorus, a disembodied voice begins uttering, rising through the smoke. We hear stray phrases evoking indoctrination and inequality as the fuming opening riff drags itself back in and the song explodes into the chorus again. Yet nothing's settled. The whistling starts up again, competing with the singer's and the band's indignations. A violent encounter. Tables are turned over in the pub. Pint glasses go flying.

And then surprisingly, movingly, and then not at all surprisingly given the album we're listening to: those soldierly whistles morph into desperate "la-la-las" that Weller sings near the top of his register, the band storming behind him, of a different, far more complex order than the wordless passages we hear elsewhere on the album. For one: what characters are chanting them? And why?—out of brutal triumph on the way home from the pub, or as a naive stay against that brutality? As many times as I've listened to the song, I've never been able to figure out the origin point of these "la-la-las," let alone Weller's reason for singing them, here, near the end of a conflagration of a song that ends in ashes. "Set the House Ablaze" is one of Weller's greatest songs and one of the Jam's almightiest studio performances: scary, righteously pissed off, unavoidable, nearly out of control.

I imagine that the singer heads back to the pub the next night, less on the lookout for his adversary than to soothe his own nerves. Yet there he quarrels with another mate who's morphing into a lesser version of himself. A bothered, rhythmically arduous protest, "Scrape Away" closes *Sound Affects* unhappily. To the singer, his friend's a victim of twisted cynicism, surrendering to hopelessness, accusing the singer of being a naive dreamer and openly mocking his idealism. Begun in the studio as a band-composed instrumental jam, "Scrape Away" never feels entirely comfortable with itself as a song. Weller wrestles his lyrics to meet Foxton's anxious, rising bass line, Buckler's obstinate drumming, and the song's odd meter, only in the choir-like held notes of the chorus finding release of sorts, as he bids his jaded friend some advice. Yet the question in the verses—what turns a young person toward cynicism?—remains, nagging, unresolved, the song fading away as a voice mutters in French and a dire siren cry issues from Weller's guitar.

"Coming home pissed from the pub and writing 'That's Entertainment' in 10 minutes, 'Weller's finest song to date' hah!" So wrote a half-grinning Weller on the sleeve notes to *Dig the New Breed*, the Jam's 1982 live album. (Twenty years later, he acknowledged that the song's lyric was based in part on a similarly named poem written by Paul Drew, who'd sent it to Weller's Riot Stories publishing imprint.) A list poem of mundane details sung in a dreamy, singsong melody, "That's Entertainment" is different from anything else on *Sound Affects*, yet is in many ways the album's centerpiece.

Playing on his acoustic guitar, complemented by Foxton's anchoring bass and by eddying backward guitar in the later verses, Weller dryly moves from one observation to the next, the song unspooling matter-of-factly. Police sirens, a crying baby, a howling dog. Walls splashed with paint, a garage band rehearsing down the street, a tacky blacktop. An icy-cold flat, a pneumatic drill outside, a torn-up phone booth. Life in all of its ordinary, graceless details, strung together in kind of threnody to the everyday. "That's entertainment," Weller sings in the chorus in a poignant blend of awe, sarcasm, cynicism, and innocence. A picture book of urban and suburban familiarity, the song echoes the album's cover art as a kind of storyboard, stark images and events strung together yet cohering: nothing *really* matters among these things, yet, as snapshots of the life we take for granted, each is profoundly significant. You want to read the song as satire or irony, yet Weller sings with such affection about blinking lamplights, boring rainy Wednesdays, kissing lovers, feeding ducks in the park—even a kick in the balls—that the earnestness is deeply affecting, and touching. "That's Entertainment" was released as a single in West Germany in January 1981, and proved popular as an import in the United Kingdom, where it reached number twenty-one on the charts. It's since become a Weller standard.

Generally a dour album, *Sound Affects* comes to life with the wry "That's Entertainment" and erupts with joie de vivre in "Boy About Town," the freest and least cynical song here. Another childlike melody elevates the story of a happy afternoon that the singer spends in the city, "on top of the world" as he glides up and down streets, window shopping and people watching. He's the guy in "That's Entertainment," now gushing about everything, the wind blowing him about ecstatically, though his ear's still tuned to minor notes. Until then, he's content watching rainbows and the folks around him "go crazy," wishing only to go his own way, where he wants, when he wants. Weller's in a great mood here, and he writes a melody and arrangement to match, the song bursting into technicolor in the instrumental break where two trumpets sing the verse melody and where a grin on Buckler's face as he plays overjoyed tumbling fills on his tom drums is practically visible. I guess that "Boy About Town" is the *third* love song on *Sound Affects*. Just before that break Weller cheerfully sings another round of "la-la-las"—it's the album's vernacular, really—and here as in "That's Entertainment" they're stripped of the complexities of those sung in "Man in the Corner Shop" and "Set the House Ablaze": joy spilling over the rim of the words we use to express it, pure language as pure song, the album's gift for its listeners.

Moving among his beloved Rickenbacker, Eccleshall, and Gibson SG guitars, Weller punches the air and adds harsh dissonance and slashing emphases to the songs on *Sound Affects*, the last great rock and roll guitar album he'd make. In 1982 he'd disband the Jam and form the Style Council with keyboardist Mick Talbot and numerous side musicians, indulging an eclectic feel for soul, funk, jazz, and R&B, and Continental fashions. His tongue-in-cheek songs become more topically political and stylistically sundry, and he seemed to have lost his interest in the sparse soundscape and fragmented, universalized songwriting style of *Sound Affects*.

Yet he regards the album with great affection. "I still feel that it was our best record," he remarked to John Harris in 2010, adding, "To me, it still sounds fresh."

Funny, what gets in and stays there.

Dialing the 9:30 Club concert line one night in the early 1980s and marveling as a few seconds of the spirited chorus to "Dream Time" burst through the phone. The Jam played Ritchie Coliseum on the campus of the University of Maryland on May 14, 1982, and maybe the club's promoters were hosting the concert, or perhaps I'm confusing this with an ad for the show that aired on WHFS 102.3 FM, my favorite radio station—I can't recall the context now, but can vividly recall those few seconds of the song surging through the air, its melody and harmonies scoring an evening or a weekend for me, the very soundtrack of my excitable adolescence. My older brother went to the show at Ritchie Coliseum, and afterward told me that they opened with "Boy About Town." I wasn't there, and still I see a spotlighted Buckler, his sticks raised over his head, counting in the song, the night, the era.

I'm hanging out with some buddies at Variety Records in Wheaton Plaza, the mall a half mile from my house in Wheaton, Maryland. "Set the House Ablaze" is playing in the store—*Sound Affects* had been out for a year or more—and my friends and I, poised at the teenage new wave punk threshold, are goofing around, wasting time, gawking at the albums we can't afford to buy. I'm startled by a *BANG* on the glass window, look in the direction of the noise, and see a punk rocker outside glaring confrontationally at me through the window. My chest goes cold. He either gives me the finger or mutters something before stalking away (in feverish retellings of the story, he does both) and I've been imprinted. I hadn't noticed the guy in the store (he had to have been in there, right?) and—moments later as the frightening march of "Set the House Ablaze" leads to the detonation in the chorus—I know I'll never forget him.

Last week, across the street from my house a girl wearing orange and black made several trips from her car to the house unloading stuff for a Halloween party. My window was open. She'd left the stereo on in her car and Tame Impala's "Yes I'm Changing" played loudly, filling the air. If I hear that song again in ten or twenty years I'll remember this girl, Halloween, and an evocative, ordinary afternoon tableau made tangible by a song. How sound affects things.

Paul Weller's 2018 performance of "Boy About Town" at the Royal Festival Hall is a gently worn paperback; the song's soft from having been carried around for a couple of decades. There are more than twenty Jam, Style Council, and solo albums and countless singles between *Sound Affects* and this moment, and the man who's singing now is a sixty-year-old fitting his hands and voice around an excitable song he wrote when he was barely twenty-two. How's that accomplished? Weller's performed "Boy About Town" fewer than twenty times as a solo artist, and to listen now is to hear a man try and plug himself back in to a young man's humming current. No longer being that young man, Weller adopts a wistful tone, inevitable given the weather in his voice and the decades removed from the shooting sparks of the song's composition. The unobtrusive accompaniment of his backing band and the tastefully arranged orchestral strings create a temperate sound far from the joyous, ardent, mod stomp of the Jam, and Weller, recognizing this, sings in a blend of melancholy and gratitude, bittersweet that the song scores a life of a lifetime ago, grateful that he still feels inspired, and is able, to sing a song about the ways in which the ordinary, daily world might still come alive to surprise us, flaws and all.

DOWN AT THE ROCK & ROLL CLUB

Amplified

I saw the Ramones for the first time after a near-fatal event in the life of guitarist Johnny Ramone. That incident grew into mythic proportions, as do even the simplest moments at a rock and roll show.

I saw the Ramones for the first time in 1984 at the long-gone Wax Museum in Washington, D.C. The band was at the tail end of supporting *Subterranean Jungle*, an album that I pulled out recently to listen to and that floored me, yet again, with its amped-up energy and great guitar sound courtesy of coproducers Ritchie Cordell and Glen Kolotkin. Like each Ramones album since *Road to Ruin*, the record has its detractors, among them the band members themselves (but then they hated everything). Some decry the slick, of-the-era production and drum sound; some lament the three cover songs; some hate the cartoonish cover. Johnny Ramone liked the guitar sound (aided and abetted by ex-Heartbreaker guitarist Walter Lure, who's thanked on the inner sleeve but otherwise uncredited), and he recalls carving out time while recording the album to watch the St. Louis Cardinals / Milwaukee Brewers World Series, and that's good enough for me. Those cover songs—"Time Has Come Today," "Little Bit o' Soul," the Boyfriends' transcendent "I Need Your Love"—are all great, as are the originals "Outsider," "Somebody Like Me," "In the Park," "Time Bomb," and "Psycho Therapy," the opening siren-wailing riff of which thrills me now as much as it did when I first heard it in Reagan America.

What I remember about the show is the scarifying ringing in my ears for a week afterward, yet there was current running through the performance that had nothing to do with the band's considerable Marshall backline. Months earlier, following a gig in Queens, New York, Johnny had been involved in a street confrontation with a twenty-two-year-old named Seth Macklin, a member of the punk band Sub Zero. According to an August 16, 1983, *New York Times* account, Ramone suffered a fractured skull during a fight "that began at 3:50 A.M. when Mr. Ramone encountered Mr. Macklin with a young woman Mr. Ramone had dated. . . . Mr. Ramone, who was born as John Cummings, was injured when Mr. Macklin kicked him in the head near the end of the fight, Sergeant Ruane said. Mr. Macklin was arrested on assault charges and Mr. Ramone was taken to St. Vincent's Hospital where he underwent surgery. The hospital refused to disclose Mr. Ramone's condition."

The following day, the *Times* reported that "punk-rock star" Johnny was in stable condition, and that "Mr. Ramone's friend" was identified as twenty-two old Cynthia Whitney; Macklin, who wasn't injured, "was arrested and charged with first-degree assault, according to the police. He was arraigned and released in his own custody." The Prescott, Arizona, *Courier* also covered the incident in its "Close-Ups" celebrity column, titling the piece "Jealous Rage." Detective Dennis Carroll reported that Whitney thought that she was in "an open relationship, and she was free to be with other people," adding dryly that Johnny "assumed his relationship with the girl was different than she thought." For his part, Macklin claimed self-defense.

Johnny didn't talk about the incident much afterward. In his posthumously published autobiography *Commando*, he devoted a single page to the incident, admitting that he remembered little of the attack that put him in a hospital bed for ten days. "I was thankful that I didn't have brain damage and that I was okay," he wrote,

> but other people said that they saw something different about me after the attack. They thought that it had changed me. I didn't feel any different, but I began to be more cautious, and looked to avoid confrontational situations. I didn't back down, of course, because New York is a confrontational place. But I watched situations more

> carefully, even people around the Ramones who might want to get too close. I did not want to get into another fight. I saw the damage that it had done. I was now more vulnerable to head injuries.

He revealed that Macklin served only a few months in jail. "I went to court and testified. I never heard from him again. I was very angry. I wanted him killed. I'm all for capital punishment," he wrote, adding, "I think it should be televised." Afterward, Johnny worried about going soft, and he peered around a bit more while on the street, bought a gun, and began carrying mace.

Many factors affect the memory of a great show: the songs and the performance; the venue; the size of the crowd; the drugs or alcohol coursing through or absent from your body. Driving or walking home afterward, a show can grow large in our retelling of it. Also graphically affecting a show are the stories that we carry inside of ourselves as we're rocking out, narratives that may or may not have happened to those guys and girls up there onstage, or next to me on the floor, but that cast the evening internally onto an even larger and sometimes permanent stage.

My buddies and I knew none of the details the night of the show, of course. Somehow we'd heard that Johnny had been fighting for his life, the result of a street brawl with some skinhead on a grimy, shadowy street in scary New York City. At the time, I hadn't visited the city since I was a child with my family, and so the imagery in my head quickly grew lurid and exaggerated, a story telling its own story filtered through Lower East Side lore. This is how the imagination works: facts are replaced by desire, what *it* wants. Before the Internet, such vivid conjuring was easy, required even. Down in D.C., because we had no corroboration of, or updates about, the fight, we re-created the incident in our heads, amplifying it to mythic proportions. The details were murky, so we brightened the story with our own internal versions. That we didn't know the incident was bound more by pettiness, toxic masculinity, and romantic politics than righteous fury or virtuous *fuckyou*s only allowed each of us to file the story under any label that we liked: most of us chose punk rock, in that the incident roiled with late-night danger, violence, and aggression in a tableau starring two punk rockers. Later, we decided where we came down on the event, on sexism, on brutal violence, on Johnny's politics, et cetera. As nearly every fact can be searched for and found online now, there's not much time left for mythology to form between an incident and its sharing, and vetting, by millions around the world. Then, what we'd heard was that his head had been shaved for emergency surgery, and afterward he sported uncharacteristically short hair. Maybe even a wig! (It didn't look like it the night of the show, but, then again, it was months after the event.)

That fall, in the tiny record store in the Student Union at the University of Maryland, I held the Ramones' new album in my hands and sensed that the band was working up a little myth of its own: *Too Tough to Die* it was titled. On the cover they emerged, backlit, from a tunnel. Inside they played faster than they ever had.

You Don't Own Me

Infamy's one thing. John Bonham used a mud shark as a sex toy! Rod the Mod had to have his stomach pumped! Paul is Dead! But when a band gets too famous, literally too big for the room, I resist. Hi. My name's Joe. I'm fameist.

I saw the Rolling Stones and the Who at the Capitol Centre in suburban Washington, D.C., in the early 1980s, and both shows were highly memorable yet occurred on the cusp of my exploding love for indie and punk, for bands, many of which were local, whose gigs take place in small, sweaty joints. I was truly baptized as a rock and roll fan in those places. Until very recently, I hadn't seen another stadium-size show, though in retrospect I wish I'd put my biases aside and gone to see Prince, the Kinks, David Lee Roth–era Van Halen, Tom Petty, Bruce Springsteen for sure, and a few others. I'm irrational: I know that fans of enormously successful artists and bands happily spend big bucks to see their favorites in arenas or at sprawling festivals; for many of them, the experience is spiritually gratifying, emotionally rich, exciting. Dwarfed by a huge crowd, one of tens of thousands, spending as much time watching a band on a JumboTron as on the stage: to me this feels like the equivalent of a hundred-person banquet dinner versus an intimate supper for five, of praying with hundreds in a megachurch versus sitting in a back pew with a dozen spiritually hungry folk in a ramshackle wooden church somewhere. I see that I'm getting carried away here: as with any doctrinaire, you can easily poke holes in my argument, call me hipster, pretentious, a sentimentalist, roll your eyes at my piousness while pointing to the sweaty, anointed kid emerging blissful from an arena, pyrotechnics still dancing in her eyes.

Randy Lewis, pop music critic for the *Los Angeles Times*, wrote recently about a transitional phase in the late 1960s when popular bands began moving from performing in revues to playing concerts at larger venues. He holds the development of professional sports responsible for paving the road. "Thanks to back-to-back league expansions by the NBA in 1966 and the NHL the following year," he writes, "a bumper crop of new sports arenas—most notably the Forum in Inglewood and Madison Square Garden Arena in New York—opened to house multiple new sports franchises: 14 NBA teams and a half dozen for the NHL in a relatively short period." Between games, these new venues were usually dark; rather than absorb financial losses, the owners thought to capitalize on off days, tapping new revenue streams by hosting large-scale concerts. An unexpected byproduct was the emergence of arena rock, "a transformation of the concert business that brought dramatic changes not just to the size of venues regularly hosting pop music's biggest names, but to its structure, content and finances."

This transformation allowed musicians literally more space creatively, Lewis observes, a liberty "that carried over into their live shows. Bands quickly began to adapt and expand their presentations to better play to the larger houses. They also were performing for audiences who were maturing with them." He cites bands such as Journey, Kansas, Foreigner, TOTO, Bon Jovi, and others that "played well to big crowds in vast enclosed spaces," indulging in larger sound systems, more stunning light shows, over-the-top costumes, trying to "capture and keep the attention of fans, many of whom sat dozens or hundreds of yards away, rather than within spitting distance," adding that "playing music live became less like an actor's subtle use of facial expression that's possible in the movies, and more like the grand gestures and booming vocal projection of acting in a play in a massive Broadway theater."

For years, I'd been deeply skeptical that a band could play in front of forty thousand people and that the experience might feel intimate, that a band could topple the figurative wall between vast stage and even vaster crowd. I'd never expected to see Green Day. I've loved the band since the mid 1990s, but have long rued that I'd missed my chance to see them in a small club or theater. Since around the time of *Nimrod*, released in 1997, I've watched videos of Green Day performing at enormous venues, and occasionally stadiums, around the world, doubting that such shows could match the informality of a smaller hall. Yet when my pal Dave scored free tickets to a show at Wrigley Field in Chicago and generously asked me along, I couldn't say no. Our seats were at the far end of the right field foul line, lower deck—during a Cubs game we would've been within heckling distance of right fielder Jason Heyward—but the view, it turned out, was pretty terrific. Yes, to be in the pit in front of the stage would've been intense, but our seats' long view gave me the perfect opportunity to see if Green Day could indeed command a stadium.

The show begins with the mock-heroic triumvirate blared over the PA at the start of each gig: Queen's "Bohemian Rhapsody" followed by the Ramones' "Blitzkrieg Bop" (the two songs recorded five months and a galaxy apart) followed by Ennio Morricone's *The Good, the Bad, and the Ugly* theme. Soon after, Billie Joe Armstrong, Tré Cool, and Mike Dirnt leap onto the stage and kick off "Know Your Enemy." Within a verse, Armstrong shows that he's regarding his crowd: he yanks up a guy from the pit who takes over for a verse (after a big bear-hug for the singer). When the song's over, Armstrong counts down and the kid takes off down the ramp, leaps into the pit, and crowd surfs.

And this was still the first song. Armstrong did this twice more, hauling up a young boy to sing a verse of "Longview" and then sending him into the crowd to surf—he looked like a cork atop a roiling sea—and then another guy to shred some guitar during the cover of Operation Ivy's "Knowledge," the once-in-a-lifetime opportunity inspiring the guy to run up and down the drum riser and to ape the end of the song. Twice. (The band happily obliged, before security hustled him off.)

I follow set list; I know that Green Day has featured such "spontaneity" at nearly every show since at least the late 1990s.

Yet there was no denying the ecstasies and laughter that those audience-participation stunts generated, a feeling of goodwill and humor that hummed throughout the park, all the way up into Section 240, where I sat with a dumb grin on my face. I rolled my eyes at the thirtieth "Hey-oh, Hey-oh" call-and-response that Armstrong bellowed from the stage, the three-too-many "HELLO CHICAGO!!" clichés, and the overly elongated songs—but the next morning I awoke and remembered even the most generic gestures with fondness. Armstrong knows that this telegraphed, well-worn, giant-stage theater works, and that when it works, accompanied with the fireworks and the flash pots and the light show, the crowd feels involved and spirited, and when the crowd feels involved and spirited, every song sounds better, every solo sounds inspired, every beer tastes better, all of that fun accumulating as the long night goes on. Armstrong is tireless; his and his bandmates' stamina are magnificent, and the band's willingness to play long and hard is tribute to their affection and respect for their fans and the great experience those fans want, and pay for.

And yet. Ideally, I'd like Green Day to play a two-week residency at, say, the Empty Bottle on the West Side of Chicago (capacity of around four hundred) so that I could watch Armstrong and his band field a smaller venue. Those days of small clubs are long gone for Green Day, and I stupidly lament that fact, though I don't fault the band their mammoth, sought-for success. (Selena Fragassi, reviewing the Wrigley Field show in the *Chicago Sun-Times*, shares my sentiment: "Though Green Day is anthems away from playing the small clubs anymore, it still makes one wonder if returning to places like Metro (which hosted a one-day pop-up shop across the street) just might be the most punk rock thing ever for a band that has gotten very used to the big time.")

Green Day played not just a great stadium show that night, but a great rock and roll show, with hooks, stirring choruses, grins, a well-paced roar of songs with the proper ebbs and flows. I knew in advance that "King for a Day" was going to blend into the Isley Brothers' "Shout"—the band's been doing that for years—but I was dubious about "Shout" blending into the Rolling Stones' "(I Can't

Get No) Satisfaction" and then into the Beatles' "Hey Jude," ancient warhorses all. Yet at that point in "King for a Day," three-quarters of the way through the show, Armstrong, lying on his back, implored the crowd to fuck politics and fuck neo-Nazis and fuck hate speech and by extension fuck Trump, and as he sang "take a sad song and make it better," with his eyes shut, he looked a little embarrassed at the song's shopworn sentimentality but also probably how he looks at home on the floor, alone, singing a song that he digs no matter how overplayed it might be, no matter how many strangers love it for different, corny reasons. It was the most intimate moment of the night—a pretty remarkable occasion considering that he's lying on the stage in front of thousands of people. It lent warmth and texture to everything that had come and everything that followed. Even in the right field stands I felt, as undoubtedly many in the crowd did, that I was crashing on the stage alongside him. Yet the best view—the *only* view for most of us—came on the giant video screens. What I was seeing was what was being broadcast, not what has happening.

On the day of the Green Day show, *Rolling Stone* published an article about *Turn It Around: The Story of East Bay Punk*, a documentary directed by Corbett Redford focusing on 924 Gilman, the Berkeley, California, nonprofit music club that spawned Green Day and many other punk and indie bands in the 1980s and 1990s. (Snippets from the film played on the screens at Wrigley before Green Day took the stage.) Green Day experienced considerable backlash from bands and figures in the small but intense Bay Area scene when they signed to a major label in the mid-1990s, enmity that only increased as the band experienced global success and ultimately a Broadway adaptation of their most popular album. "There was a very vocal few that sort of blew it out of proportion and we felt it," Armstrong said. "But I think the majority of the people in the scene were wrapped up in their own lives, and doing their own thing, you know? Most people were just like, 'You're going your way, and I'm going my way.'"

Still, I couldn't help but think about the many miles that Green Day's trekked from playing weedy Berkley backyards and tiny clubs in front of dozens to enormous stages around the world in front of millions. Back then, Armstrong and others on the scene surely loved the Isley Brothers, the Beatles, and the Stones, but would they have acknowledged it, or played their songs in any way but ironically? At Wrigley Field, Armstrong, a genuine ham, but also a genuine rock-and-roll fan who gets it, ran that gauntlet of sixties classics with love, affection, and an instinct for pleasure. "This is fucking awesome," he said at one point, surveying the phone-lit crowd and ancient Wrigley. "Let's just celebrate this."

A few weeks later I drove east past Illinois farmland on Route 38 through DeKalb and Kane Counties to see the Detroit Cobras at Brauer House, a small pub and eatery in suburban Lombard. The Cobras' patented tipsy strut through obscure, badass rock-and-roll songs was warmly received by a decent-size crowd. It's well known that you roll the dice when you see the Cobras: other times when I've caught the band, lead singer Rachel Nagy, she of the superbly emotive and impossibly timeless voice, had staggered on to and eventually off of the stage. At Brauer House, she was all there: confident if a bit self-conscious in the opening numbers, forgetting some of the words to "Out of This World" ("Because I'm old!" she grinned at the crowd), pausing at one point to indulge herself with a face-bury into the ample cleavage of a besotted fan at the front of the stage. She was fully committed to each bracing song, from the rocking to the "slow skate" ballads, from the silly stuff to the momentous. Whether she's husky close to the mic or rearing back her head and belting from the back of her throat, Nagy inhabits the songs she sings, renewing each of them out of their obscure past, and the decades-old songs feel as relevant as the contemporary rock and roll played over the PA before the set.

The rest of the band were loose, in good humor throughout the night, clearly enjoying themselves and the proximity of the tiny crowd. (A bucket of iced-down Miller High Life's onstage always helps.) The intimacy of the club encouraged banter among the band members and with the crowd; we were all eavesdropping. Songs were spread over the band's several albums, and a new number, the terrific "Feel Good," rocked the joint. The Cobras play only covers of vintage R&B and soul (with the exception of the original "Hot Dog (Watch Me Eat)" from 2004's *Baby*; "'Hot dog' means 'slut' in Detroit," Nagy helpfully informed us), and they play eternal chord changes and song structures so lovingly and with such loose, informal pleasure that they give the impression of summoning the crowd to come crash on the floor with them as they rifle through their great album and 45s collection. At the club that night, such an invitation seemed plausible. The phrase *I Know Where You're Coming From* is emblazoned on the band's drum set. I know exactly where the Cobras come from, too, but on this night they showed that old rock-and-roll songs can sound like they were cobbled together yesterday, in the van.

Watching the Detroit Cobras in a small joint weeks after seeing Green Day in front of tens of thousands was less a study in contrasts than in alternate universes. As professionally rousing as Green Day was, exhorting a packed baseball park to rise, stay risen, and cheer, the Cobras played the room; the band was indivisible *from* the room. Near the end of the set, Nagy ordered a "fire brigade" to bring her a Grey Goose and soda, a feat accomplished with enthusiastic brio by a line of well-oiled fans; the bar, where before the show I sat two stools down from Nagy, who was chatting amiably with a couple fans, was maybe a dozen feet from the stage; I saw band members alight from their van out back and duck in and out of a fluorescent-bathed hallway, at the end of which was their dressing room, which probably also doubled as the bar's stock room. Before the show I practically leaned over Cobra guitarist Mary Ramirez's shoulder as she tuned her instrument and then taped down the set lists; earlier, I'd peered into the other guitarist's case, lying open at the foot of the stage. It was intimate, like reading someone's diary. Nothing can replace the nearness of you, rock and roll.

Nagy died in 2022. The summer before her death, I'd complied a 740-plus playlist of Detroit-area bands for a cross-country drive. Over the course of many hours of that trip, it seemed as if the Detroit Cobras popped up every few songs, grinning emcees to the party, hard-won emissaries of the Detroit rock and roll ethos that they represented so well. I couldn't have asked for better company on that drive. Nagy's voice was ours—by *ours* I mean the rabid community of lifer fans of under-the-radar bands, musicians who write, or in the case of the Cobras, bring to life, the songs that star our interior Top 40, in the alternate reality we fans live, where rock and roll has vital currency.

I'm coming at all of this with some perspective. I played Madison Square Garden on September 3, 1966, with my band J.P. and the Writers in front of a crowd "estimated over 50,000 people." That figure comes from the back of *J.P. and the Writers: Live at Madison Square Garden*, an album rush-released on Capitol Records later in the year. Ignore the fact that the Garden holds about twenty thousand people for a rock concert. And didn't open until February 11, 1968.

Confused? Allow me to provide some (equally apocryphal) context: "On May 4, 1942, Joseph William Bonomo was born at Columbia Hospital at 1 AM. At 10 lbs. Joe was a strapping infant, with a radiant smile that could light up a room. His parents, Philip and Catherine, were proud of their boy and took him home with them to their house on 612 Kanawha Street in northwest Washington, D.C. He grew up in a healthy, normal atmosphere with his three brothers and one sister. On November 9, 1945, his parents brought home Paul Anthony Bonomo from the hospital. Joe took instantly to his little brother and the two grew up in love."

This is the origin story of "Joe Bonomo, Rock Star" as I wrote it when I was eleven or twelve. I can't recall now how this fantasy began, but sometime when I was ten and my brother was seven we concocted a fictional band. We were already besotted with the Beatles, the Monkees, the Partridge Family, Top 40 radio, and the various 45s that our older siblings and their friends brought into the house. Naturally we used the Beatles as our historic model. J.P. and the Writers were alternate-reality American competition to the Fab Four, and our careers spanned roughly the same era: we formed in the early 1960s and broke up in 1970 (though we re-formed in 1973 and played for five or so more years). Paul and

I possessed a cheap gold-foil drum set my parents bought us from Sears (or maybe they purchased it secondhand, or it might've been a hand-me-down from a neighbor), a guitar (actually a toy ukulele with plastic strings called Mr. Banjo), and a desktop tape recorder. We wrote actual songs, dozens of them, and recorded them in our basement, childishly forging verse, bridge, and chorus, faking studio "fade-outs" by slowly walking away from the tape recorder and singing quietly until we stood in the far corner of the room; then we'd rush back to turn off the recorder.

We begged our parents to buy us large sheets of white poster board and inexpensive, three-pack Certron cassettes from Dart Drug, and with kitchen scissors we cut out record covers, and I painstakingly drew the cover art for each album. We eventually upgraded from "Mr. Banjo" to a cheap, child-size electric guitar with a nothing-watt amp that my parents bought me for Christmas at Montgomery Ward (it was bright red and to our ears sounded as loud as if roared through a Marshall stack). We began composing slightly more sophisticated songs on the family piano in the rec room, upstairs from the basement, recording ballads with our lyric sheets and the tape recorder balanced precariously—hoping against hope that our dog Molly wouldn't sneeze or bark during the precious final few moments of the song. She often did.

We stuffed our lyric sheets into a psychedelic-swirl-designed folder, which I still have. As the band's unofficial archivist, I also possess the cassette tapes of our albums, housed in a Dick Tracy lunch box in my basement as they'd resided for years in the basement of our house in Wheaton, Maryland, suburban Washington, D.C., the center of the rock and roll universe.

In the rec room, I spent many afternoons laboriously typing out the official J.P. and the Writers biography on the family IBM Selectric II, cribbing from Roy Carr and Tony Tyler's coffee-table book *The Beatles: An Illustrated Record*: "When Joe was seventeen and Paul was still a ripe fourteen years of age, they started playing together in local diners and rec centers, gathering up whatever money they could and honing their skills. Featuring a wide assortment of material, the two would play anywhere they could. About this time, Joe found a new interest in drumming. A friend in D.C. had shown him his drum set, and soon Joe was banging away on his own. The boys' parents marveled at their talent and were quick to urge it on." By the early 1960s, the duo had a surprisingly large wealth of original material, and "they inched their way up the Washington, D.C., club circuit under the name The Spacemen. It was still just the two of them, but the tightly packed and loud crowds loved the way they rocked in their own special way. One club they were particularly popular at was The Riot where they often would play till the wee hours of the morning, much to the chagrin of their parents." The Spacemen came to the notice of Charley McMilian, a "local businessman who had already signed two groups to contracts on the famous Capitol Records, where he had his job." (Here, I helpfully added, "The year is 1963, and Capitol had already taken a chance on distributing Beatle records in America.") On the fateful day—imaginary, I again remind you—of October 4, McMilian ventured into The Riot, and liked what he saw very much: a "spark and energy in the music compounded with a cache of good original material. He met the boys backstage and talked with them for an hour or so. Within a month, Charley McMilian was their manager."

I have no idea where I'd learned the word "cache" at age eleven. Fast-forward: Joe and Paul win a local newspaper poll as best local band, pocket five hundred dollars in a Battle of the Bands contest, and audition with Capitol Records in New York City, where they "went through the motions for George Best, head of Capitol, who remained expressionless throughout the twelve-song set. Dismayed by Best's ambiguity but comforted by McMilian, Joe and Paul returned to a heroes' welcome in the Nation's capital. The two were beginning to enjoy their success, and at this time Joe began to express the initial stages of the egotistical rampagings that would eventually disintegrate the group. On February 27, 1964, word came from New York: the boys were in. A recording date for their first single was set. The boys hurriedly said goodbye to everyone at home, and headed to the Big Apple."

On the flight, Joe and Paul discussed the band name. The Spacemen was out; J.B. and the Rioters came next but received a flat no from Paul, who sensed his older brother's controlling ways. J.*P.* and the Rioters? No, they decided, their sound wasn't that energetic. They finally settled on a name originally suggested by McMilian in order to minimize the fact that the band was a duo, quartets being all things gear in 1964. The plane touched down in Kennedy Airport, and off walked J.P. and the Writers.

Well, that's how you would've imagined it all, too. At least I gave the destructive and rampaging ego to myself and not to my brother.

Most of the cassettes with our songs have survived. A couple of decades ago, Paul and I attempted to digitally convert them, but even fortified with drink we got through only four "albums" before we could no longer stand the sound of our precocious singing voices. That, and we were laughing so hard we could barely operate the CD-R unit. I'm afraid the tapes would snap if I tried to play them again, so they sit down in the basement, in the dark. The dozens of songs remain, mostly about girls—a subject neither Paul nor I had any inkling about yet knew was the rightful, the just-about-only subject for rock and roll—but also about magic, stars and clouds, numbers, music, and 'lil doggies. We rewrote Gordon Lightfoot's then-popular "Wreck of the Edmund Fitzgerald" as "Fight for the Battle of Sea Time," our own poor boy's epic ballad. We eventually added to the band two imaginary members, a bassist and a drummer, each from England. Concocting a group that was ostensibly a contemporary of the Beatles, we nonetheless suffered hilarious, inevitable anachronisms: the band members I drew for our midsixties album covers looked suspiciously mid-seventies (think Grand Funk, not Herman's Hermits); we covered Beatles songs, not strange in itself, as many 1960s artists covered the Beatles, yet somehow we knew how to play the trippy "Blue Jay Way" three years before George Harrison wrote the song, our version having miraculously appeared on our 1964 debut; we also wrote a patriotic song, "Colonial Days of '76," to celebrate the Bicentennial that was occurring the summer we first began composing songs, yet with no indication that we were supposed to have been writing when LBJ was president, not Jimmy Carter. Etcetera.

But for a couple of kids, we got a lot of things right. The dynamic of fame and success, for starters. During the recording of J.P. and the Writers' *Live at Madison Square Garden*, my brother and I faked the deafening roar of the crowd by pointing a Radio Shack walkie-talkie at the tape recorder, and turning the static up and down before and after songs—squint your eyes and it sounds like a real crowd (minus the occasional frequency interruptions from the WTOP AM radio transmitter located a couple of blocks from our house). To us, a successful rock band played in front of fifty thousand or more people. That was the goal, the pinnacle. At Wheaton Regional, a sprawling public park near our house, Paul and I would on occasion stand on the modest band shell and, having made sure no one was looking, pretend J.P. and the Writers were playing for thousands and thousands of fans, the sea of their undulating bodies and waving arms stretching away for miles. In my feverish eleven-year-old fantasizing I saw things from the other side: how infinitesimal we looked to the fans, and how immense. Paul and I exhaled the crowd's roar into our cupped hands, gave shrill whistles of adulation. The immense adoration, the glory. They were tiny. We were stars.

Remote, celestial, glittering. For centuries we've looked up at them, spun myths about them, read our fates by them. Ingenuity and smarts have allowed us to approach them, circle them, never land. They're too distant, too hot. "Reach for the stars," we're urged with earnestness; the dirty secret is that you likely won't get there. We call someone a star because she's elevated, or her ascension comes with the title. Her light obscures those closest to her, the steps leading toward her. We call someone a star because he's out of reach, and the purer for it. A star is held together by its own luminous gravity, has amassed so much density in its very starness that it needs no one, nothing, only admirers, mythmakers. A star's distance is what makes it so stunning. Starlight. Star shine.

We need telescopes to see them, yet they remain enigmatic, epic. Otherworldly.

Distance and elevation come at a price. "I have to admit I've found myself doing the same things that a lot of other rock stars do or are forced to do," said Kurt Cobain. "Which is not being able to respond to mail, not being able to keep up on current music, and I'm pretty much locked away a lot. The outside world is pretty foreign to me."

Patti Smith: "It was always my belief that rock and roll belonged in the hands of the people, not rock stars."

I never thought I'd see Billie Joe Armstrong live in person if he weren't projected on hundred-foot-tall LED screens beneath smoke bombs and strobe lights. I was wrong. Ever restless to make music, in late 2017 and early 2018 Armstrong ducked into an Oakland studio and recorded a batch of new original songs on which he did everything: sang and played guitar, bass, and drums. He digitally released an EP, an album, and then a clutch of singles, billed the outfit the Longshot, recruited a bass player, drummer, and a second guitarist, and hit the road for a small-club tour. My buddies and I snagged tickets for the show at Black Cat in Washington, D.C., and in late May I stood in a packed, sold-out club with roughly seven hundred others, a dozen feet away from a musician who'd long kept his distance from me.

The Longshot put on one of the better rock-and-roll shows I've seen in years. Liberated from having to roam and command an arena, vibing off the proximity of his sweaty bandmates, Armstrong focused on the pit in front of him and delivered a stirring set of tunes, his and others', obviously pumped that his band's righteous noise was roaring back at him off of near walls and a low ceiling. Exhorting so many massive crowds for so many years seems habitual to Armstrong now; he still couldn't resist the hammy "*hey-oh, hey-ohs*" and *Clapyourhands!* commands at Black Cat, but those jumbo-size gestures were minimal. Instead, Armstrong seemed genuinely inspired by the push and crush and nearness of the crowd. As the show began, I hung back a bit; by the end, turned on and delivered by the melodic, anthemic, eighth-note rush of the Longshot's hooky power pop and garage-y three-chord riffing, I was right up front of the stage, drenched by beer and sweat, elbowed by giddy fans, many of whom were in their teens and twenties blending raucously with older, 1990s-era and *American Idiot* Green Day lifers.

During "Stay the Night," one of two Green Day songs the Longshot played, the figurative wall between the band and the crowd, blissfully thin already, began to come down, and by the end of the tune and into and during the next, a cover of Bobby Fuller's "I Fought the Law," the distinction between the stage and the floor in front of it vanished. One by one, two by two, fans began climbing onto the stage, surrounding Armstrong as he played and sang, eventually filling the stage end to end. On the floor even feet away as I was, jostled and elevated in the scrum, singing along and snapping the odd photo, I lost sight of the band: the crowd had taken over the stage. Armstrong could barely play; he had to leap in the air and swivel midjump to see his drummer to figure out how to end the song. As at Wrigley Field, fans took the opportunity to stage dive, and at Black Cat the leaping fans gave the impression of guffawing kids at a public pool springing off of a diving board. By the end of "I Fought the Law," the crowd of underagers, teenagers, and older fans looked as if it would gladly stay for breakfast onstage if the club would stay open. The vibe was giddy, homey, utterly democratic: fans of all shapes and sizes had taken over the stage, head-banging, selfie-snapping (for many of which Armstrong posed grinning, guitar in hand), smiling, pogo-ing, taking turns singing badly into the mic, gossiping. An undulating organism, collective fist in air. New Orleans R&B and rocker Larry Williams: "Rock and Roll has no beginning and no end, for it is the very pulse of life itself."

At one point in "I Fought the Law," a moment poised between verse and chorus, a young fan leapt into the crowd at Armstrong's prompting. It doesn't matter that such spontaneity happened the night before and the following night, too: this kid will never forget this moment. And if there had to be a point to the mayhem and fun, that was it.

What does a band owe me? Nothing. I feel churlish in my cute, self-diagnosed fameism, as if I'm begrudging a band or an artist their coveted mass success and subsequent distancing from me. I'm drawn perversely to the cramped room, the tiny stage. At what cost? That a band stay small for me? Childishly, I tug at the bond between me and a favorite band, demanding that they stay close. I remain blissfully unaware of the sacrifices made by the band that never makes it beyond the bar but desperately wants to, by the artist who's reaching for the stars but is destined to remain bittersweetly earthbound, where I stay.

In June 2001, I drove around with a New York garage rock-and-roll band in a rented van as they swung through five cities in the Northeast and Midwest on a small tour. The band was unofficially celebrating their twenty-fifth anniversary, but the crowds, as they have been in the States for decades, were thin. In the van one day, naturally curious (well, I'm a snoop), I reached into the open glove compartment and retrieved a folded sheet of paper.

"Oh, lemme have that," the guitarist snapped from the back seat.

"Oh, sorry." I gave the sheet to him.

He hesitated only a moment before shrugging and handing the sheet back to me. "Whatever. I don't care."

The paper was a printout of that night's club's financial guarantee for the band. The figure was small. He'd been mildly embarrassed, and then realistic: *this is what it is*. That night, the band played for a small crowd as if they were playing in front of thousands. I was glad to be part of the phantom many.

On *Exhibitionism*

Can rock and roll be "enshrined" without losing something mysterious and joyful in the process? The Rolling Stones aim to find out.

The tiny flat at 102 Edith Grove in West Chelsea, London, sits in a district that was derided centuries ago as the "World's End." The name still seems apt: from the looks of things, I could push my fist through a water-damaged wall pretty easily, but I'm scared of what I might find living behind it. Small lamps in a few corners offer dingy light. Food-encrusted dishes and sticky glassware are stacked in the sink and on most available surface areas, soiled hand towels of dubious purpose and dozens of half-smoked cigarettes and butts abound, wallpaper is streaked with dirt, days- or weeks-old milk bottles gather like so many low-rent science experiments, trash cans overflow, half-empty beer and liquor bottles waft stale scents of earlier good times. On the three unmade single beds, sheets are stiffened into dioramas.

Stilled in time, just beyond protected glass, these rooms archive a curious blend of chaos and stillness, pungency and airlessness, laddish mayhem and scholarly attention. I'm in Festival Hall B at Navy Pier, in Chicago, attending *Exhibitionism*, the extravagant, multimedia, nine-gallery tribute to the long, successful, apparently never-ending career of the Rolling Stones. The Edith Grove flat, shared by Brian Jones, Mick Jagger, and Keith Richards in the early 1960s, is staged between the "Experience" and "Meet the Band" rooms, appropriately early in the exhibit, as the curated rooms evoke a sense of heedless nowness and of a future erupting, of kids living on their own for the first time indulging in all sorts of youthful obsessions, including absorbing music. The in medias res stereo console in the living room and the various records placed carefully so as to seem strewn about the place—scratchy LPs and 45s by Muddy Waters, Chuck Berry, Bobby Bland, Willie Dixon, et al.—reflect the boys' deepening immersion in the blues, rhythm and blues, and rock and roll, loud music played loudly all day and all night among friends. These meticulously created re-creations capture all of this—this *living*, these smoky hours of giggles and reverence—quite well, and surprisingly so, since they're based not on photographs but on memories of the roommates and of visitors at the time, including Bill Wyman and Charlie Watts.

What am I doing here? I'm a skeptical fan, drawn to the exhibition by my longstanding love for the Stones and their complicated, fascinating career, and by positive word of mouth. Though I natively resist rock and roll under glass, the thesis that music might be dramatized and evoked by objects, truth be told, the amateur archeologist in me is curious. Amy and I visit the exhibit on a beautiful, bright day in May. The breeze is chilly off of Lake Michigan, the choral seagulls above our heads in perfect voice. The sunny pier is full of strolling natives and countless tourists, many lining up in queues for the Seadog or Spirit of Chicago boat tours of the lake, some pushing strollers or leading small children by the hand. There are many young couples, and handfuls of folk enjoying lunch and drinks in the open-air restaurants. At my fanly insistence, Amy and I take the requisite photos of each other posed alongside the several oversize inflatable Rolling Stones tongues outside, dotting the century-old jetty, leading toward the exhibit doors.

How do the Stones attract attention to themselves inside? At the start, with floor-to-ceiling lights and cranked decibels and many, many bright flashing screens blinking image-moments of decades of band and cultural history. In addition to the Edith Grove re-creations, the galleries are stocked with over five hundred career-spanning artifacts that took three years to gather, including dozens of the band's guitars and keyboards; Watts's Ludwig Sky

Blue Pearl-Keystone Badge drum kit, which he played in the studio and onstage from late 1965 through the middle of 1968; bulky analog recording decks and mixing boards; a mock-up of a studio; recording session notes and tape boxes (including some from the band's famous mobile studio); concert handbills and posters; original handwritten lyrics and diaries; album art in-process; miniature, to-scale stage sets and the design history thereof; Warhol lithographs; candid and promotional photographs; a room devoted to a frantically edited dash through the band's music videos, and another room featuring a short film hosted by Martin Scorsese, who holds forth on the artistic quality and cultural value of several Stones tour films; a brief history of the creation and design of the band's tongue logo, featuring a floor-to-ceiling model that changes colors and prints; and dozens of extravagantly over-the-top costumes, primarily Jagger's, worn in promotional photographs and onstage, spanning decades (and tastes!).

Near the end of the exhibit, one enters a taped-off, all-access mock-up of a backstage area, complete with posted set lists, snaking power cords, and piles of roadie equipment and tools. Though corny in its staging of faux authenticity, the room's instructive in demonstrating how Jagger prepares preshow (a small makeup mirror, bottles of Evian water, a steam inhaler), and is frankly thrilling, to this spectator, for the proximity it allows to Richards's and Ron Wood's road-worn guitars, freed from under-glass specimen duty. (Yes, I believe I could've touched Richards's beat-up 1953 Fender Telecaster, were I That Guy at a Museum. And I wanted to be.) The small "backstage" crowd is then ushered by a heroically enthusiastic museum employee through black "stage doors" into a tiny room, where we receive 3D glasses, turn to face a wall-size screen, and watch film of the band tearing through a deafeningly loud performance of "(I Can't Get No) Satisfaction," the encore from a show at Hyde Park, in London, on July 6, 2013. The 3D enhancement is, as is usually the case to my eyes, kind of silly; if it weren't for the occasional foregrounded mic stand or speaker stacks or the millions of descending rose petals, I wouldn't have noticed much. This version of "Satisfaction" (I believe it's the band's 11,375,298th performance of the song) is decent, energetic and elongated with call-and-response Yeahs! from a tireless Jagger, and features as a guest Mick Taylor, the band's lead guitarist during the 1969 to 1974 peak era, who during the band's 2013–14 "50 and Counting Tour" appeared with the Stones onstage, at the historically minded band's invitation. After the song, doors open on the opposite side of the room from where we entered. Departing, we dutifully hand back our 3D glasses and enter a penultimate gallery featuring several more rare, glassed-off objects, including Watts's National Jazz Band "London Outfit" traveling toy drum kit, circa 1930, and the Phillips cassette recorder that Watts and Richards used to record the lo-fi, raw, timeless "Street Fighting Man," in 1968.

We discover that we can't return to the exhibit. We're funneled into the last, and in many ways most revealing gallery room, the gift shop. ("A great department store, easily reached, open at all hours, is more like a good museum of art than any of the museums we have yet established." —John Cotton Dana)

In 1997, Alan Artner, art critic for the *Chicago Tribune*, wrote "In Defense of Elitism," in which he hoped to restore the luster that had been stripped of that term in the twentieth century. "Can anyone recall another word that has been so completely reversed in meaning?" he wonders.

> Less than a half-century ago, aspiring to the elite in any field was among the most honorable of life's endeavors. An intellectual elite earned our trust for having surpassed everyone else in the uncompromised pursuit that is learning for its own sake. An artistic elite inspired our awe for having created on a level so far above the rest of us that only a word with magical associations—"genius," which originally meant a guardian spirit—adequately described them. How did a faith in the highest and most desirable come to be understood among Americans as something ugly and exclusionary?

Artner pivots toward museums, which, when founded in the United States in the middle of the nineteenth century, "operated on the same elitist principle. They were not built for visitation by the many. It was understood that few people at any time truly seek to perceive what challenging artists are up to. This was unfortunate for artists who during their lives did not enjoy such understanding. But it's the way things were, are and will be. Many are called, few are chosen."

By the end of the nineteenth century, art museums, shaken by evolutionary theory, stirred by challenging philosophies, and mindful of growing audiences, began embracing aesthetics, "a 'religion of art' that raised up and ennobled the faithful."

> This led to the misunderstanding that art, like diet or exercise, was a way toward mass self-improvement. . . . A few people did have positive reactions, though only after repeating the experience several times, learning something about the artists, understanding the range of their outputs, perceiving its relation to that of other artists and grasping their relative mastery of techniques and styles. But even then, aesthetic pleasure being different from moral or intellectual betterment, the exact nature of a supplicant's change remained unquantifiable, mysterious.

He continues, "There lies the late 20th Century myth that one of the most profound experiences in life, the meaningful perception of art, is an American birthright. The highest order of artistic experience is for everyone. This has been the message of museums in our time, though it is patently untrue. The art that can give such experience should be available for everyone, but that's something different. Availability and understanding—one does not automatically lead to the other." The larger and more expansive museums became, Artner feels, "the more they propagated the myth, as they required more and more visitors to keep in business. If the click of the turnstile was not as quick as expected, something was wrong, but surely not the guiding principle. The highest order of artistic experience was supposed to be for everyone."

Yet, Artner argues, artistic experience is *not* for everyone.

> But because for so long we said it was and still it has not turned out to be so—think of children who were given every educational and financial advantage yet as adults could not care less about high

> culture—we now say lower the order, it's too elitist. Funders tell art museums to give people more of what they already know. Substitute what easily succeeds with the many for what arduously has succeeded with the few.
>
> In that way, museums will assure their own continuance. But what for? So they can provide a cornucopia of fun experiences? The finest works of art, no matter their continent of origin, are not fun. They do not give themselves at once, by osmosis, as visitors stroll past as in a shopping mall, for diversion. The finest works of art lead away from the immediacy of fun to a more gradually achieved condition of pleasure—which calls for a process requiring work.

Later, Artner argues that great art "does not excite us like sports or entertain us like movies. It does not titillate us like the Web or get us moving like rock music." He's clearly insisting on a stark, value-laden difference between, say, high art and pop music, between expression of the highest, most challenging order and low, body-driven impulses. The considerable limits of his argument aside, a worthwhile question surfaces: Is there a place for rock and roll in a museum? (And is it a problem if you're having fun there?) After my one and only visit a couple of decades ago to the Rock and Roll Hall of Fame in Cleveland, Ohio, I fantasized about a marauding group of (good-natured) juvees who, once assured that the building is empty after closing, blow up the place. At the time, that seemed a more appropriate rock and roll gesture to me than entombing hundreds of objects behind glass, not to mention the tiresome, narrow-minded politics involved in who does and who doesn't get voted into the Hall. (I've since evolved a bit in my thinking about the place. More open-minded about its cultural value, I no longer wish to see it leveled, but I doubt I'll ever go back.)

Who, or what, is *Exhibitionism* for? Navy Pier, Incorporated, certainly ("the click of the turnstile"). The band's fans, of course. The Glimmer Twins and Company's coffers, yes, and I don't begrudge the band and their vast numbers of employees that; the cash registers were bulging on the day I visited the exhibit. Are the Stones' strutting cannon and unruly spectacle too low for a museum? Of course not. The history and cultural context in *Exhibitionism* are worthy of the kind of sustained survey and elevated status common to museum exhibitions. The Stones have written and recorded songs that have moved people, literally and figuratively, as urgently as any other human expression has, and they were pivotal figures in the popular, politically complex midcentury synthesizing of Black influences, expression, and culture, in the collapse of the divide between so-called High and Low Art, and in the broadening chasms between and among the generations.

But the real issue for me is what I'll call the index of mystery, and what Artner calls the unquantifiable: there will always be a tantalizingly narrow gap between what an exhibit about rock and roll might do, and what a rock and roll show can do, a gap somewhere between control and chaos, between structure and unpredictability. "There's some incredibly interesting things that go along with the Rolling Stones, and it's not actually the members themselves," Richards remarked in 2015. "All of the bits and pieces, and technology, and instruments and stuff—the things that have passed through your hands in that time. Very interesting—at least to me, because half of them are stolen!" I love this observation, where Richards nails both the appeal and the limitations of *Exhibitionism*: the guitars "and stuff" versus a bandit's thieving spirit, the sexy, maybe dangerous essence of rebellion. Simple to catalogue the former. But the latter?

When I saw the Rolling Stones on their 1981 *Tattoo You* tour at Capital Centre in Landover, Maryland, I was in the second row, and Jagger flew over my head in a cherry picker, dispensing flowers. He was so close that I could see the makeup caking on his sweaty face and momentarily peer into his eyes, which looked disinterested, "far away," as the guys sang on *Some Girls*. Now when I recall the first moments of that show's opening song, "Under My Thumb," the thrill and fear in my chest return, the impossibly loud lines from Richards's Fender and the boom of Watts's snare ringing and reverberating from the inside of my body out. The heady smell of sweat and weed, the sight of knocked-out girls around me in tight Stones jersey-tees, the sudden plunge of the (long gone) Capital Centre into darkness, the slowly revolving stage revealing a prancing Jagger, the ear-ringing sound and spectacle. It's all there, still, when I conjure or hear those opening notes. Such sensuality is difficult, if not impossible, to re-create materially; only in my memory and imagination am I brought fully back. The 3D film of "Satisfaction" tries to emulate a concert experience, but missing are the flying elbows, the flirty glances, the sweat and the smells. We stood in an airless room with paunchy tourists and watched a short film.

The coolest attractions in *Exhibitionism* are Watts's drum kit (the very set he played on some of the band's greatest recordings) and the "mixing boards" a couple of galleries over. Here, on small screens, you can access recordings of eight of the band's songs—"Rocks Off," "Start Me Up," "Miss You," "Angie," "Undercover of the Night," "Doom and Gloom," and live versions of "Honky Tonk Women" and "Sympathy for the Devil"—track by track, raising or lowering digital faders to isolate vocals, guitars, drums, keyboards, horns, et al., or to blend, or "mix," any group of tracks in any arrangement you wish. Tethered to headphones, we got off on these boards, jamming and dancing around as we set off Jagger's raggedy street vocals on "Miss You" against Watt's spare, funky drumming, dug the raw rhythms of Richards's guitar riding the choppy waters of "Rocks Off," or marveled at the prettiness of the piano and the acoustic guitars in "Angie," stark and lovely echoing intimately on their own in a distant studio. These mixing boards offer sounds of something real, of moving hands on frets and throat muscle and sinew and bum notes and fuckups—the nowness of making music, the ensemble playing of this great groove band ironically highlighted by attention paid to the individual parts, the guitars' wandering reined in by the drumming, the vocals given dimension and cushion by the bottom-end bass playing. *Exhibitionism* felt the most alive, not to mention the most fun, to me here, at my fingertips, as I allowed myself the fantasy of moving around parts of a spontaneous creative process that the rest of the exhibit kept sealed off from me. I was curating, arranging my own exhibit in my own ears. (I have new respect for how a song and an album are mixed.) I wish they'd included more songs. I was barely aware of anyone else around me; I could've spent hours doing this. ("A record is a concert without halls and a museum whose curator is the owner." —Glenn Gould)

Every once in a while, you stumble upon the right rock and roll band playing on the right night—right for them, and for you. This has happened to me more than once, happily, but never quite as urgently as on a night more than thirty years ago when I caught the Oysters at the 9:30 Club in Washington, D.C. I don't remember what drew me and my buddies to the show; I know I hadn't heard their debut album yet; probably it was just a random night out; maybe they were opening for Lyres. (Both bands hailed from Boston.) Whatever the reason, there I was, drunk, young, ready for anything, and the Oysters blew me away. I was astonished at their coming-apart-at-the-seams playing, their literal crashing into one another onstage, the tuneful, anthemic noise, their beery grins often fading to desperate looks when it sounded, and likely felt, as if everything was going to fall apart: the song, the band, the friendships, maybe a romance, maybe my night. But the Oysters held it together for a show that's remained secure on my list of all-time favorites.

If I'd seen the Oysters the night before or the night after, would they have sounded and looked as if they were saving rock and roll, as they did the night I saw them? Maybe they were really on (or desperately off), maybe I was in the right place at the right time to have rock and roll grace bestowed on me. One image stands out: the bass player J. R. leaping and then landing on the band's crashing note at the end of some sloppy song—or was it the ragged opening of another?—a messy grin on his face, *We pulled it off!* He looked like a kid who'd made a half-court shot, or like a younger brother who'd begged the band to let him play with them, *Just for tonight!* When I later picked up their one and only album (*Green Eggs and Ham*, released on Taang! in 1985; the band broke up within a year), there was J. R. in a group shot, wearing his guitar and more or less the same expression. I was happy to see that.

The album disappointed me—it had to. The drums sounded smaller, the guitars less raucous, the indefinable and unpredictable maelstrom of a show—sweat and girls and beer and a night without end and the surprise of being surprised by a great band, the threat of all of that—couldn't possibly be reproduced. But that's okay. I have the memories. I did write a review of the show for the late great D.C. punk zine *WDC Period*, but my copy of the issue is long gone. That's okay, too: all I need is what I saw, though it's disappearing a little over time: a young band of reckless kids hitting a stage, plugging in, and taking everyone and themselves down a shockingly steep hill that bottom of which is both blessed and regretted.

Around this time, I went to see the hardcore punk band Government Issue at the Sanctuary Theater on Columbia Road, in D.C. Afterward, a bulky, locally legendary skinhead named Lefty chased me and my friends up 15th Street and tossed rocks at us, loudly denouncing my sport jacket and skinny tie. I was in my mod phase. "This ain't prom night!" she yelled. The rumor was that she put a guy in the hospital in Philly. We were scared to death, and ran.

I conflate this show with another from around this time, the ska band Bad Manners at the 9:30 Club. Afterward, out on F Street, my friend Marty and I removed our vintage, old-man baggy suits we'd bought at a thrift shop that day and, guffawing, wrung sweat from them as if they were dishrags.

Exhibits from the Rock and Roll Museum of the Ineffable.

In the short film at *Exhibitionism*, Martin Scorsese mentions that as a young filmmaker, and a fan, what drew him to the Stones' music was the contact it made with the "dark nature of human experience." (Scorsese often uses the band's songs in his films; think "Jumpin' Jack Flash" and "Tell Me" in *Mean Streets*, "Monkey Man" and "Memo from Turner" in *Goodfellas*, "Can't You Hear Me Knocking" in *Casino*, and "Gimme Shelter" in *The Departed*, songs that soundtrack joyful depravity, desperation, and menace.) Scorsese cites *Cocksucker Blues*, the still-unreleased documentary of the Stones' 1972 American tour directed by photographer Robert Frank, whose grainy, grittily surreal black-and-white work graced the cover of the band's *Exile on Main Street*, arguably their greatest album. Over time, the film became legendary for its furtive, myth-creating absence. After watching it, band members allegedly were mightily embarrassed and, fearing the potentially incriminating material, lobbied to have the film shelved permanently; eventually a court ruled that, beginning in 1979, Frank could screen the film, at first with a Stones-edited and -approved version, but no more than four times a year and only when he himself was present in the theater. One of these rare screenings, with a Q&A with the director, took place at an art film house in D.C. in the 1980s, but I couldn't attend.

I regretted this for years afterward. Envious, I hung on every word of my older brother's friend who saw it, and marinated in my head lurid re-creations of the movie's scenes, of topless girls with lidded eyes and explicit smiles. What I'd heard about the film was pure raunch: hard drug use, of the smoked, snorted, and injected variety; groupie gang-bangs on planes and in hotel rooms; television sets launched out of high-rise windows; and, yeah, some great live rock and roll. You can find snippets of the film on YouTube, but act fast, as they're usually removed swiftly. The few scenes that accompany Scorsese's comments at *Exhibitionism*—drunken stumbling about; laughing girls' tops being yanked off; dazed women wandering pants-free up and down plane aisles; Richards and a buddy, the sax player Bobby Keys, tossing that TV set out the hotel window—offer glimpses of the debauchery. The rumor that gained the most traction down the years was that during group sex on the plane, one of the band members accompanies the goings-on by banging on a tambourine. That kind of stuff.

Yet, the myth that is *Cocksucker Blues* was deflated a bit when news leaked that some of the sex scenes were staged. The Stones, who have a long history of courting a particular rough-boy, outcast image, were charged with re-creating—with curating, really—their own nastiness in the spirit of cinema vérité. In 1977, *Rolling Stone* reported that Frank had approached a groupie during filming and said, "We want a chick to fuck someone on the plane for the movie." As Charlie Finch writes at *Artnet*: big deal, right? "The tiresome Stones publicity machine has beaten the dead horse of the famous airplane pussy-eating scene as being 'staged,' conveniently forgetting that, as Truman Capote, who makes a brief appearance in the film with [New York socialite and fashion icon] Slim Keith and [Atlantic Records cofounder and president] Ahmet Ertegun, pointed out, 'everything the Stones do is note for note exactly the same night after night.'" One might see the sex on the tour plane, manipulated for camera lenses, as one sees the Edith Grove flat re-creation at *Exhibitionism*, manipulated for lines of attendees: reality staged, bottle by bottle, girl by girl, note for note.

> "If someone wants to know what I did in 1965, they can look it up on Wikipedia."
>
> —MICK JAGGER

Three and a half miles south of Navy Pier, at 2120 South Michigan Avenue, stands the modest building that from 1956 to 1965 housed the Chess label and studios, "hallowed ground," as Richards describes the place in his 2010 memoir, *Life*. (In the early 1990s, Willie Dixon's widow, Marie, bought the building, renovated it, and reopened it in 1997 as Willie Dixon's Blues Heaven Foundation, which offers tours, a concert series, and educational scholarships.) In the second week of June in 1964, the Stones stopped in at Chess to record a handful of tracks, positively knocked out at visiting the label on which so many epochal records had been issued by artists they revered, among them Bo Diddley, Howlin' Wolf, and Muddy Waters. The band was in the middle of an American tour, between gigs in San Antonio and Minneapolis, and were well-oiled, loose, and eager to record. "There in the perfect sound studio, in the room where everything we'd listened to was made, perhaps out of relief or just the fact that people like Buddy Guy, Chuck Berry and Willie Dixon were wandering in and out, we recorded fourteen tracks in two days," a still-amazed Richards recalls, songs including, over the two-day sessions, "Don't Lie to Me," "I Can't Be Satisfied," "It's All Over Now," "Time Is on My Side," "Around and Around," "Confessin' the Blues," "Down the Road Apiece," "Empty Heart," "If You Need Me," "Look What You've Done," "Reelin' and

Rockin'," and their grooving instrumental tribute to their place of worship, "2120 South Michigan Avenue."

Also at Chess on that first day, a myth emerged. "Some people, Marshall Chess included, swear that I made this up, but Bill Wyman can back me up," Richards insists. "We walked into Chess studios, and there's this guy in black overalls painting the ceiling. And it's Muddy Waters, and he's got whitewash streaming down his face and he's on top of a ladder." He adds, "And also Bill Wyman told me he actually remembers Muddy Waters taking our amplifiers from the car into the studio. Whether he was being a nice guy or he wasn't selling records then, I know what the Chess brothers were bloody well like—if you want to stay on the payroll, get to work."

Here's Bill Wyman's take on that visit, from his exhaustively detailed 2002 chronicle *Rolling with the Stones*: "The next day we helped Stu [Ian Stewart] unload the equipment from the van, when who should appear beside us but the great Muddy Waters himself. We were staggered, lost for words. What shook us even more was when he helped us carry our things into the studio. Muddy very definitely was not up a ladder painting the studio, he was a major star at this time and had been for years." Wyman is well-known as the band's archivist—a hoarder, the lads affectionately call him—having over the decades obsessively collected and itemized scores of Stones memorabilia. There's a wide gap between archive and legend, between the certainty of a document and the desire of memory. Here, the collector contradicts the myth spinner. Whom do you believe? Whom do you want to believe?

ROCK AND ROLL MUSEUM OF THE INEFFABLE: A TRIPTYCH

FIRST PANEL

Chicago's Ukrainian Village. I was feeling placeless and lonely. I'd arrived early for a show at the Empty Bottle, and learned that the headliner wasn't hitting the stage until midnight. So: between sampling the opening bands, I sat in my car for an inning or two of the

White Sox game, hit a couple bars along Western Avenue, walked. I'd driven in from DeKalb, far enough from home that I was obligated to linger in the city—a favorite pastime of mine, yet on this night, inexplicably, a somewhat sorry sentence. I gazed up into silent, yellowed windows on the upper floors of brownstones along Oakley Boulevard and on Cortez and Thomas Streets, gnawingly possessed by a blend of self-pity, curiosity, and grimly acknowledged fate that I recognized from adolescence, when I'd slowly drive alongside the impossibly gorgeous and stately homes and sprawling apartment buildings along upper Connecticut Avenue in D.C. and pine for the imagined lives inside, feeling them so beyond my reach as to be fictional. In "Street Haunting," Virginia Woolf, having walked the streets of London one night, possessed by a similar, moody wanderlust, writes, "And what greater delight and wonder can there be than to leave the straight lines of personality and deviate into those footpaths that lead beneath brambles and thick tree trunks into the heart of the forest where live those wild beasts, our fellow men?" Woolf returned home that evening, changed; most cities in which I don't live stir this *What might have been* in me—it happens to you, too, I know. But this night felt different, a gathering of doubts and missed opportunities that created a burdensome gray internal weather. Hours later in the club, standing on the top step of the landing at the far edge of the dance floor, a beer in hand, my forlorn mood began lifting as I watched the eternal routine of band members hauling their gear to the stage, plugging in, tuning up, exchanging small talk and jokes with the sound guy and with the previous band members now straggling off, taping handwritten set lists to the monitors, opening a couple of beers or water bottles, huddling and muttering among themselves, shading their eyes and peering hopefully into a room now subtly charged and changing by lowered house lights, the modest gathering of people moving toward the stage, curious, alive.

SECOND PANEL

The assignment in Introduction to Creative Writing was to write a sensory snapshot poem. I tried to capture a moment that occurred at the end of the long hallway in the 9:30 Club when, as I was waiting in line to get tickets, the thick glass doors opened and closed and in the interval out poured—stormed, charged!—a couple seconds of the Slickee Boys playing, a key moment in their tune "Here to Stay." I was angry that I was missing the show, the divide between me and the song made so graphically vivid, hopelessly large by that moment of amplified rock and roll, which also brought with it and into my body the smoke and weed and beer and cocaine and promises made and broken and the darkness dotted with lights and roiling with movement and the melancholy of the drive back home up 16th Street.

THIRD PANEL

High on a great show, my ears ringing a bit, I'm in a slowly moving mass of people, all pressed together closely, shuffling our feet, inching toward the exit doors. A woman in front of me reaches behind and grabs my belt near my zipper, slips her fingers in the loop and pulls me up against her butt. In a moment I know what's up. "Ooops, wrong guy, you've got the wrong guy," I say to the top of her head. She glances behind and, appalled, let's go of me and wraps her arms around her chest. "God, I'm sorry. That's so embarrassing," she says, searching over my shoulder for her boyfriend, a dude or two behind me. "No problem. It's packed in here." The moment was very sexy, a surprise of intimacy, two strangers pressing against each other. I was her man, for the moment. If this had happened to me when I was younger, I would've gone home that night and tried to write a poem or a short story about it, and fail epically.

"Actually meeting your heroes, your idols, the weirdest thing is that most of them are so humble, and very encouraging. 'Play that lick again,' and you realize you're sitting with Muddy Waters. And of course later I got to know him. Over many years I frequently stayed at his house. In those early trips I think it was Howlin' Wolf's house I stayed at one night but Muddy was there. Sitting in the South

Side of Chicago with these two greats. And the family life, loads of kids and relatives walking in and out. Willie Dixon's there . . ."

That's Richards in *Life*, vibing on the warmth and brotherhood of a long career experienced and on occasion shared with the great bluesmen he's idolized since he was a teenager. In 2015, Netflix released *Keith Richards: Under the Influence*, a documentary made to accompany Richards's album *Crosseyed Heart*, and in it Richards shares an anecdote with the director Morgan Neville. He brings Neville along to visit Waters's old house in Chicago, and remembers a night when Willie Dixon accompanied him to a party there. "It was a lot more vibrant last time I was here," he says in front of the dilapidated home with a padlocked front door and the word "Muddy" and a pink flamingo painted on each door window pane. "It was rocking when I got here, I remember that. It's leaving I don't remember!" He's smiling now. "I crashed out here, but I woke up at Howlin' Wolf's house. I don't know what happened—I got carried away. The party continued, and I went with it!" I searched *Exhibitionism* in vain for the gallery that showcased this rock and roll journey from legend to legend creating legend in the forgotten dark.

Let's Have a Big Fuckin Party

And check your common sense at the door.

In March 1993, the Devil Dogs—guitarist and singer Andy "The Fabulous Andy G" Gortler, bassist Steve Baise, and drummer Mighty Joe Vincent—gathered with the Fastbacks' Kurt Bloch at Egg Studios in Seattle to cut *Saturday Night Fever*, an album that re-creates the sonic blast of a crowded house party in all of its beery, humid, ear-ringing glory. The idea feels a little dangerous these days, no matter that it was put over with a half grin. Folks inside drinking, rocking, and yelling only feet away from the band? Not during COVID, sadly. But on the prowl in the mid-1990s, I needed this album, and return to it when I'm jonesing for a dose of lo-fi, amped-up, three-chord rock and roll, especially now as the memories of sweaty, packed clubs grow dim. The band having plugged in to something eternal back then, the album never disappoints.

The Devil Dogs turned to Bloch following an unhappy experience with their previous record, and their first with Vincent, *We Three Kings*. "We really had great songs on that LP," Baise told me, "but the mastering got screwed up, and we took the heat for it." That record had been the third Dogs album produced by the Raunch Hands' Mike Mariconda, and as the band was already planning out *Saturday Night Fever*, Mariconda suggested that they consider doing the record with someone else. "That was odd," Baise acknowledges now, "but we love and respect him. He knew we had a great one in us and he knew enough to step aside and allow someone else to take us there." After returning from a tour of Japan during which they'd dug Supersnazz's album *Superstupid!*, produced by Bloch, the Dogs knew who they wanted manning the boards for *Saturday Night Fever*.

By the time the guys arrived at Egg Studios, they were primed. "We rehearsed the shit out of those songs for months," Baise says, "then did an eight-week tour ripping those songs a new ass for two weeks before Seattle." He adds, "I believe we recorded four ten-hour days straight, and played three nights live." The Devil Dogs had no trouble acclimating themselves to the homespun charms at Egg. Gortler told Eric Davidson in *We Never Learn: The Gunk Punk Undergut, 1988–2001*, "They talk about these famous studios—the Hit Factory, the Power Station, Olympic Studios in London. The places that I work in are like in some guy's house, in the basement, next to the recycling bin. That's what Egg Studios is, Conrad Uno's basement. But Kurt really did know his shit. It sounds great!"

"The idea for the Live Party atmosphere was Andy's," Vincent told me. "He wanted it to sound kinda like the *Beach Boys' Party!* album, like the vibe of 'Barbara Ann.'" Bloch concurs: "It was their idea to make it a party scene—We Are the Devil Dogs and You Have Been Invited to a Party!" That was the idea." Says Baise, "We always treated what we did as a special occasion. Andy orchestrated when everyone yelled or screamed." When Capitol Records hyped *Beach Boys' Party!* in 1965, the label distributed bags of potato chips featuring the album's cover art to record stores and radio stations. One can only imagine what Crypt Records might've sent as a promotional item with *Saturday Night Fever*: a shot glass? A bottle opener? A barf bag?

Vincent acknowledges that *Saturday Night Fever* was the Dogs' "most planned and concentrated effort." The majority of the material was written and demoed at a studio in Brooklyn, and then battle tested on that long cross-country trip from New York to Seattle. "We were going to treat the recording just like another gig," he said. "Just set up in the studio with Kurt and rip through our set. Then we saved an overdub track where we were gonna put backing vocals and tambourines and stuff for the party. So on the last day we invited everyone we knew in Seattle to come to a party at Egg, which was not a very large room, got a bunch of beers, and had everyone making noise and getting drunk in the background. We got them to sing along on some stuff too." The Dogs cut twenty songs, fourteen for *Saturday Night Fever*, the remaining six spread over an EP and a single. Bloch recalls a highly productive week of orchestrated carousing. "The party was probably the last night of the session," He told me. "They'd invited their Seattle friends over for beers and a listening session. We must've had a pretty good idea of the album's running order, and they'd done a Seattle gig and a Bellingham gig during that week so we managed to load up the tiny recording room with likeminded revelers." Bloch and Gortler each had to don a poor man's conductor hat, as the party hadn't heard the record yet, "so it was hard for them to know where to clap along without some corralling, but it worked great!"

As Egg was set up in the basement of a house, "we'd have to be finished by ten p.m. each night due to the neighbors," Bloch remembers. "No-one really up and running very early in the day-times. But what a raging session. Once they got warmed up and rolling, there was no stopping them. And so goddam funny they were. Nonstop slapstick. Glad we recorded everything the way we did, 'cause there wouldn't have been nearly enough time to have done it any other way." The Dogs laid down the scorching tracks, live, with all involved working and hollerin' in the same room, "kinda the modus operandi of all good sessions," Bloch feels. "A few guitar overdubs and some vocals. It was all their raging energy that made it as killer as it is."

Saturday Night Fever starts with idle party noise: some high-spirited chatter, stray handclaps to urge on the band who's taken "the stage" (probably the floor, feet away from the partygoers). Someone remarks that he could seriously use some beer. Just as someone else gets up the nerve to ask the girl next to him, "What did you say your name was?" the plugged-in Dogs count in, hit a deafeningly loud chord, and Gortler steps to the mike: "It's so good to see all my friends down here tonight, and I know—I *know*—everybody's ready to have a good time, yeah!" "We are!" someone retorts, and after Gortler compliments everyone for looking good, the set rockets off with the evening's theme song, the stomping "Big Fuckin Party"—part one, that is. The song's reprised at the album's end. "I think that was Kurt's idea," Vincent says. "We recorded it as a whole and I think it clocked in at over four minutes! That is absolutely forbidden in Punk Rock world, and certainly in [Crypt Records honcho] Tim Warren's world! So it got split in two sections which open and close the album. I thought that was a brilliant touch."

The album detonates one killer cut after another—sounding, as in the best rock and roll, that each song might implode before it finishes, that the band is letting the music play them rather than the other way around, all of it sent to the ceiling by a boisterous gang of partying friends. "I was worried that someone would break something down [in the basement]," Bloch said, "but I think it was all fine. Not the first drunken party in that room, that's for certain."

The band threw in a few covers: the Victims' "Dance with You Baby," Gary Glitter's "Shakey Sue" (left off of the CD version), Gene Pitney's "Backstage," and a quickly arranged take on the Rolling Stones' "It's Not Easy" (Baise: "Andy said it could be done in five minutes, and he was right, as usual.") Each cover slotted in nicely next to snarling yet catchy originals such as "Gonna Be My Girl," "I Don't Believe You" (my personal fave from the record), "Back in the City," "6th Avenue Local," and "Sweet Like Wine." The band's take on "Backstage" is especially great, a desperate, heart-on-sleeve ballad about the loneliness of a rock star's life. No backstage in this joint, maybe a tiny bathroom off of the hall. The guitar's loud and distorted, the drums and bass rumble, yet the songs' considerable hooks are strong enough to withstand the assault. Everything's played at breakneck speed yet as tightly as a Swiss watch, sung with half grins and that intangible urgency that arises when a band knows it's locked in.

Just before the Dogs reprise "Big Fuckin Party," a reveler shouts "Uh oh, somebody's in trouble!" while another asks "Hey, what's in the box?"—a little off-stage narrative mystery and a great touch of drunken verisimilitude, reminding the listener that at every party there are always a few smaller parties working the room, all kinds of fun and drama catching fire, blazing, and burning out during the course of the long night. Alas, we'll never know what was in that box . . .

"All the memories [of the session] are great," Baise says. "We were so ready to record that record," he says, adding, "We were taken care the whole time by really fucking nice, cool folks. I will say we always minded our shit and always kicked ass." Vincent added one more thing, "which sounds kinda name-droppy, because it is. After the album came out, one of the dudes from the Sinister Six was at a party in Seattle and Eddie Vedder was there. The guy put *Saturday Night Fever* on the stereo and Eddie *loved* it!"

The next day, the guys found a note slipped under the door that read:

> Thanks for turning me on to the greatest Rock'n'Roll record EVER!
> Your friend,
> Eddie

Let's hope the cops don't show up.

RANDOM PLAYS AND B-SIDES

"I'll Get Her!"

After Van Halen finished recording "Everybody Wants Some!!" during the 1979/1980 sessions for *Women and Children First*, the band could've looked at each other, collectively shrugged, nodded, and as the dust settled in the studio, muttered, *Yeah, well, we're never gonna top that.* From its primordial, crawling-from-the-ooze opening, "Everybody Wants Some!!" sounds like the very birth and cry of The Rock and Roll Song. So simple and elemental is the song's preverbal rumble, so perfect is its humor, winking earnestness, strutting, mock-heroic, man-on-the-make spectacle, gigantic, hooky guitar riffs, throbbing drums, and universal sing-along chorus that, in it, Van Halen perfected itself, and, arguably rock and roll, too. Why the hell continue to write? Play a last enormous pay-per-view gig somewhere, end with this tune, and call it a career.

Of course, had Van Halen indulged my little alternate history, we wouldn't have had the epic "Mean Street" or "Unchained" from *Fair Warning*, "Top Jimmy" or "Hot for Teacher" from *1984*, and whatever your post-1980, David Lee Roth-era Van Halen favorites are. And we wouldn't have had "Panama," maybe Van Halen's greatest rock and roll song—certainly one of the great rock and roll songs of the 1980s—a sonic statement of purpose from a larger-than-life band, and another one that was pretty damn hard to top. Roth would split the band in 1985, taking with him his grab bag of swagger, self-importance, hilarity, sparkly scarves, insecurities, and intuitive grasp of spectacle. The band was never the same again.

I courted my wife Amy with mixtapes and cheap drinks, not with a cool car. Never a gear head or a big automobile dude, I drove a piece-of-shit Ford Taurus, the two-liter engine of which whined mournfully as it bravely ascended the hills of Athens County, in Ohio, where Amy and I met. The engine never sounded particularly sexy; it sounded needy. But it got us around. (I did manage once, when we were parked, to get both front seats to lean back simultaneously with teen-sex-movie panache, but that was mostly luck.)

Though I didn't fantasize about cars or car culture, like anyone else I bought into the myth. I marveled at the Duke Boys' General Lee Dodge Charger stock car as it leaped over swamps, gators, and hapless cops. I can still feel the vividness of the *tough* that some kid behind me muttered in the movie theater, where we sat in the dark watching *Smokey and the Bandit*, as the Bandit's Trans Am sexily slithered into view. (I also took close note of Sally Field's evolving reactions to the car. And to its driver.) I goofed on Ed "Big Daddy" Roth's Kustom Kulture cars that I'd see on the "Weirdo" T-shirts worn by the public school kids, or in the back of comic books. The zany cartoonishness of Rat Fink and Roth's other hot rod characters was more my speed. I drove a boat-size Ford Gran Torino station wagon to high school toga parties, read *Musician* magazine, not *Car and Driver*. I left cool cars to cooler guys. But that didn't mean that I couldn't get off on a car song. I loved Chuck Berry. I loved the Beach Boys. I understood the dirty jokes in "Drive My Car." Soon I'd hear the Modern Lovers' stirring "Roadrunner" for the first time and feel the pavement beneath me move.

"Panama" is about a car and a girl, but it's mostly about the feel of the roar and the heat of combustion. It's really a song about an engine, how it motors the mind and the body and can elevate us off the ground. The back story: while in Las Vegas attending a drag race, Roth had seen a car called "Panama Express." Aware that his band had never written a car song, or having had it pointed out to him—he changes the story—he worked up some lyrics. (Roth later named one of his own cars "Panama" and mounted its bumper and hood in his front foyer. The lyrics may or may not also be about a stripper he knew.) The words' imagery and tone are well-worn: fast car + fast girl x sex = checkered flag! But Roth's best lyrics are typically clever, and funny, too. The car (or is it the girl?) is a "model citizen" with "zero discipline." She'll take off around the corner, but he'll catch her. One of Roth's best lines—about the on-ramp comin' through his bedroom—makes the smut so absurdly clear that by the time we reach the band's trademark breakdown after the guitar solo it feels redundant. But who the hell cares? As with all peak-era Van Halen breakdowns, and the schoolboy comic opera that is "Hot for Teacher," the monologues are delivered by a young, lucky guy, poised between just right and too much. Roth's stage and studio patter are fun because the guy who's doing it is funny and he's having fun. She's blinding. He's flying. Got the feeling, power steering, pistons popping, *ain't no stopping now!* and we're at the final chorus. The song stops on a dime, as all well-made cars do.

Famously, during the recording of "Panama" the guys drove Eddie Van Halen's 1972 Lamborghini Miura S to 5150 Studios in Studio City and miked the exhaust pipes as Eddie revved the engine. On the recording, the band's grins are virtually audible; in rock and roll, all teenagers' late-night fantasies come true. Yet, as taped and mixed for the song's breakdown, the gunned Lamborghini somehow sounds less like a motor than Eddie's playing does; his astonishing guitar work turns a stock lyric into a sports car. With bassist Michael Anthony and drummer Alex Van Halen having built the chassis and engine block, Eddie creates a combustion chamber. (At the Roland website, Josh Munday does a helpful job of explaining how Eddie obtains his tone, via a humbucking pickup, a Marshall Plexi amplifier cranked to its loudest levels, and effects.)

Among the many great archeological artifacts found on YouTube is the isolated guitar or vocal track, usually reverse-engineered from master recordings. There are tons of these online, and listening to them allows you both to geekily imagine that you're in the studio mixing (or playing!) and to marvel at how a song is built from the foundation up. There are several of Eddie's isolated tracks online. Listen to "Panama." Eddie's a longtime admirer of the sadly departed Malcolm Young, rhythm guitarist in AC/DC, and as everyone knows, there was a surreally thin line between *literally* and *figuratively* in the engine that was the AC/DC rhythm section: you don't need hallucinogenic drugs to envision Malcolm's right and left hands as gears or pistons. The engine that Eddie builds for "Panama" is just plain wacky, as high-energy and funky as his red and black-and-white striped "Frankenstrat" Fender Stratocaster, which he infamously jerry-rigged early in the band's history by ham fisting the double-coil pickup of one manufacturer's guitar onto the body of another manufacturer's guitar. Eddie wanted a guitar that felt like a Strat but sounded like a Gibson. The thing looks like demented craft project: some paraffin wax; a piece of vinyl shaped into a pick guard; three screws for five mounting holes; some double-sided masking tape; a quarter jammed in as a shim; red Schwinn bicycle paint. Mad science.

A self-described "tone chaser," Eddie takes his guitar to exhilarating places in "Panama," as he does in his best work in the band. Isolated, his playing assumes dimensional shape—raw, rousing chords in the intro and chorus, lidded-cool idling during the verses and the breakdown, and swooping, diving leads and fret board tapping in the solo. I marvel every time I listen: his playing has so much personality that it's a band in itself. Eddie's rightfully lauded as a mold-breaking lead player yet, as the only guitarist in Van Halen, he's also the rhythm player. What's remarkable is how he alternates—morphs, really—between lead and rhythm in any given song. He was hardly the first to pull off this style—there's a reason why Eddie is spoken in the same breath as Jimi Hendrix and Jimmy Page—yet coupled with an outrageous frontman, the giddiness of the songs, the blend of raw rock riffing and pop hooks, and the mass, international commercial successes of his band, it sounded, looked, and felt as if Eddie was doing something new. To my ears, his rhythm/lead tandem playing on "Panama" is especially outrageous. I listen to the isolated track, close my eyes, and (this would feel likely even if I didn't know the origin of the song's lyrics) I see churning gears, I smell gasoline and oil, feel heat, thrumming, throttling, elevation. Above all I feel *speed*. This guy's telling a story with a beat-up, cobbled-together guitar. Indulge me:

he's writing the imaginary theme song to an imaginary documentary. *How an Engine Works!*

Van Halen's rhythm section is solid; with Roth and Eddie upfront, there's little room for more flash. Yet, Alex and Anthony are capable of surprise. In the full band version, listen to the four-bar bridge into the chorus: Roth has just bragged that she's coming home with him but he's worried that he'll lose her in the turn ahead. "I'll get her!" he yelps, as Alex, Anthony, and Eddie steer the song through a tight S-curve, the passengers airborne and guffawing in the back seat. It's maybe my favorite moment in the song (and that's saying something, given the righteous chorus) because I can't hear it without seeing—*feeling*—a car careening down a road toward the head-on damage of a hairpin turn and, for a frightening but elating second, lifting off the ground en route. Amusement park fear and the fun of all that. Ohmygod we're gonna tip over! Whoa-oh! Nope! "Panama!"

The iconography's indelible. Roth's aloft via a wire rig, swung to and fro across the stage, wearing shades, pantomiming swimming while holding a boom box; Anthony, too, is flying about the stage, laughing and dearly clutching his trademark custom Jack Daniels bass; Alex's pounding his drums and peering through stockinged female legs; Eddie's blowing smoke rings at a piano when he isn't clutching his Frankenstrat, darting about the stage and sliding on his knees like a first grader in Rock School. Everything in the "Panama" video, codirected by Roth and Peter Angelus, is eighties bright, hair-sprayed. The concert scenes show a loud band on the top of the world having a blast in front of a worshipful crowd. Partly filmed during a sound check and show at the Providence Civic Arena (now the Dunkin' Donuts Center) in Rhode Island on March 17 or 18, 1984, the shoot captures the band a third of the way into their mammoth, 101-date *1984* tour through the United States and Canada, and they're loose, well-oiled, and in fine silly/hokey form despite the toxic differences among certain members.

Writing for the *Awl*, screenwriter and producer Stephen Falk (*You're the Worst*, *Orange Is the New Black*) nails the appeal of the video for a particular audience, a twelve-year-old boy: "This video had it all: a cool airplane, jumping, kicking, spandex, karate, cops, chest hair, head hair, hot chicks, motorcycles, booze, screaming fans, rhythm gymnastics. It was the perfect music video for the confused sexuality of puberty," he wrote, adding, "To me, Eddie and David were what I hoped an adult male friendship could be: driving around in an awesome car, drinking, acting like goofs, but also leaning on each other tenderly while singing. Aside from epitomizing the androgynous frat boy bonding of the best hair bands, Van Halen spoke to the pure dumb fun of being a guy. No one wanted Van Halen to think." Repeatedly watching the video on VCR with his buddy, Falk felt as if he were "let in on what this at-the-time unknown, scary void of impending adulthood and sexuality and being a man was all about."

I was on the cusp of college when the video aired. I've never been crazy about it—it's awfully corny—but that has to do with my general shunning of most mainstream popular culture beginning in my late teens, which I semiregret now. I'm an admitted fameist (I might need help) and the "Panama" video is a vivid lesson in showy excess: the mile-long stage, the props, the light show, the over-the-top theatrics, etcetera, reminded me then that I'd never see Van Halen playing "Panama" in a small packed club or an intimate theater. They seemed so far away, so worldwide, that I could barely imagine them as real people. After Roth departed Van Halen, the subsequent dull blur: Van Hagar; the Wilderness Years; rehab; infighting; public posturing; silly on-again/off-again reunions. And then a surprise: 2012's *A Different Kind of Truth*, a Roth-led Van Halen (minus Anthony) revisiting and filling out some early demos and half-finished songs. The thing smokes, and, a little like R.E.M.'s *Accelerate*, if you're of a certain age and can look past the nostalgia, the songs remind you of how great Van Halen once was back when they seemed ahead of the pack, gunning it for the finish, laughing all the way. "Panama" is one of the emblematic tracks from that careening, downhill era.

Thirteen Ways of Thinking about the Cramps

1. "Some guy had just climbed the World Trade Tower and the headline in the *Post* that day was 'Human Fly Climbs Tower.' I was out walking along the street at about six in the morning. It felt like *Night of The Living Dead* the way all the people were wandering around. Somebody had jumped off the roof of the building next to ours and they were scraping him off the sidewalk. All of that made me go home and write the song."
2. In 1972, Erick Lee Purkhiser and a buddy picked up a woman hitchhiking near Sacramento State College in California. Erick and the woman, Kristy Wallace, later ran into each other on campus in an "Art and Shamanism" class. They hung out, soon fell in love, and commenced indulging mutual obsessions with early American rock and roll, B-movie imagery, and trash-pop aesthetics. They wanted to start a band and play rock and roll, so Purkhiser snagged a stage name from an automobile ad—"Lux Interior"—while Wallace was vouchsafed "Poison Ivy" in a visionary dream.

   Following a two-year stop in Lux's hometown of Akron, Ohio, Lux Interior and Poison Ivy moved to New York City, and in 1976 the Cramps were hatched on The Bowery with Lux on vocals, Ivy and Bryan Gregory on guitars, and Gregory's sister Pam "Balam" on drums. They'd change drummers a couple of times—Miriam Linna replaced Pam, Nick Knox replaced Linna—and when their lineup settled began playing regularly in the burgeoning NYC street rock scene. (Several personnel changes would occur over the following decades.) They stomped, growled, and grooved at

CBGBs, Max's Kansas City, and other area venues, celebrating horror movies and junk culture, mutating R&R and blues-based garage punk and rockabilly into something uniquely theirs: raw, morbid, and difficult to categorize. Lux dyed his jagged hair night-black and, often half nude, writhed onstage in high heels wearing daring, painted-on low-rider black leather pants, pushing his body past its limits, fellating the microphone when in the mood, hiccupping, moaning, yelping, howling. Ivy sported a flame-red teased-up hairdo, fishnet stockings, and go-go boots, on other nights a form-fitting dress or tight red latex pants or a mini, wielding her guitar like a talisman. Eyeliner ruled the night. The Cramps mesmerized audiences with their "sexed up, swampy cocktail of swagger and spook."

3. In 1958, 20th Century Fox released *The Fly*, a science fiction horror film about the dangers of playing God. André Delambre (David Hedison), a brilliant scientist living in Montreal, is working on a molecular transporter. He's buoyed by early, successful experiments, and is eventually able to transport a piece of pottery by reducing it to its atomic level and then reconstructing it in a receiver across the laboratory. Emboldened, Delambre attempts to teleport himself, but a common fly enters the transporter during the process. Delambre's and the insect's atoms combine, and when André emerges from the machine he has the head and left arm of a fly. The fly, in turn, is cursed with Andre's miniaturized arm and head, and burdened with André's self-awareness.

André keeps the disaster from his wife Hélène (Patricia Owens) for as long as he can, though she eventually learns of the incident. She and her son, who's innocent of his father's ghastly transformation, attempt to catch the fly—identifiable by its tiny white human head—in order to try and reverse the teleportation process, but they fail to do so.

Aware of the impossible fact of his mutated self, that he's a creature never to be understood or accepted, a mutant fit only to be destroyed, André convinces his wife to help crush him to death in a hydraulic press.

4. The Cramps cut a handful of songs in October 1977 down at Ardent Studio in Memphis, with Alex Chilton producing. Among the batch was Lux's "Human Fly."

   "It's not easy to get that sound—that 'on the edge of distortion' sound we had on 'Human Fly,'" said Lux. "The trick is to use bad microphones."
5. "Human Fly" is a song about a man who's part insect. Or is he fully man-insect? (A mansect?) No origin story is offered, as he's buzz-buzz-buzzing at the start, and though the song's sinuous and sexy, there's menace beneath the surface: he/it is a self-described "reborn maggot using germ warfare," and his self-worth is made clear as his "garbage brain" drives him to the brink of madness. The winking reference to his "unzipped fly" and to ? and the Mysterians' classic "96 Tears" elevates the mood a bit, as does the guitar's trebly surf leads and the fuzzed-out rhythm section, which turn the freak's lament into a dance floor jam: rock and toll transmogrifies into rockabilly mutating into psychobilly.
6. In an early experiment, André attempts to transport the family's beloved cat, but the test goes horribly wrong and the cat vanishes into thin air, suspended bodiless and unseen, its cries echoing in the laboratory.

   Later, André confesses to his wife, explaining that the cat "disintegrated perfectly, but never reappeared."

   "Where's she gone?" an appalled Hélène wonders.

   André sighs, gazing at the ceiling. "Into space, a stream of cat atoms," he replies, adding, "It'd be funny if life weren't so sacred."
7. How to categorize the Cramps? They waded through the muck of garage, R&B, surf, and Link Wray rawk over the course of their career but early on popularized the term "psychobilly," which stuck.

   Ivy: "We never meant [psychobilly] as a style, different from rockabilly, it was just like a dramatic word. 'Rockabilly voodoo' is a phrase that we invented too. All it means is the magic of rockabilly."

Lux: "That's one of the prime ingredients of rockabilly, is that it's got to be psychotic to begin with."

Ivy: "The really good, lesser known and obscure rockabilly from the fifties was very psychotic in its day and really stands up as being psychotic by today's standards—so all good rockabilly was psychobilly originally."

Lux: "I've always thought of us as surrealists, right from the very beginning. I think anytime anybody gets too comfortable or decides to cleverly pigeonhole 'the way things should be' . . . an artist is going to come along and turn the whole thing upside down. That's always healthy. That means people are thinking; they're not just doing what they're told. It means they're being moved by a spirit. . . . Gauguin said there are two types of artists: revolutionaries and plagiarists. We're revolutionaries."

Gothabilly? *Punkabilly*? *Hellbilly*?

Ivy: "We're the Kings and Queens of Rock and Roll."

8. The tagline on *The Fly*'s movie poster was "The Monster Created by Atoms Gone Wild!," which could've been the name of a Cramps song.
9. Are the Cramps too funny for Goth? They trade on kitschy sex and cartoonish evocations of midcentury horror and sci-fi imagery with a half grin and a wink against the gloom. Some find it hard to take the Cramps all that seriously given that their humor's so out front and over the top, no matter how ghoulishly presented. There's little that's foreboding or sorrowful in the Cramps' songs, and what feels ominous is usually leavened with camp. Representative song titles from their twenty-five year recording career: "Garbage Man," "I Was a Teenage Werewolf," "Goo Goo Muck," "Don't Eat Stuff off the Sidewalk," "Can Your Pussy Do the Dog?," "Bikini Girls with Machine Guns," "Two Headed Sex Change," "It Thing Hard-On," etcetera. The band does earn a full entry and a mention in the "Gothabilly" note in *Encyclopedia Gothica*, though editor Liisa Ladouceur acknowledges that for some Goths, the Cramps are just too much fun.

Lux: "If people think that we're funny—I kinda feel sorry for them because it means that they think it's a joke. We've spent our lives searching out incredibly wonderful things that most folks just don't know about yet." Elsewhere, asked if rock and roll must be dangerous to succeed at, Lux remarked, "We like the unexpected. Dangerous almost means that someone's gotta get hurt or it's not rock 'n' roll. . . . Rock 'n' roll's supposed to be fun. It isn't supposed to be: See what kind of damage you can do to yourself or others. We're asking [people] to come and be crazy and they never stop thinking up new ways to be crazy."

Ivy: "We don't take life seriously, we take ourselves seriously, and what we do, we're just totally committed to it."

10. "I think 'Human Fly' is an anthem—an anthem about being a human monster."
11. The other victim of André's tragic experiment—the tiny fly with the scientist's head and arm—evades capture by Hélène and her son, only to inevitably fly into a spider's web, where, immobilized, it waits in terror as the spider moves slowly toward it. "Help me!" it screams, so faintly to our ears that it sounds like nothing but a buzzzzzz. *"Help meeee!"*
12. Lux: "All my life people have told me I was a pest, something that looked ugly, smelled bad and ought to be gotten rid of, something that spoiled everybody's planned-out fun."
13. In April 1978, the Cramps, armed with two hundred bucks, produced a promo film for "Human Fly" that went unseen for decades, acquiring legendary underground status. Allegedly, neither Lux nor Ivy possessed a copy. The video surfaced online in 2015. Filmed on a rainy Saturday morning by Alex de Laszlo, it's superb lo-fi horror, *Nosferatu* meets MTV. De Laszlo was a high school student who'd made a few sixteen-millimeter experimental films, one, using Velvet Underground on the soundtrack, shot in "stark black and white, with jagged imagery and very much in the tradition of adolescent surrealist mischief," de Laszlo recalls, adding, "The din of the Velvets soundtrack only added to the generally robotic and disturbed narrative."

A friend introduced de Laszlo to Steven Blauner, the Cramps' first manager. De Laszlo was already a fan of the band, having dug them several times at CBGBs in late 1977 and early 1978. (He remembers Lux whipping out a *TV Guide* from his back pocket, whereupon some wag in the crowd asked, "What's on TV tonight, Lux?" and Lux would proceed to read a listing for a "4am, bottom of the barrel, Z grade, low budget horror film, complete with a lurid *TV Guide* description.") Blauner arranged for de Laszlo and Lux to speak on the phone, and "he talked about the movies he had made as a kid, his love of cheap horror movies, and how he wanted the film to look," de Laszlo remembers. "He conveyed to me an aesthetic which I already appreciated and understood, having seen them perform and having been raised on a steady diet of surreptitious Late, Late Show TV viewings of *The Incredible Crawling Eye* and *Attack of the Mushroom People*."

De Laszlo borrowed a Bolex sixteen-millimeter camera and a couple of movie lights, and from MERC, a nonprofit film collective for independent and student filmmakers, snagged some midcentury military surplus film stock. Not only was this film cheap, but it approximated the lousy reception on a TV. "The excessive age of the film stock meant taking a risk," de Laszlo says, "but once Lux heard '1950's,' 'low definition,' and 'grainy,' he was all for it." De Laszlo met the Cramps at their rehearsal space near the Bowery, and went to work. In the film, Lux injects himself with serum that turns him into a monster; a transistor-radio-bopping Ivy accidentally trespasses Lux's underground lair—cue the dangerously descending opening guitar line in "Human Fly"—where he and the other Cramps emerge from the shadows and initiate her into their dark ways. "Most of the footage was shot in very dank, dark, and close quarters, very little in the way of set design was required," de Laszlo remembers. "Four hours later, we had our footage." The film dramatizes the threat inherent in the song, but in B-movie irony. The glimpse of an Alfred E. Neumann poster on the wall says it all: this is terrifying stuff, yet it's also the Cramps.

Nowhere

The album should've been called *Really Fucked Up*, though that likely wouldn't have cut it with Reprise Records.

In the event, the title Green Day came up with for their fourth album was just as apt. *Insomniac*, released in October 1995, hit number two on the *Billboard* 200 chart and would eventually be certified double platinum in sales. Since its release, the album has sold over two million copies in the United States alone. A blockbuster, to be sure—though relative to *Dookie*'s monster sales from the year before, a bit of a commercial letdown. The singles "Geek Stink Breath" (released in September 1995), "Stuck with Me" (December), "Brain Stew/Jaded" (July 1996), and "Walking Contradiction" (August) performed well, each detonating in the Top 40, yet the album's a dark affair, stuffed with lyrics about anger, sickness, mental and physical distress, addictions, abuse, disappointment, rejection, bitterness, panic attacks, and disorientation. The pop hooks, brisk pace, and melodies ultimately set *Insomniac* apart from the still-trending grunge movement—in 2014, Billie Joe Armstrong lamented what he'd felt had been excessive "whining in rock" at that time, adding, "By nature we're extroverts"—yet the album's still pretty brutal. Its success ensured that songs about despair and self-disgust would play in high rotation in millions of teenagers' heads.

By 1995, Green Day was mentally and physically exhausted. (In many interviews from this period, Armstrong, Tré Cool, and Mike Dirnt look equal parts bushed, messed-up, and surly.) Armstrong and Cool had each recently become first-time dads, and were wrestling not only with unprecedented professional demands but familial ones. Like all new dads, Armstrong was up nights with the baby, grappling with fatigue, and on top of that was dealing with insomnia, likely in part a result of commercial pressures and the unwelcome intrusions of fame—all while writing a new album in the crossfire of burdens from his label and accusations of selling out from folks in the East Bay punk scene.

Several songs on *Insomniac* suggest that there were other wearying factors at play. The lyrics to "Geek Stink Breath" read like a scattered journal scribbled at rehab. The song's an indolent lope through confession cut with denial that begins with a sick moan and ends by slightly speeding up, from either a real high or longed-for one. The video, aired late at night on MTV, included graphic scenes of a tooth pull. That the lead single from *Insomniac* was an ugly, explicit tale of the ravages of meth abuse indicates just where the fatigued, contrary band's punk head was at, gazing at a *Billboard* Top 40 peopled with the likes of Seal, TLC, Faith Evans, and Hootie and the Blowfish.

The geek with the stink breath no doubt knew well the thrill seekers, hooligans, and mannequins partying up at "Tight Wad Hill," the nickname for Charter Hill, which overlooks California Memorial Stadium at the University of California, Berkeley, notorious for the free view of football games (hence its nickname) as well as being a haunt for druggies. "A lot of tweakers come and hang out up here, the crank victims and stuff," Armstrong revealed in a 1995 *Rolling Stone* cover story. His song's a clear-eyed take on the hollowed-out devastation awaiting users there: begging for fixes, turning tricks, burning daylight. The lyrics feature a classic Armstrong-esque paradox, the kind he loves to knot up his songs with: the kid's having a blast yet hating every second he's alive. Such tensions sweated out in the margins between sensations and oblivion have always appealed to Armstrong. Misfits and punks know "how to express themselves better," he said in *Rolling Stone*, adding, "Besides, I always thought anger was a lot more interesting than feeling good about yourself."

The opening line describes a simple problem: *I can't sleep*. The chords drag you under. The cycle's despairing. After the fifth chord, we're hauled back to the first, and the misery deepens.

"Brain Stew" has long been considered Armstrong's anti-ode to his insomnia. (Before it became the album's title, "Insomniac" was the working title for the song; "Brain Stew" was also the nickname of James Washburn, a longtime buddy of the band's.) The new baby, the growing impositions of fame, the pressures of having to produce, the fallout from the Gilman Street drama (addressed on this album in "86") all conspire to keep the singer up until his bleeding eyeballs bulge. Fans, many doubtful that 3 a.m. feedings and a fussy infant were the song's sole inspirations, have been unpacking the lyrics since the album's release. Talking with *Rolling Stone* last year, Armstrong came clean, as it were. "The song is about methamphetamine, not being able to sleep, and staying up all night," he acknowledged. "It was something that was creeping into our punk scene at the time, and I definitely did my experimenting with it. It's just such an evil drug." The code officially broken, the lyrics assume their rightful place on *Insomniac*'s Goya-like canvas. No one had to puzzle much over the reference in the first verse to *crosstops*, the speed pills infamous for their cross-shaped grooves. Is the singer zooming, or crashing? Though he's spun out, the ponderous chord progression and the sickening march when the band kicks in suggest a comedown, a withdrawal, jonesing, or all three. Armstrong's guitar scraping in the spaces between the power chords mimics the gnawing anxieties. It's all a waking nightmare: dry mouth, numb face, delirium. After the 9/11 attacks, Clear Channel Communications (now iHeartMedia), the behemoth landlord of U.S radio stations, included "Brain Stew" on its list of "lyrically questionable" songs sent to stations that were then urged to drop them from playlists. Even as an instrumental the song might've made that list, so distressing is the mood.

It's especially agonizing that "Brain Stew" lacks a bridge or chorus that might deliver the singer from the anguish; there's no musical change to reflect—and to bring about—a mental change. Armstrong's a devotee of classicist rock and roll, and knows (and loves) the mood-changing power of a good middle or refrain. Yet "Brain Stew's" locked in place, sweating out its fate on the mattress with no hope of reprieve. Dirnt's harmonies only add irony. The chords are hammered repeatedly, helplessly, as the song comes to a merciful close without resolving a thing. (*Here we go—again.*) Cool wallops at his snare drum during the final few bars, willing the nightmare to end, yet the song's a perpetual motion machine with no hint of dawn.

Then, something startling occurs. If you were to read the lyrics to "Jaded," the song that comes charging out of the distortion of the final held chord, you'd be forgiven for thinking that they were extended verses of "Brain Stew"—both deal in despair and disorientation, and "Jaded," with its nervous, apocalyptic dread, feels like the kind of worrying you mutter toward the ceiling on a sleepless night. But sonically we're in a different place altogether. "Jaded" is pure thrash, the band locked in and the arrangement supertight, among the fastest songs that Green Day's cut in the studio. (*Nimrod*'s "Platypus" beats it by a hair; *American Idiot*'s "St. Jimmy" is up there, too.) At ninety seconds, it makes "Brain Stew's" three minutes feel like the long, anguished night it is. Charging at your heels, snarling, "Jaded" is impossible to ignore, and feels like an inevitable punk roar.

"Jaded" tears open "Brain Stew's" emotional straightjacket with a chorus, a lurching change that tries to leave anxieties behind, only to get tangled up in another of Armstrong's bitter paradoxes. The chord changes elevate things to an even higher pitch, yet the two chords trade punches in the last line of the chorus before settling back. The chorus offers an insight, if you can hear it in the noise, but it's complicated, promising that a straight line goes nowhere, that if you find a home, it's in nowheresville. At the song's stuttering close, a lyric in the final verse rings in your ears.

Inertia versus Eruption. If "Brain Stew's" about staying down, "Jaded's" about getting up. "Brain Stew's" stuck in horizontal. "Jaded" moves forward. Is "Jaded" an answer of sorts to the lethargy of "Brain Stew," or, if the speed's coming from another dose of meth, is it fucking things up again? Pete Townshend's been credited with observing that "Rock & Roll might not solve your problems, but it does let you dance all over them." The brilliantly sequenced pairing of "Brain Stew" and "Jaded" tests the limits of that promise to its near-breaking point.

The video debuted on MTV in the summer of 1996. Directed by Kevin Kerslake, who'd worked with Iggy Pop, Sonic Youth, Bob Mould, Prince, Nirvana, R.E.M., Dinosaur Jr., Stone Temple Pilots, and the Rolling Stones, the video, like the songs, moves between two worlds. "Brain Stew's" bleached in a sepia tone and inhabits a hallucinatory landscape, while "Jaded's" a more conventional, if unconventionally filmed, band performance. "The plan all along was to keep the videos married together, just like the songs appear on the album," Kerslake told me. "As far as I can recall, there wasn't a specific mandate to drive one or both in any specific direction, but 'Brain Stew' steered my brain into some absurdist no-man's land, image-wise, while 'Jaded' tugged it more in the direction of band performance. With a wet finger in the electrical socket."

The "Brain Stew" portion is an antinarrative hellscape. In a dump somewhere in Nowhere, Armstrong, Cool, and Dirnt sit on a shitty couch (meant to evoke the similarly ratty sofa in the "Longview" video) pulled bumpily through the trash by a bulldozer steered by an old, tobacco-spitting driver. "The imagery was inspired by a good many things," Kerslake said, "including the lyrics, the sludgy riff, and the band's East Bay punk rock roots." He added: "But the idea that got the motor running was that the couch from 'Longview' somehow ended up in a dump, and the band along with it." You want to look away but the imagery's mesmerizing: close-ups of roiling mealworms; a line of benignly smiling hula dancers; a stray dog; a central-casting schoolmarm mouthing the lyrics; a horse writhing on its back in the dirt. "From there it was simply a matter of inviting alien figures and ideas into the picture, juxtaposed against the humdrum, day-to-day banality of life in the dump," Kerslake said. "Nothing in the sandbox fit together on paper, deliberately, and it was fun finding ways to make all those things feel like they fit together in the edit. Not in any rational sense, necessarily, but on some level."

Kerslake and his crew built the junkyard in Los Angeles ("out in the valley somewhere"), a trash heap for the band slouched glumly on the couch to be trapped within, moving randomly but not really getting anywhere. Armstrong adopts a meditation posture complete with a Gyan mudra (he's sincere or goofing on it, it's hard to say) but that doesn't seem to provide much harmony against the ugliness of the landscape and the bizarre terrors of the clashing images.

As Cool's drums are crushed beneath the bulldozer and the horse rises and runs off, the band launches into "Jaded" and the video moves from sepia to full, loud color. The cameras fly about a small room (a soundstage in Hollywood) filming the band in absurdly tight closeups and jittery, distorted angles, trying to keep up; the impression is that Kerslake and crew tossed their equipment into the mosh pit and then ran out of the way. "I just figured if we're going to get into some of the bratty punk stuff, to do ["Jaded"] really crude and raw, almost like Super-8," Kerslake said to Gillian G. Gaar in *Green Day: Rebels with a Cause*, adding, "And I simply wanted to distinguish between the songs; if I was going to go into the garage phase, with tweaked-out colors, I thought it might be cool to play with a more antiquated look in the first part, giving it a look like found footage, like somebody pissed on the film can and it's been lying in the sun for decades. That was the feeling that I was shooting for."

Kerslake remains proud of the video, which captures not only the songs' moods but an era. "There's nothing in it that wants to make any sense," he remarked to Gaar. "It feels like it's giving you the finger, or giving any sort of straight talk the finger. And that's cool, to have that sort of teenage rebellion."

> Sometimes you do videos, and you want them to be really smart or tell a great story, or just have a great performance, and sometimes you just want to throw paint on the wall and let the splatter stay. Or just go into a certain realm and just want it to feel grim. And I feel like that's in there too, just this bleak hopelessness, that I was happy to keep. It's not necessarily that you have to exaggerate, or go to great

> lengths to say, "Oh, woe is us, life is fucked, we can't make sense of anything," just embody it in the flow of images or the disconnect from one image to the next. So it happens on a more subtle level.

I asked Kerslake if he was aware of the drug abuse imagery in "Brain Stew" before he worked on the video. "Since I wasn't interested in story, I never explored the precise reasons for his insomnia," he responded. "I figured the less it was tied to something specific in the video, the better."

"Things were getting really scary. I'm such a dedicated songwriter and musician, and when *Dookie* got so big—it was on par with becoming one of the biggest pop records of all time—I really wanted to be like, 'I'm a rocker. I'm a punk rocker. That's what matters to me more than being some kind of pop star.' That sort of fueled that record." This is Armstrong in 2020, talking about *Insomniac*. "Everything was happening. I got married, I had a kid, I was 23 years old, and people were climbing in my trees to look inside my house. It was the scary side of becoming a rock star, or whatever. You can't control the outcome of your life. I wanted to show the uglier side of what Green Day was capable of."

A couple of years ago, Armstrong revealed to Ian Winwood in *Kerrang!* that *Insomniac* "is the most honest record I ever made at the particular moment that it was written and recorded." Startling and vivid, "Brain Stew/Jaded" remains unnervingly evocative of a soundscape nowhere, cast in 4 a.m. shadows. Even punk thrash can't deliver you from that joint.

“It’ll All Be Over Soon”

So this is what the end sounds like.

But first, a beginning. James Osterberg Jr. was born on April 21, 1947, in Muskegon, Michigan, a small town on the Lake Michigan shore. He grew up with his parents in a trailer park in Ypsilanti, just west of Detroit. He dug rock and roll, started playing drums when he was around eleven, made a lot of noise in that trailer. In school he was, by the looks of things, a pretty average teenager. Clean-cut, cleanly dressed. Debate team. “Most Likely to Succeed.” Yet things were always seething below the surface.

Here’s Osterberg in a poignant scene from *Gimme Danger*, Jim Jarmusch’s 2016 documentary about the Stooges. He’s recalling a time when some kids from school paid a visit to his family’s trailer. “They were a group of the slightly more popular, slightly more physically aggressive guys in my class,” he said. “And there were about four or five of them at the time. I’d been to one or two of their homes, I used to eat french fries with them across the street from school.”

> So one of them had a car his daddy’d given him. They came out, they did three things. One of them said, “Yeah, look, his dad drives a Cadillac and he lives in a trailer. The car’s bigger than his house!” A few of them got together: “Let’s see if it shakes!” And they started pushing it and trying to shake the trailer on its foundations—which it would not, but you did feel, you could feel it. Yeah, I wanted to be friends with these guys, and I admired certain things about them. One of them jumped in the bathtub and made some sort of remark about the size of the bathroom.

He adds: "And ever since I've been out to get 'em. Ever since. You know? I'll bury those guys."

By the early 1960s the Kingsmen (Lynn Easton, Jack Ely, Mike Mitchell, Bob Nordby, and Don Gallucci) had been banging around the Pacific Northwest for a half a decade, and they were itching to cut a record. They dug Rockin' Robin Roberts's cover of a Richard Berry 1957 B-side, an R&B/cha-cha number called "Louie Louie," marveling in some club they were visiting in Seaside, Oregon, one long night as the song came roaring from a jukebox. They didn't know what the hell the song was about and they couldn't understand the words, but they knew this: the tune got whoever was listening up and moving. Other bands were picking up on the number, and it was becoming wildly popular on the local scene. Inevitably, bands were going to try to nail a version of "Louie Louie" and put it out as a record, and soon.

The Kingsmen wanted in. On April 6, 1963, they met at ten in the morning at Northwest Recorders, a small recording studio in Portland. Because "Louie Louie" never failed to rouse and move a crowd with its three-chord stomp, its super power, its stumbling charm, the night before the session the Kingsmen had played a delirious ninety-minute version of the song at a gig. The band arrived at the studio wearing an uneasy blend of exhaustion, nerves, and ambition. Like many local bands, they'd rearranged the song after Roberts's version, clumsily de-Latinizing it in the garage rock tradition and retaining Roberts's unhinged *okay let's give it to 'em right now!* launch to the guitar solo. Their manager Ken Chase was nominally producing.

Dave Marsh, in his essential *Louie Louie*—and I've got to supply the book's epic subtitle here, *The History and Mythology of the World's Most Famous Rock'n'Roll Song; Including the Full Details of Its Torture and Persecution at the Hands of the Kingsmen, J. Edgar Hoover's F.B.I., and a Cast of Millions; and Introducing, for the First Time Anywhere, the Actual Dirty Lyrics*—picks up the story: "They went inside and set up their gear as quickly as possible—studio time cost money, and the clock started running when they walked through the door. But then there wasn't that much equipment to set up and Northwest Recorders, while the best facility in Portland, was pretty primitive itself. The band moved a large backdrop curtain and rolled up a rug. Within a half hour, engineer [Bob] Lindahl began placing the microphones." As Marsh notes, this became an issue. Rather than on a stand or in a vocal booth, "Northwest Recorders' vocal mike hung from a large boom stand, and it was so unwieldy it remained well overhead. Jack Ely was forced to stand on tiptoe." Other reasons for Ely's slurred delivery? "He wore braces on his teeth, and the "Louie" marathon had been cord-crunching."

After a false start, Chase pivoted and asked his boys for a simple run-through of the number so that Lindahl could check and set the sound levels. Marsh: "Easton counted the song off and again kicked into *duh duh duh. duh duh.* Ely squalled upward at the mike as hard as he could. The band was nervous; this may have been a rinky-dink setup but it was their Shot."

> Ely yawped like Donald Duck in a rage on "Okay, let's give it to 'em, right now!" The others' nerves showed, too: Just before the vocal came back in, Lynn Easton clacked his sticks together and cussed, "Fuck!" Although Lynn was off-mike, he said it loud enough to register slightly on the tape, and never quite recovered the beat, stuttering and stumbling throughout the rest of the take. When they got to the guitar break, Mike Mitchell fumbled his way through his Rich Dangel–inspired solo as if he'd never heard of the song before.

Ely blew his vocal entrance on the last verse. The drums were sloppy. The band hated it and wanted to rerecord it. Chase loved it and wanted it on the radio. "Louie Louie" was released as a single on Jerden in June 1963 and then reissued on Wand in October 1963. Soon the world would *duh duh duh, duh duh* on its axis.

First came an FBI investigation into the reputedly dirty lyrics (the Bureau's final verdict: "unintelligible at any speed"), then the innumerable obligatory garage band covers. Then a kind of cultural obsolescence, then John Belushi and *Animal House*, then a retro revival, and (finally?) Irony. (Dave Marsh lists over one hundred and fifty different recorded versions of the song in an appendix in *Louie Louie*; the list is ongoing.) By the midsixties, a few Detroit-area bands had gotten their hands on the song and, to the growing concern of local officials, would mildly dirty-up the lyrics onstage at teen dances. Osterberg's first band, the Iguanas, for which he grinningly banged the drums and which would be the origin of his lifelong nickname "Iggy," played ramshackle versions of the song. Osterberg interpreted the Kingsmen's interpretation of Roberts' interpretation of Berry's sailor's glee at returning to his Jamaican girl by turning it into Midwest smut, making far more explicit the bawdiness rumored to be lurking in the swamp of Ely's slurred vocals on the Kingsmen version.

By the time Jim Osterberg adopted his stage name and persona Iggy Pop and his band the Stooges got around to recording "Louie Louie" in 1972, they had two crucial, groundbreaking rock and roll albums behind them, their self-titled debut (1969) and *Fun House* (1970, produced by Kingsmen organist Don Gallucci), each of which stiffed commercially. Their shows were legendary—Iggy prowling the stage and hurtling himself into the dark mayhem of the crowd, the Asheton brothers, Ron on guitar and Scott on drums, stripping an already minimal groove to its bones, Scott pummeling his kit or riding steady, glowering, while Ron fuzz-riffed, wah-wah'ed, and slashed on guitar.

Their record label Elektra eventually gave up on them, unhappy with their poor sales and anxious about the band's active mutation into a druggy muddle. Bass player Dave Alexander was booted in 1970. After some lineup shuffling and a brief breakup, during which Iggy, under David Bowie's generous wing, relocated to London as a Columbia Records solo artist, the Stooges reassembled with fellow Michigan native James Williamson on guitar and Ron moving over (he'd later say "demoted") to bass with Scott back behind the drums. This is the lineup that cut the ferocious *Raw Power* album in 1973.

In the studio in London in the spring of 1972, with the members' drug use and interpersonal anarchy threatening to derail everything, the Stooges fired up "Louie Louie." It isn't much, really, a run through, a loosening-up job. Williamson's riffs are loudly assertive and Scott Asheton, playing an open high-hat, tries to inject some swing into things, but the band sounds uncharacteristically tentative, a little distracted, maybe bored. This version calls to mind the Paleolithic arrangement that the Sonics played for their 1966 cover of the song on their album *Boom*, Larry Parypa's guitar a pummeling jackhammer relative to Don Gallucci's loose-limbed organ riff. Iggy's voice is a ragged mess. He's half-faithful to Berry's original lyric in the first verse, then in the second verse steps into the lewdness that he'd regularly amplify onstage—she's not the kind of girl he'd bring home; it's a fuck-and-go situation; in front of a rabid crowd he added more indecorous details—but the thing's finished in a couple minutes, and never really transcends its workmanlike vibe. Based on this lone studio recording, it's safe to assume that the song came alive onstage for the band, Iggy reveling in just how far he could push the filth and shock a crowd inside an innocently beery frat-rock standard.

> "If all else fails, do 'Louie,' right? That's what you learn playing in a fraternity band for five years. Play 'Louie Louie' and it will always get you outta anything."
>
> —IGGY POP

The legendary status conferred on the Stooges' first three albums obscures the dire situation that the band was in by early 1974. Addictions, commercial irrelevance, and internal animosities were gnawing at the band, dragging them from any mainstream connection they might've secured with rock fans and igniting their increasingly sporadic shows with dangerous consequences. Always an audience-baiter ("I'll bury those guys"), always a self-harming *provocateur*, Iggy was by 1974 a genuine danger to himself, smack-addicted, 'lude-lost, alcohol-abusing, willingly, loudly courting violence on and off the stage. Some of it was indeed "an act"—the Stooges' fan base expected and in some ways demanded it—but much of it was Osterberg's inner turmoil in action. "It was an act for a long time," Ron Asheton acknowledged to Paul Trynka in *Iggy Pop: Open Up and Bleed*, "sincere, wholesome emotions that made him be Iggy. Then it spilled over. To where he could not separate the performance from his real life." (In the mid-1970s, Iggy would enter a Los Angeles hospital for treatment for heroin withdrawal, and intense psychiatric evaluation. He left relatively healthy and more committed to his career.)

The events between February 4 and 9, 1974, have assumed mythic proportions in Stooges history. This frigid Michigan week saw Iggy and his band bottom out in violence, ennui, and grim comedy. As with many legendary stories handed down from participant to participant, witness to witness, fan to fan, dreamer to dreamer, the versions of these incidents have been altered down the years. "I am trying now to exaggerate the essential," Vincent van Gogh wrote to his brother Theo, "and purposely leave the obvious things vague." The obvious things? The Stooges were all but finished when they took the stage at the Rock 'N' Roll Farm in Wayne on a Monday night, and Iggy was a strung-out mess. Soon after the show began, hostile patrons began throwing stuff at the stage. The essential? Iggy, wearing a floppy flowered hat, a leotard, and ballet slippers, got his clock cleaned by a biker.

Iggy and others have been sharing their versions of these iconic events for decades. After a hailstorm of eggs hit the stage, Iggy stopped the show, demanded to know who was responsible, and leapt into the crowd, wild-eyed for confrontation. "Lo and behold, the waters part and hundreds of people spread apart," Iggy tells Anne Wehrer in his careening 1982 memoir *I Want More*. "And there before me, about 75 feet yon, really just standing there like man-mountain Dean, just grinning, feet squarely planted, toes out, was this ENORMOUS youth with the most, the biggest, happy smile I've ever seen."

> Really, it was a wonderful smile, cause he *knew* he was king and was about to kick my ass (I'm hoping not too badly), with long flowing red hair. He must have been 6' 5", huge shoulders, had this large plaid lumberjack shirt, this big grin. And this one arm had a knuckle glove on—a KNUCKLE GLOVE that went ALL THE WAY UP the arm, studded

at the knuckles. He was carrying one of those dozen-egg cartons—his weapon. He's clearly got his act and he's just standing there, a hand on his hip, just leering at me, you know, and in a deep, resounding voice he says, "Hello."

He brought Iggy down with one mammoth punch to the head.

A decade later, speaking with Legs McNeil and Gillian McCain for their oral history *Please Kill Me*, Iggy slithers away from the story a bit, claiming that the guy "didn't deck me, he couldn't knock me down, it was real weird." (He'd also claim that this was the guy's "initiation for a motorcycle gang, to egg Iggy for the Scorpions!," an assertion that, needless to say, has been uncorroborated.) The storied studded knuckle glove reappears each time that Iggy tells it, as recently as his sprawling conversations with Jeff Gold for the Stooges biography *Total Chaos*, published in 2016, yet Skip Gildersleeve, a fan who was at the Rock 'N' Roll Farm show, is quoted in Trynka's biography remarking, "I've heard how the biker was supposed to be wearing studded gloves or a knuckle duster. He didn't." He adds dryly, "He didn't need one."

(Uncontested is a hysterical chain of events immediately following the gig: a woman whom Iggy had been seeing spirited him away to the safety of her house in the suburbs where she was living with her parents; the next morning a dazed Iggy endured—and probably charmed his way through—a quiet breakfast with the girl and her mother while still clad in his ballerina outfit and slippers. Iggy, laughing to Gold: "I met her mother in the fuckin' tutu." Perhaps out of deference he removed his floppy hat, but nothing could've been done about the dried blood and welts on his sorry face. He'd bear a lifelong scar between his eyes.)

Whatever the precise events of February 4, Iggy remained bruised but unbowed, crowing about the incident a day or so later on WABX, promoting the Stooges show at the Michigan Palace on the ninth and daring the biker and his gang to show up. "I went on the radio," he related to McNeil and McCain, "and said, 'The Scorpions sent this asshole down to egg me, so I say, come on down, any Scorpion, let's have it out and see if you're man enough to deal with the fucking Stooges!'" According to Trynka, "no Scorpions seemed to show up" at the Palace, en masse anyway; in the event, the Stooges had prepared reinforcement backstage in the form of God's Children, a biker gang associated with Detroit legend John Cole. As it turns out, *Scorpions vs. God's Children (featuring Iggy Pop)* was averted.

But there was still plenty of violence onstage. "People were throwing stuff at us from the very beginning of the show," Iggy told McNeil and McCain, "cameras and compacts, expensive shit, a lot of underwear—then came beer bottles and wine bottles and vegetables, stuff like that. But I had an arsenal backstage and a few throwers, so I had them all come out and whip stuff back at them." Prowling through their set list, the Stooges played to menace in the combative air, half-aware that this might be their last gig. The then-unreleased "Open Up and Bleed" (during the ominous start of which Iggy asks for applause from everyone "who hates the Stooges"; they oblige) and "I Got Nothing" (a.k.a., "I Got Shit") are intense and urgent, Iggy's harrowing, brutally honest lyrics about feeling used and wasted, about being down harder than he'd been strong, delivered in desperation. The tension between the stage and the crowd is palpable.

But the insulting "Rich Bitch" and puerile "Cock in My Pocket" ("a song that was co-written by my mother") follow, and the despair and urgency devolve into adolescent smirking, pseudo-outrageous riffs that might've worked if they were funny. Reading the unruly crowd, Iggy seems to feel that his band's time is up, in more ways than one. "Anybody with anymore ice cubes, jellybeans, grenades, eggs they want to throw at the stage, c'mon. You paid your money so you takes your choice, ya know," bellowing hoarsely, "It'll all be over soon!" Band introductions follow—the end is near—as Iggy anoints himself "your favorite well-mannered boy." Responding to a sarcastic jibe from the audience, or from inside his own head, he yells into the darkness, "I *am* the greatest!" It's hard to know whether the band's endless tuning throughout all of this requires Iggy to fill time by baiting and insulting the crowd, or whether it's the ambient soundtrack for it. He ridicules the audience for missing him with their continuous stream of eggs ("Listen, I've been egged by better than you!"), and narrates a new incoming hailstorm of light bulbs and plastic cups ("Oh my, we're getting violent!"), before admonishing the audience: "I think a good song for you would be a fifty-five minute 'Louie Louie.' Would you rather we just ran through our programmed set and looked real slick, or would you rather we just relaxed and did Louie Louie'?" Without waiting for an answer, Williamson impatiently kicks off the riff that Iggy's loved since he was a teenager, and as his band lurches into the song Iggy yells at the crowd, "I never thought it would come to this, baby!"—in disbelief or irony, it's impossible to know in the moment. "Just want to fuck, don't want no romance," he had sung in "Cock in My Pocket" a few minutes earlier, a taste of the lewdness that would come oozing from "Louie Louie." Iggy reaches back for his well-worn X-rated take on Richard Berry's words, but who knows if howled references to menstruation and appeasing blow jobs, if slut shaming, bare tits, and a black ass have any effect on the jaded crowd anymore. It's 1974, not 1964.

Following the collapse of the song on its final, weary chord, Iggy addresses the crowd for the last time: "Thank you very much to the person who threw this glass bottle at my head. You nearly killed me, but you missed again. Keep trying next week!" The last sound on tape is a bottle landing on the stage with a crash.

We can eavesdrop on the wretched grandeur of the Stooges' show at the Michigan Palace because a young man in the crowd named Michael Tipton recorded the performance on reel-to-reel. Those tapes would change hands a couple of times before being released by the Paris-based Skydog label in 1976 as the infamous *Metallic K.O.* (coupled with tapes from a 1973 show at the same venue; the album's been reissued in expanded versions numerous times). Following the Stooges' implosion, this sought-after album became the stuff of legend, and would ultimately be as influential on the midseventies U.K. and U.S. punk rock bands as the Kingsmen's "Louie Louie" had been on midsixties garage bands. The cover features a photo of Iggy from the show—you can see the top of his Danskin—allegedly knocked out cold on the stage.

"Can't remember how I found out about [the album]," Iggy told Gold, "but the first thing was, I thought was, 'Hey, I love the picture.'"

The Kingsmen found a home in "Louie Louie," the decades-long durability of which probably amazed them. Some days I listen to the Stooges' deconstruction of the song and it sounds like a bad joke, a desperate pose in the face of hostile indifference, a house of cards I could blow over. On other days their song sounds, and feels, like performance art of the highest order. On those days, what fascinates me is the movement from the mystery in Ely's vocal to the transparency of Iggy's, a move from wide-eyed innocence to heavy-lidded jadedness that's nothing short of a lesson in cultural history. The Kingsmen's song wasn't explicitly dirty, but playground and high school hallway rumors would have none of that, and desire took over, told *its* story, all manner of lascivious imagery and blue phrases filling the heads of kids all over the place. (A side note: the Kingsmen's insane "Little Latin Lupe Lu," released as a single in 1964, has always sounded to me *much* filthier than "Louie Louie." Recorded "dirty" with tons of distortion at what sounds like a single-bulb basement-party, the excitable percussion and rumbling floor-toms are impossibly sexy, and nearly pull the song down. *Shake it, shake it, Lupe.* I don't know how the thing was released sounding as unbuttoned as it does.) Iggy Pop squeezed the mystery out of "Louie Louie," making what was kinda-sorta heard (and certainly desired) into explicit, poor man's porn, and that aggressive, bullying move was punk as hell, if unsubtle. Iggy and the Stooges Did It Themselves. What both versions of "Louie Louie" can't extinguish is the mystery in the music, the eternally renewing three-chord majesty, the perpetual motion machine those chords create, the primal hip shake of it all. "Louie Louie" will never end.

Of course, this wasn't the end of the Stooges, either. Remarkably, the band re-formed in the early aughts, first with Ron Asheton and then, after his death in 2009, with James Williamson on guitars. With Minutemen/Firehose bassist Mike Watt they toured internationally to venues packed with adoring fans and awestruck critics, and released two albums, *The Weirdness* (2007) and *Ready to Die* (2013).

Since the mid-1970s, Iggy has been shepherding a solo career through sundry sonic highs and lows, experimenting across styles, bands, and labels, eventually earning the sobriquet of "Godfather of Punk." In 1993 he released his eleventh solo album, *American Caesar*, a strong collection following the commercial and artistic success of 1990's *Brick by Brick* (which gave him a hit with "Candy," a duet with the B-52's Kate Pierson). At the request of his label, Iggy hauled out "Louie Louie" one more time. He blew off the dust and whatever else was sticking to it, and found himself at home again, revising the lyrics two decades after the Michigan Palace cave-in to narrate "life after Bush and Gorbachev" when "the wall is down but something is lost." His band struts confidently behind him but there's nothing dirty here, just "the news," as Iggy describes his favorite song, acknowledging how much the remarkably simple, eternal "Louie Louie" has given him over the decades, a sturdy if beat-up suitcase he's lugged around the world since he was a teenager. He can stuff so much inside of it, yet it never falls to pieces.

Halfway through, he nails what might be the perfect epitaph for this remarkable performer, this punk rock and roll lifer: *thinking about the meaning of life, I just hafta sing "Louie Louie."*

No Heroes

Can the call to writing be dramatized? Should it be?

Jessica Blank and Erik Jensen's play *How to Be a Rock Critic* begins with Lester Bangs on the toilet. Thankfully, we don't see this. We hear Bangs, played by Jensen and directed by Blank, offstage, cursing a lousy order of Kung Pao Chicken, and then a toilet flushing. Enter: Lester, opening random cans of sudsy Schlitz, bitching about a deadline and writer's block. We're facing Bangs's apartment, a mess, with a couch at center stage flanked by a chair, an ottoman, and a writing desk stage right, and a messy table on which sits a stereo, stage left; strewn across the stage are many albums (some crated, most in towering stacks), several cough syrup bottles, tossed books and magazines, the requisite open Chinese food takeout box on its side.

The production at Steppenwolf Theater's 1700 Theater in Chicago is very intimate; the space is tiny, and at the Saturday matinee my wife and I attended I counted twenty heads as the lights went down. Jensen used this nearness to address the crowd, first imploring us to remain in the hall outside his apartment, then tossing audience members cans of beer and vintage copies of *People* and *Rolling Stone* magazines to read before he settled in, took a deep breath, belched, and launched a ninety minute monologue/rant/statement of purpose about music and writing and the appeal and despair of both, with occasional backward-looking glances at his fucked-up childhood and adolescence, a fractured account of his move from California (where he wrote for, among other outlets, *Rolling Stone*) to the Lower East Side (*Village Voice*) via Detroit (*Creem*), and random spins of his favorite records—the Troggs, the Count Five, the Carpenters, the Velvets, the Stooges, the J. Geils Band, the Ramones, Van Morrison—all the while sipping beer, swilling Romilar cough syrup, and chugging straight gin. Jensen being Lester being Lester.

I'm not exactly sure what *How to Be a Rock Critic* is, or who it's for. Bangs apostles who attend will likely find themselves in one of two camps: among the Besotted, nodding along in recognition of the play's lines and the stories adapted from Bangs's work, and getting off on Jensen's tightly wound portrayal of the sloppy hero made flesh; or the Skeptical, in love with Bangs's words and his charged calling, but doubtful of the need to dramatize them so theatrically. Those new to Bangs or only slightly familiar with him might feel as if they're trapped, lectured by a well-meaning blowhard. In a way, each response is valid, as each registers somewhere along Bangs's character and intentions and the reactions that his writing—and his oversize personality—often got.

If there's a narrative arc in the play, it's Bangs's search for Van Morrison's *Astral Weeks* album; he's literally looking for it throughout the play, promising the audience that they'll love it if he can just find the damn thing, and also figuratively searching for the momentary transcendence that that music provided, and might again. The play is also bookended by Bangs's narrating of two events he witnessed: when a groupie was viciously attacked by a Hells Angel member during an orgy; and when a fourteen-year-old fan of the Clash was assaulted by a member of the band's retinue.

In both cases, Bangs did not intervene. Jensen plays these two accounts as sources of great guilt and shame for Bangs, who seems to find a parallel sense of ennui and helplessness in the face of corporate rock and bloated professionalization of rock criticism of the early and mid-1970s prepunk era. As Bangs often did, Jensen moves between ecstasy and despair—he foams at the mouth, leaps about, jumps on the coffee table and the stacks of records to make his points, and ends the performance dissolute, drunk, and high, nodding off on the couch as the Van Morrison album plays. In a nice bit of directing, the album jump-cuts to the last song, stuck in a perpetual skip as the play ends.

People who knew Bangs well said that he could be a long-winded and a loudmouth bore, that he could be very mean, especially when drunk or high, and that you often felt like a captive audience when he was holding forth. "Lester was this big, swaying, cross-eyed, reeking drooler," Richard Hell recalled in the *Village Voice* in 2003, "smiling and smiling through his crummy stained mustache, trying to corner me with incessant babble somewhere in the dark at CBGB's, 1976 or so. He was sweet like a big clumsy puppy, but he was always drunk and the sincerity level was pretty near intolerable." He added, "Of course it's easier to like a good-hearted, hard-working dead person, the extremely edited Lester, than the obliviously intrusive physically present one, but Lester has made way more friends than most since he died." That sense of being stuck with an ecstatic as he proselytizes and careens between earnestness and bombast is well dramatized in the intimate space of the 1700 Theater, and Jensen milks his center-of-attention status well. Bangs could be annoying; so is Jensen playing Bangs. Bangs was also brilliant, talented, funny, and deeply caring; Jensen moves among those poles, as well.

Do we really need more Lester Bangs myth forty years after his death? Didn't he provide enough of that when he was alive, and haven't his followers stoked the legend? Jim DeRogatis's terrific biography *Let It Blurt* (2000) and Raul Sandelin's documentary *A Box Full of Rocks: The El Cajon Years of Lester Bangs* (2013) are sturdy, clear-eyed takes on Bangs's life; Blank and Jensen are interested in the Theater of Bangs, the dimensional space that his writing inhabited in all of its hyperenergy and essayistic galloping about. These are Bangs's words and rambling sentences; it's up to Jensen to adapt them and to act them. For the most part, actor and director succeed in dramatizing Bangs's mania, which was both genuine and fuel for his self-conscious persona. A few times the production stumbles: Bangs's epiphanic moments of reflection are precious and often telegraphed, Blank making Bangs's unhappiness and depressive hopelessness obvious. Bangs was rarely subtle, a personality trait and writerly aesthetic he seemed to lack or be deeply skeptical of, but often on the page, especially in his more autobiographical writing, the energy and drive of his sentences did as much to describe his ill-fated mania as do Jensen's wounded, over-the-shoulder glances to the audience.

Blank and Jensen also get it right, most often when Bangs holds forth about the music he loves. His description of driving around with a blissy, spaced-out girlfriend as the Troggs' "Wild Thing" plays on the radio wonderfully captures the way that simple, unadorned rock and roll—Bangs's favorite kind—can open doors to overstuffed rooms. Near the end of the play, as Jensen's admirably paced alcohol- and cough syrup-high is cresting, Bangs takes on Elvis, persuasively proving that the boy from Tupelo who seemed to come from outer space was both a local turd and a larger-than-life force of nature. *Why can't he be both?* Bangs wonders. (I bristled at Jensen's mimicry of Elvis's moves as Bangs imagined eating the drugs from Presley's intestines after Presley died; it's one of Bangs's greatest, most insanely inspired riffs, and Jensen's play-acting trivializes it.) Before he nods off to Morrison's "Cypress Avenue," Bangs ruminates on the power of music that once gave him a glimpse into something remarkable, something that refreshed him and gave him hope. His confessing to spending the rest of his life trying to rediscover and renew that moment is the most potent and moving dramatization—and description—of Bangs's life and career that the play achieves.

As any fan of Bangs's writing knows, even in his pay-the-rent shitty album reviews and profiles, he was rarely writing just about music; he was writing about what it means to be a living, breathing human who didn't choose to be here and is now stuck looking for justification. Bangs writes about how being alive blows and is also the greatest gift—45s and album cuts were simply the moving parts that got his words to the page.

Still, I'm on the fence, somewhere between my gratitude for Blank and Jensen's commitment to a great writer and my skepticism about whether music writing can be fully dramatized. After the performance, I wondered half-seriously if maybe the best thing Blank and Jensen could've done would've been to have Jensen-as-Bangs sit on his couch, drink, get high, and play the entirety of the Carpenters' *Close to You*, or all four sides of Lou Reed's *Metal Machine Music,* while half grinning, leering, and crying and—oh, and here's Bangs on *Metal Machine Music*: "As a statement it's great, as a giant FUCK YOU it shows integrity—a sick, twisted, dunced-out, malevolent, perverted, psychopathic integrity, but integrity nevertheless"—not saying a word. He's staying here. After all, we've got his books.

A Groovy Way to Grab a Musical Bag That Turns On the Sounds of Today

In the 1970s, the Pickwick label released a slew of albums featuring Kings Road, a studio-concoction "group" that recorded sometimes inspired, mostly inept versions of current hit songs. I listened to these records as a kid, with the dawning realization that I was being ripped off.

Rediscover Records, Elgin, Illinois. The voice to which I'm only half-listening sounds familiar, but something's off, also. I look up blankly from the records I'm riffling through and realize that I'm hearing Elton John, one of his well-known hits from the early seventies, but I haven't heard this version before. Is it a demo? An early take? A scratch vocal? Elton sounds pretty awful, as if he's poorly imitating someone imitating him. That, or he has a cold. I ask the cashier what's playing. She points to the album sleeve propped on the counter.

Turns out that I'm half correct. It is Elton. And it isn't. *Elton John Rock Hits* was released in 1975 near the tail end of the pianist-singer's half decade meteoric journey across the Top 40, but John was nowhere to be found in the studio when the album was concocted. The songs here, those that momentarily confounded me in the record store—"Goodbye Yellow Brick Road," "Daniel," "Rocket Man," "Don't Let the Sun Go Down On Me," et al.—were performed by King's Road, an anonymous group of session musicians and singers whose catalogue by the midseventies was bulging. Between 1970 and 1975 they issued twenty-three albums, nearly all on the Pickwick label (their career would be finished by 1976).

King's Road wasn't a band so much as a hologram—a holoband, a hollow band—a one-dimensional image of a group whose sole purpose was to imitate, gamely if at times ineptly, the well-known hits of the day. King's Road was a bad joke, a cut-rate impressionist. King's Road was the best at being the worst.

Pickwick Records was founded in 1950 by Cy Leslie, a Harvard-educated World War II veteran who understood the dynamics of the wallet. He'd started Voco Records, an audio greeting card company that branched out to children's albums. After further success with the Cricket label, he began issuing cheaply priced albums through Pickwick, initially based in Long Island City across the East River from Manhattan. Through the 1950s and 1960s, Pickwick specialized in low-cost albums that were designed to move swiftly from studio to retail/discount stores to family rec rooms.

In the 1970s Pickwick began acquiring albums that had been deleted by record companies, including RCA and Motown, and proceeded to flood the market with one cheaply packaged reissue after another—think of the cut-rate Elvis albums you've been seeing in used record stores and thrift shops for decades. Pickwick would eventually purchase a sizeable pressing plant and enter into profitable agreements with various retailers, most notably Musicland, which agreed to hawk Pickwick products in their stores (known as "rack jobbing operations"). Thus as John Broven observes in *Record Makers and Breakers: Voices of the Independent Rock 'n' Roll Pioneers*, "Pickwick controlled content, manufacturing, distribution, and points of sale." Leslie might've been jeered at as the "King of the Cheapies," but he was no dummy.

In 1970, Pickwick's *Plays Today's Pops* appeared in stores, featuring the Beatles' "Hey Jude," Dion's "Abraham, Martin, and John," Ohio Express' "Chewy Chewy," Judy Collins's "Both Sides Now," and others. But who's performing them? According to the liner notes on the back sleeve, "a group of today's musicians taking today's music and making it their thing." That's unassailable, if wildly misleading. Further elucidation follows, including the origin story of King's Road:

> Formed in the swinging summer of '68 in London, their music bag is from all over. "King's Road" is a moving, shifting group. It swirls and reforms itself, into the frenetic patterns of today's musical sounds. The multi talents of the group are colorful as their way out gear, and as diversified as the sounds they create. Many were classically trained, others self taught by the big beat that throbs through the boutiques & bistros the length of King's Road, Chelsea—the centre of swingin' London.
>
> This is their bag. The sounds of today made their way . . . The groovy feeling of being young, being now, are what today's hip composers created in this record.

The writer signs off with that age-old query: "Dig?"

Let's unpack. To describe the turbulent summer of 1968 as "swinging" might be an historical inaccuracy, but we can forgive that—they were confusing times—yet describing King's Road as "moving" and "shifting" as it "swirls and reforms" smartly pegs the group's raison d'être: they're faceless, nameless studio musicians hired to reproduce familiar songs, and required beneath a ticking studio clock to move swiftly from one song style to the next. "Multi-talented"? Probably. Some are "classically trained," while others are "self-taught." Who's to argue? We don't know who the musicians are. As the comprehensive crowd-sourced database Discogs shrugs of the entire King's Road cannon: "No credits anywhere."

Presumably, *Plays Today's Pops* sold well enough to warrant a follow-up. *Let It Be,* also issued in 1970, contained versions of Tony Joe White's "Rainy Night in Georgia," Santana's "Evil Ways," Ashley and Foster's "House of the Rising Sun," the title track, and others; later that year, tracks from both albums were gathered with several new cuts for *18 Top Hits By The King's Road*. Common to *Plays Today's Pops* and *18 Top Hits* was a front- and back-cover photo of a Carnaby-Lite mod couple emerging from a paisley pink-orange-red swirl, she wearing heavy eyeliner, a fur-trimmed vest, bright red slacks, and a headband, he a goatee, a multicolored scarf, a red jacket to match his girl's, and oversize sunglasses in the shape of the Union Jack. (I guess his scarf was multi*coloured*.)

Then came the flood of *Super Hits* compilations, ten of them issued between 1971 and 1973, each gathering King's Road's versions of current hit songs, each sporting a smilingly flirtatious young woman on the front and back covers and retailing, as the ubiquitous liner notes promise, "for just over a dollar and change." The albums are interchangeable, a collective barometer of early to midseventies pop. From Crosby, Stills, Nash & Young, T. Rex, and the Carpenters to Steely Dan, Wings, and the O'Jays—with Sly & the Family Stone, the Faces, and Bread among many others making noise—the artists and groups featured on the *Super Hits* series spanned widely disparate tastes and styles, a broad swath of Top 100 Nixon-era daylight. The albums, like many of Pickwick's low-budget releases, were stocked in discount department and convenience stores, ready to move.

Once teenagers got past the groovy typeface and eye candy of the front cover, they didn't have to drop the needle to learn the hard truth, they merely had to read the liner notes, as by the second album a certain "Keith Wood," posting from Pickwick International, was pretty clear about what was going on. Before signing off with "Love & Peace," Wood urged buyers to send him titles of songs they wanted to hear on future albums, care of an address in Long Island City. In later albums he gave shoutouts to the fans who wrote in, inevitably girls "with a little bread for a little rock," and those names—"Vicki Mulchi in North Carolina, Debbie Kuell in Chicago, Donna Fischer in Cedarburg, Carrie Charters in Canada, Bianca Gonzalez in California," et al.—were likely as fake as his own. ("Keith Wood?" my wife said. "Sounds like a mashup of Richards and Ronnie to me.") His name might've been bogus, but his aim was true: "What we're doing on this record is to cherry pick the charts for the hits and the heavies, record them to sound just like the original high priced spread, and rush the whole works straight to you at the crazy low price marked on the front of this jacket," adding for good measure, "Instead of spreading your bread thin to get all the goodies you're hearing on the radio, just look for the Superhit album of the month."

On the second *Super Hits*, the band's described as a "ragged, lovable talented crowd of kids" now "loosely tagged" as King's Road. By the ninth *Super Hits*, the jig was up. Flatly, Keith Wood calls the band Pickwick's "resident rip-off group."

The members of this house con band may be lost to history, but they toiled within a long-standing tradition. (Lou Reed, pre-Velvet Underground, worked as an uncredited songwriter and studio musician on a couple of Pickwick and its subsidiaries' albums in the early and midsixties. And funnily enough, before he hit it big and inspired rerecordings of his own hits, Elton John labored, without credit, on many soundalike compilation albums released in the United Kingdom in the late 1960s and early 1970s.) Session musicians have routinely been stripped of their identities, their names absent from labels or sleeves, their hard work and gifts distinguished only by the music itself. Even at massive databases such as AllMusic or Discogs, the latter of which exhaustingly documents the names of recording personnel, session musicians depend on the kindness of labels to provide proof of their existence. For every group of studio musicians such as the Muscle Shoals Rhythm Section, the Wrecking Crew, the Funk Brothers, or the Nashville A-Team, some members of which have become well-known and rightly celebrated (if not always compensated fairly), there are countless unnamed backing singers and instrumentalists, paid by the hour, who've shuffled anonymously in and out of studios. These musicians, on the clock in large and small studios, recording a film score or an advertisement or behind a hopeful nobody, on 48 tracks or 4, master the arrangements of songs that aren't theirs, contributing their expertise and chops with the expectations that their input won't showily intrude, won't run against the grain of the song as the writer or writers present it. A session musician has a clear job to do.

King's Road's trade was far murkier. Like the mood ring or the pet rock, they were very much a product of their era. Their charge wasn't to play songs, exactly, but to reproduce them. They weren't a conventional cover band, nor were they a tribute outfit. They didn't write and perform original songs that milked a fading trend in the hopes of commercial relevance. (Think of forgotten late-era-Beatlemania groups, KISS' 1997 "grunge" album, and the like.) King's Road weren't deceitful scammers, as their game—"Played and sung like the original hits"—was clearly emblazoned on the front and back covers. The songs themselves weren't counterfeits, out to fool the ear in the way that a seasoned forger dreams of bilking an art dealer out of millions. I can't locate the many members of King's Road. If I did, I'd ask them where their own artistic ambitions fit in the Cy Leslie/Pickwick assembly line, whether inside another's Top 10 hit they felt, and either resisted or indulged, an urge to express themselves creatively, a vocal manner or a guitar line echoing the original's language but written in their own hand.

Few would pay a hefty admission fee to a museum that hangs only reproductions of art—*Painted and Framed Like the Original O'Keeffe!*—yet Pickwick found a way to attract an audience hungry for product by capitalizing on both the shifting sands of Top 100 and the surging album market, marrying the two at a low cost. Because the label wasn't compiling original songs, it didn't have to pay for the privilege of doing so, dodging millions of dollars in licensing and copyright fees. Pickwick seemed to simply duck the lawyers for as long as it could. Infamous for operating with a low-budget mentality, label executives discovered a gray area somewhere between securing copyright permissions and paying out mechanical royalties to release cover songs. Hence the spate of *Super Hits* in your local discount store, an inexpensive boon to parents on the hunt for birthday presents for their moody teenagers. As Keith Wood enthused on the back cover of album after album, Pickwick delivered a "lotta rock for a little bread."

In *Record Makers and Breakers*, Broven notes that Cy Leslie's budget volume business "was shunned by serious record collectors," but that "their narrow niche was not his concern." The latter's true enough; in a 2005 interview, Leslie explained that Pickwick's goal was to "keep a good reputation; that's important," yet first and foremost was "to keep overhead as tight as you can."

Yet despite—or because of—its shoddy elan, Leslie's product has not gone ignored by collectors down the years. One such fan is Shelley Pierce, a longtime DJ at KMSU at Minnesota State University, Mankato. She owns more than two hundred such soundalike compilations, mostly on Pickwick (similar records have been issued on Springboard, Modern Sound, and Mountain Dew Records, among other labels). "I started picking them up for the covers. There are so many things to love about these records," she says. "The labels clearly did not pay for the rights to release them and they would slightly alter some aspect of the song to get away with it. But at the same time they strove to sound as much like the original as possible. I love hearing the bad imitations as much as the really good ones. If they were at a loss for how to sing a hard part or hit the high notes they would give it off to a guitar solo instead or even have a woman sing it instead of a man." A favorite moment of deception for Pierce occurs on a soundalike song of Yoko Ono's, where the band approximated her singing style with . . . a trumpet.

The enduring mystery of the nameless personnel has enthralled Pierce, as well. "I've rarely found a record that actually has credits of any kind. A few might have photos of some players, but no names. Or if there were names they were clearly made up names. Why? If they included the actual names of the musicians would that be a giveaway to consumers that it wasn't the original artists? Was it a simply cheaper to pay the musicians a set price and send them on their way?" She wonders if they might've been too embarrassed to admit that they played on these knockoffs. "I honestly don't think we'll ever find out."

Pierce is also drawn to the fact that these records were "straight up con jobs." A record store employee in Mankato, she's continually amazed that these albums, with their dated covers and of-the-era panache, manage to dupe unsuspecting buyers. "Just the other day someone was buying what they thought was the *Grease* soundtrack, but it was actually sung by a soundalike group called The Cruisers." She remembers being nine years old and coveting the *Star Wars* soundtrack for her birthday. "My mom went out and bought the first record she saw that had *Star Wars* on the record sleeve, without paying too much attention to the artist. In this case it was Meco, not John Williams."

Poignantly, the deception didn't matter all that much to Pierce: "I was a kid and it sounded like the *Star Wars* music I remembered from the film. Perhaps the audience for these kind of records were kids as well? Or those who weren't too picky and didn't have the money to spend on the real deal? I suppose it was all of these."

At a theater in my town last month, Liverpool Legends, a Grammy-nominated Beatles tribute band, performed their "The Complete Beatles Experience!" The group was allegedly fashioned by none other than George Harrison's sister Louise Harrison, who hand-picked the four musicians and actors herself. "Each member of the group is so close to the originals," she gushed in a press release, "that I often feel like I'm transported back in time with the lads." I didn't attend. But I'm not a cynic about such things. I understand the appeal and nod respectfully at the endurance of the highly lucrative tribute band circuit, the nights of genuine pleasure offered fans who want to ride back in time to whatever mop-topped, be-fringed, or mulleted world those songs and those singers created, and these tributes revive, for them. No guilty pleasures there.

The time machine appeal of the *Super Hits* albums is something different. Hearing the songs, I'm taken back to a time in cultural history when deception met dollars, when your not-really-favorite hits were dished up by a smiling woman in a halter top. When I was a kid and Pickwick's *Super Hits Volume 10* and *The Beatles 1962–1970* ended up in my family's suburban basement, I rejoiced. The Pickwick Beatles album appeared the same year the Apple label released the epochal "Red" and "Blue" Beatles compilations, their arrival a seminal moment in my music life, and millions of others'. Pickwick's compilation was clearly a cash-in. It bizarrely extended into the Beatles' members' solo careers, its fourth side including versions of "Maybe I'm Amazed," "My Sweet Lord," and, fantastically, John Lennon's emotionally painful "Mother". Yet it and its generic front- and back-cover art design are perversely dear to my heart. My brothers and I knew within seconds of dropping the needle that we weren't listening to the Beatles. The deceptiveness of it was unnerving but mostly hilarious, and not absent a dose of adolescent melancholy. "Listening to King's Road," I wrote a decade ago, "I felt unnamed pity for the musicians even as I was making fun of them. . . . What was meant to sound like earnest tribute and celebration fell on my ears as desperate and embarrassing. This much I understood as the album spun around and around: King's Road were the weary substitute teachers of pop music."

I pouted as a kid when listening to the Edgar Winter Group's "Frankenstein," the Who's "Pinball Wizard," and Steely Dan's "Reeling in the Years" on *Super Hits Volume 10*—imposters all—and yet I'm surprised at how decent are many of the soundalikes, especially those that I'm hearing for the first time. Sly and the Family Stone's "Family Affair" and Isaac Hayes's "Theme from *Shaft*" from volume 4 are much looser and funkier than I would've ever imagined, the musicians syncopating with some style, evoking the grooves and vibe of the sublime originals. And on the second volume, the version of Cornelius Brothers & Sister Rose's slinky, irresistible "Treat Her Like a Lady's" not too shabby either, the band sliding under the snug arrangement with ease, and T. Rex's "Hot Love," though the singer's overmatched by Marc Bolan's original vocal—who wouldn't be?—evokes that band's spacey glam and smiling, heavy-lidded sensuality in ways that honor the song's uniqueness, not simply imitate it.

But many King's Road attempts miss the mark. Though it's rude to poke fun, it's also too fun not to. Consider the Rolling Stones' "Tumbling Dice." The singer's take is howlingly inept, and the lyrics are wrong—so wrong that one wonders if they were transcribed by a dude who was tripping while lip-reading Jagger through snowy television reception. The lyrics on *Exile on Main Street* were notoriously difficult to figure out, so I think King's Road just said, *Screw it, we'll write our own* (which are also tough to figure out, so I guess they went for verisimilitude of a sort). And while it's unfair to expect any group of musicians to match the well-worn, in-the-pocket groove of sounds caught in that humid basement in Villa Nellcôte, King's Road, with their cardboard guitars and plodding arrangement, seems to have aimed for a bar-band-on-a-dare vibe, not that the stakes were particularly high.

Sadly, I've yet to come across Pickwick's *Excerpts from the Rock Operas* in the record store wilds, a 1973 double album on which King's Road offers selections from *Tommy*, *Jesus Christ Superstar*, *Hair*, and *Godspell*, but I did recently reacquire *The Beatles 1962–1970*, and I urge you to track down a copy, as it's a model of the genre. King's Road comes off sounding like somewhere between a *Beatlemania* cast rehearsal and a half-committed soundcheck by Sire Records–era Flamin' Groovies. On several tracks—"I Want to Hold Your Hand," "Get Back," "Can't Buy Me Love," "My Sweet Lord," one or two others—the singers fairly approximate the lead Beatle singer, but what's glaringly absent is that ineffable spark the Beatles created as they played. The probability of a group of session musicians capturing that is so laughingly remote that my instinct is to feel as if the whole thing's a send-up. The harmonies in "Please Please Me" and the famous opening chord of "A Hard Day's Night," are merely copied, in "Hello Goodbye" the psychedelic mischief only hinted at, the arrangements throughout the album so wooden and unimaginative as to suggest a first-take/best-take work ethic burdening a band with little time for rehearsal.

The true oddity here is Lennon's "Mother," a song so harrowingly personal and complexly dark that it beggars belief the track was even on offer to King's Road, let alone selected for the album. Lennon wrote "Mother" after intense primal therapy sessions with the psychotherapist Arthur Janov in an attempt to purge himself of his grief, anger, and pain of abandonment. Though faithful to Phil Spector and Lennon/Yoko Ono's minimal production and arrangement, including that haunting reverb, King's Road's version pales, and is poorly sung, a sonic equivalent of a spotlit teen actor puffing his chest to emote adult stuff. I can only imagine each potential singer clearing his throat and pointing to the others when this song came up for recording—who'd want to tackle a performance so raw and private, not to mention infamous and epochal? (Interestingly, "Mother" has been covered several times, by Barbra Streisand, Shelby Lynne, Lou Reed, David Bowie, and others.) I don't know who the singer is, of course, and my embarrassment for him is relieved somewhat by his decision to not try and match Lennon's anguished and cathartic screams during the fade, opting instead for a few affected moans. He didn't need the therapy, I'm guessing.

By the end of the decade, the writing was on the wall. In 1977, Pickwick was purchased by the American Can Company. (A manufacturer of tin cans—the irony, given the "inside of a tin can" quality to King's Roads' recordings, is fitting.) American moved the corporate headquarters from Long Island City to Minneapolis, Minnesota, and sold its assets to PolyGram the same year. PolyGram folded Pickwick for good in 1983.

The death knell for the soundalike records, and for King's Road's career such as it was, had tolled a few years earlier. After the *Super Hits* compilations dried up in 1973, Pickwick issued a few more "played and sung like . . ." albums, one each of Neil Diamond, Simon & Garfunkel, Neil Sedaka, and Elton John (including the record that baffled me momentarily in the record store), and a couple of TV show themes, before the line ended, and with it a certain Zeitgeist. "I suspect these kinds of records came to an end when the record business started to pay attention to paying for the rights to record the songs," Pierce says. "Perhaps there was a ten-year loophole that soundalikes took advantage of? I'm afraid this will all remain a mystery unless someone in the record business who was involved with soundalikes decides to share their experiences," she said, adding, "In the meantime I will just keep collecting them and enjoying the crazy covers."

As reported by Zaria Gorvett for the BBC a few years back, anatomy researcher Teghan Lucas, equipped with a collection of photographs of U.S. military personnel and the assistance of colleagues from the University of Adelaide, studied the faces of nearly four thousand people,

> measuring the distances between key features such as the eyes and ears. Next she calculated the probability that two peoples' faces would match.

> What she found was good news for the criminal justice system, but likely to disappoint anyone pining for their long-lost double: the chances of sharing just eight dimensions with someone else are less than one in a trillion. Even with 7.4 billion people on the planet, that's only a one in 135 chance that there's a single pair of doppelgängers. "Before you could always be questioned in a court of law, saying 'well what if someone else just looks like him?' Now we can say it's extremely unlikely," says Teghan.

It seems to me that the *Super Hits* albums buck those slender odds. Badfinger, Neil Young, the Bee Gees, Carole King, the Doobie Brothers, Jim Croce, Harry Nilsson, Bread, et al.—haunt your local record stores and thrift shops and you'll find spirit doubles of them all, ghostly doppelgängers, other Selves of songs. They sound uncannily close to their twin strangers, and yet something's not quite right in the performance.

Shopping for her family of eight in the 1970s, my mom chose to buy knockoff sodas rather than name brands. Thus, I grew up on Cragmont Cola, Safeway supermarket's house brand, not Coke, which nearly all of my friends drank. Yet I grew to love Cragmont. If I were to taste one now I'd likely reel with nostalgia for an ideal childhood. I think about what it might have been like had I grown up, pre-Internet, on a remote outpost somewhere, a thinly populated island, or a one-light town in far northern Greenland, wherever radio and commerce and pop culture would perish on their way to, and the only records I owned were a few *Super Hits* albums that made their way to my local one-stop shop. If all I knew in my life were King's Road songs, would I have loved them? Would they have moved me as profoundly as so many of thc original songs have, changed my life in countless ways, given me hours and hours of deep pleasures? Raised on the merely adequate, I might have become a different person, less robust, undernourished, and yet unaware that I was subsisting on a meager, lesser diet, the *Super Hits* albums soundtracking my life in shades of grays. Fortified by King's Road, I might've taken fewer risks, offered only lukewarm advice to friends and strangers, shied away from pursuing that girl, shrugged my shoulders at a sublime sunset.

Then I imagine myself at Rediscover Records hearing for the first time not Pickwick's Elton John cash-in album, but *Honky Château* or *Goodbye Yellow Brick Road* or *Madman Across the Water*, astonished by the differences, but maybe scoffing lightly, finding Elton's songs fussy or baroque, his band too busy, Paul Buckmaster's arrangements over-the-top. Would the store around me gradually, without my barely taking note, brighten, the world outside waiting for my deliverance into a more authentic, rich life? Or would I prefer the ersatz, content in my sentimental love for the off-key singing, pedestrian arrangements, and dull musicians of the songs that scored my adolescence? King's Road were the million-sellers in an alternate universe. I raise a Cragmont Cola to them.

Dispatches from the Past Present, or Dick Clark's Face

Dick Clark was omnipresent when I was a kid, a genial, smiling face that promised good times and good cheer. The *Dick Clark/20 Years of Rock n' Roll* double-album soundtracks the unruly early and midseventies while also looking back in nostalgia.

Spring 1973. Chuck Berry, Bo Diddley, Little Richard, the Shirelles, Bill Haley, and other acts popular in the 1950s and early 1960s are playing to big crowds on Richard Nader's wildly successful "Rock & Roll Revival" tours. Nader, a former radio deejay, had pined for the earlier, less complicated days of popular music, and, a born promoter, he sensed that the average American was, too. A feature on Nader in an October 1970 issue of *Record World* reports that in the late 1960s, he'd faced an uphill climb, enduring "scant success in convincing anyone that the revival would occur. But today, niteries around the country are offering oldies nights, the major record labels have been purchasing old catalogs and radio stations are programming more oldies shows than ever."

Nostalgia's in the breeze. "When people bumped up against the nineteen seventies there were many things that made them very uncomfortable," Nader remarks to the *New York Times* in 1973. "Comfortable, secure, warm, accepted—that's all nostalgia is." He adds, "All I did was give them the key, music of the fifties that made guys my age in the seventies comfortable and secure. They were running to my show, not to applaud The Five Satins or Bill Haley or Chuck Berry, but their own memories and associations. They were getting back into the irresponsibility, the carefreeness, the fun they had before they got married. They were crawling back into the womb of Madison Square Garden."

At Nader's Rock 'n Roll Spectacular Volume VII show at the Garden in October 1971, Ricky Nelson, the former "teen idol" who'd played a popular character on *The Adventures of Ozzie and Harriet* in the 1950s and who'd scored many Top 40 hits, dutifully performs a scattering of his oldies. He's warmly received until he moves across the stage to the piano to play his take on the Rolling Stones' "Honky Tonk Women," a song that was then only a couple of years old. "When he sang his hits, everybody loved him," Nader tells Gary James. "I tell you, there were standing ovations, one after another." He adds that the twenty thousand people who were at Madison Square Garden that evening, however,

> were not there to hear contemporary music. They were there to escape it, the Vietnam War and the '70s. They were seeking to slip back to the euphoria and comfort of oldies Rock 'n' Roll . . .
>
> When he started to sing "Honky Tonk Woman" [sic], that disrupted the ambiance of the evening. The euphoric sort of cloud that was in the Garden became disrupted because here was a current song that jarred people from the '50s to the '70s and back to reality. They booed him because of that.

The boos begin softly, first "a ripple," and then "louder and louder to the point where Rick was just bewildered. He's in the center stage of twenty thousand people, sold-out, and he's being booed. So he went back, put his guitar on and sang his signature song and left the stage. So we continued on with the show."

Nelson, a writer-performer looking backward and forward simultaneously, finding his way, will write the song "Garden Party" in response to these boos. "After the people have heard ["Garden Party"] a few times, they begin to listen more to the words and discover what it's about," Nelson will remark to *ZigZag* magazine a couple of years later. "Some people, though, think that the song is about some desire I might have to return to the Fifties. It's really just the opposite, of course—I'm trying to put a stop to all that."

Meanwhile, in the summer of 1973 David Bowie records *Pin Ups*, an album of covers of 1960s U.K. songs, and a few months later in Los Angeles John Lennon commences sessions for his ill-fated *Rock 'n' Roll*, an album of covers of late 1950s and early 1960s songs, coproduced with Phil Spector.

On February 25, 1972, an episode of *Love, American Style* titled "Love and the Television Set" premieres, which, we'll learn later, was the unsold pilot episode for *Happy Days*. (In the episode, an American family in the 1950s purchases their first television set.) Film director George Lucas is inspired by the episode to cast young Ron Howard as Steve Bolander in his film *American Graffiti*, set in Modesto, California, in the summer of 1962. The movie's a massive success, encouraging ABC to revisit and to ultimately greenlight *Happy Days*, which will run for eleven seasons and two hundred and fifty-plus episodes, never moving beyond its 1950s and 1960s plotlines. Production of the first season begins in 1973 as *American Graffiti*'s becoming a sleeper hit, while Chuck Berry's duckwalking his way across stages from the past to the present and back again.

On June 1, 1973, eight OPEC countries raise the price of petroleum by 11.9 percent. Two days later, John Dean informs members of the House Judiciary Committee that he'd discussed the cover-up with President Nixon at least thirty-five times. Back to reality, *boooooooo*. So, the national mood is complicated. Executives at Buddah Records wonder if Americans over the age of thirty want to hear the songs from their collective childhood and adolescence, songs that scored long afternoons and gentle twilights, songs that didn't call attention to the darkly complex currents in the air.

By the 1970s Dick Clark has been "America's Oldest Teenager" for quite some time, having hosted *American Bandstand* for many years, helping to create and exploit the youth market that gladly opened their collective allowance-fed wallets. In 1972 he produces the first of his *New Year's Rockin' Eve* countdowns in Times Square, assuming hosting duties two years later, and in 1973 he begins hosting *The $10,000 Pyramid* game show, assuring that his genial face and well-scrubbed demeanor will charm folks in their kitchens and living rooms on a regular basis for decades to come.

Buddah Records, meanwhile, is facing some rough times. Having ridden high on the charts only a few years before with innocuous bubblegum singles such as "Simon Says" and "1-2-3 Red Light" (by the 1910 Fruitgum Company) and "Yummy Yummy Yummy" and "Chewy Chewy" (the Ohio Express), the label's now reckoning with rapidly changing album and radio markets, foreboding changes in the weather as the teens who smacked gum at the local public pool and devoured disposable 45s are growing up, following their daring friends and older siblings into the murky waves of progressive music and hard rock. By 1973, though Buddah's still delivering singles and albums in the charts, the writing's on the wall; head honcho and hits-creator Neil Bogart will depart the following year to found Casablanca Records—the name of which conjures disco, KISS, and piles of blow, indelible markers of the end of the tumultuous decade far removed from the innocent sunniness of bubblegum.

One of the last records Buddah will release during their glory years is *Dick Clark/20 Years of Rock n' Roll*, a gathering of thirty "original hits" aimed at those eager to turn away from the amped din of acid rock and power trios, Nixon, and fuel shortages. An image of a smiling Dick Clark (is that redundant?) is splashed on the album cover, his toothy grin saying, *It's ok*. Just over his shoulder looms an image of Clark from the 1950s that says, *Look, good things can last.*

20 Years of Rock n' Roll arrived at my family's house in Wheaton, Maryland, shortly after its release. I recall sitting with the double album down in our rec room—in other memories I'm in the basement—poring over the images on the sleeve, and yet my siblings assure me that we never had the LPs, rather we had the 8-track tape, and we probably selected it from the Columbia Record Club, that mail-order bonanza that delivered many an album to our home. However it arrived, and in whatever format, *20 Years of Rock n' Roll* became a formative album for me as a kid.

As I look closely at the album now I recognize that Buddah packaged it with a slightly more complex approach than Clark's simple, beaming face suggests. Bookending Clark on the left are newspapers clippings about early rock and roll and Beatlemania, on the right about Woodstock and biker gangs—a lot of history between those images remains untold, but Clark's face *is* the real news here, the reason we bought the record (or the tape or the 8-track), his smile papering over darker, more unsettling news. Open the gatefold sleeve and the narrative told by the headlines gets a bit more complicated. Clark's face pops up several more times (Dick's the album's emcee, the guiding spirit, he's what holds the center) as you read about the Jets and the Mets' amazing wins and the moon landing, yet also stories about rock and roll as a "communicable disease," the Pill, Kennedy's assassination, Johnson's decision not to seek reelection. Watergate.

Flip over the album and we retreat again to midcentury quaintness with a montage of black-and-white images—sock-hopping teenagers, a Dick Clark *Caravan of Stars* tour bus, a scene from the set of an *American Bandstand* episode, nearly everyone gleaming, buttoned-up, white. The present returns as your gaze drifts to the center of the sleeve, where there's Clark again, standing in what looks like a studio backlot. In an oddly meta move he's holding a copy of the very album I'm holding, his collars, lapels, and pants legs seventies-wide, his face grinning the grin, offering a gift from the past that both celebrates and obscures that past.

"A good portrait ought to tell something of the subject's past and suggest something of his future." That's photographer Bill Brandt. I see little of the past in Clark's face other than what he wants me to see, a made-for-TV version of history, his and the country's, and you can dance to it. What does his face say about the future? I still havc to remind myself lhat he died (in 2012, following a stroke), so permanent a fixture was he in my childhood, on TV, on album covers. If Clark's preternaturally youthful, smiling face suggested anything about his future it was that that future might never come.

Record executive, journalist, and producer Richard Robinson enjoyed a long and rich journey through popular music. He ditched his studies at Yale a few months before he was to graduate to form a band, and by the end of the 1960s was writing a syndicated music column and spinning discs late at night on WNEW-FM in New York City. He married the music journalist and author Lisa Robinson, with whom he cofounded *Rock Scene* and edited *Hit Parader*. He later found work as a producer of the Flamin' Groovies, Lou Reed, and David Johansen. A record executive at Buddah, he was involved in various design and production duties, such as composing the occasional liner notes, which included the knocked-out space age copy on the back of *Journey to the Moon*, an of-the-era album celebrating the moon landing with "hip" music by Sound of Genesis.

And he cowrote Dick Clark's autobiography, *Rock, Roll & Remember*, and wrote the copy to the twenty-three-page *Yearbook* booklet that came with *20 Years of Rock n' Roll*, stuffed with yet more promotional photos of artists and bands and even more headlines. Cartoon stars light up every page. The text is essentially a potted history of popular music from the Crew Cuts and Bill Haley to Alice Cooper and T. Rex, but because Robinson was an intuitive and knowledgeable music writer and cultural historian, he's keen to weave in national and international events—television's ascendency, the Korean War, Hollywood flicks, Sputnik, the Israeli/Arab conflicts, Vietnam War protests, the Bobby Kennedy and Martin Luther King assassinations, and the rest. But any attempt to add historical dimension to the sounds of Top 40 is flattened into a Wikipedia-like litany of events, history as bullet points. Dick Clark's face appears on nearly every page: he's interviewing and posing with musicians, he's a smiling floating head the high wattage of which bleaches away troublesome news, conflicting narratives of racism, sexism, and payola. Robinson clearly understood his remit from the Buddah execs, as *American Bandstand*'s history and Clark's role in it are offered as a kind of origin story of popular music, our host's pleased countenance a through line from start to finish. Richard Wagstaff Clark, without whom . . .

Dick Clark's face revolving, revolving. This is no fever dream. *20 Years of Rock n' Roll* came packaged with a "special bonus record," a cardboard flexi disc emblazoned with, naturally, Clark's cheery face. (The record plays at 33 1/3 rpm, and in an unnerving design bug the spindle hole nailed Clark right between his eyes.) On the record, he shares a handful of memories. "You know, I got to thinking," he begins in his impossibly relaxed, amiable manner, "there isn't any way I'm going to be able to ramble about the past twenty years of my life in and around rock n' roll and get it done in any reasonable length of time." He chuckles. "Too much has happened, I've had so many great memories I'd like to share with you."

So he focusses his lens, talks about "close personal friends" in the music business, that one "girl singer" (Connie Francis), the fabled "Fabian shot," a close-up on the heartthrob singer employed to capitalize on his "sensual good looks"—Clark remarks with fatherly pride that the Fabian shot is still being used "on Donny Osmond, Mick Jagger, Paul McCartney, Alice Cooper" (Alice Cooper??)—and the time his talent coordinator hesitated in booking the Mamas & the Papas because "they don't look like our kind of people, they're just not right." Ever the even-tempered, cool-headed host, Clark urged her to book them anyway. "And she did," he chuckles.

Listening now conjures an image of a group of long-haired teens, a captive audience sitting at Clark's feet, one kid clutching a Led Zeppelin album, another an Isley Brothers album, a little bored with the old guy as he reveals star after star who made their debut on *American Bandstand.* Stoned eyerolls all around. Clark's monologue's more than corny, to be sure, with more than a hint of self-aggrandizement, yet Clark pulls it off completely, so disarmingly lured are we into cottony complacency and feel-good vibes by the folksiness of his voice, his gee-whizz enthusiasm, his earnest eagerness to please. Dick Clark's face rotates at forty revolutions a minute and a spell is cast.

20 Years of Rock N' Roll did big business on its release. "With the nostalgia craze at full storm, this album is a natural," gushed *Billboard* in its "Top Album Picks" column in the June 30, 1973 issue, adding that "the worldwide name value of Dick Clark is also a winner." The verdict? "Best cuts: All of them." Two months later, Buddah took out a full-page ad in *Billboard* congratulating Clark (and themselves) for selling more than a million copies of the double album.

If you're reading this in, say, your twenties, your conception of *a half century* is wildly different from a person who's reading this in their sixties—the absurd weight and surreal pull of time. If a day is a microcosm of a life, I think of the decades I spent during any given afternoon of my childhood listening to *20 Years of Rock n' Roll*, an album that we're as far away from now as the album itself was from 1923.

I loved *20 Years of Rock n' Roll* as much as any other record when I was a kid. The thirty songs have lodged in my musical DNA, as essential to my genetic identity as my height and handedness. The record's my internal Big Bang, and I've carried the songs inside of me for decades, the first years of which especially intensely, as they essentially soundtracked my childhood, the complicated moments in the classrooms and hallways and on the school playground at St. Andrew the Apostle, during my long solo allowance walks or bike rides, with my family around the dinner table or down in the basement, alone upstairs in my room. This music was the weather I walked through. Along with the Beatles' "Red" and "Blue" albums, *20 Years of Rock n' Roll* laid the foundation. A half century later I still know the sequencing by heart, the expectations in the clicks-and-pops between tracks, the next song beginning before this one ends. *20 Years of Rock n' Roll* stuck by me, stuck inside me, coloring everything I did.

Within a few years of the album's release, St. Andrew's introduced a late-morning "folk mass" on Sundays where young parishioners with (amplified!) acoustic guitars and a piano sang up-tempo hymns, dragging the grave solemnity of the ten o'clock mass into the present with singalong pop. Such transformations were in the air in dioceses across the country; it was the era of declining interest among youth, *The Cross and the Switchblade*, the "common language" Good News bible translations, missalettes and sermons with secular shadings, the arrival of female altar servers. The folk masses, with their smiling singers and occasional eighth-notes punctuating the churchy air, added a lively, upbeat charge to Mass, and were not well-received by the more conservative parishioners at St. Andrew's. I didn't care much; I was preteen cool to the whole controversy. Yet I couldn't help noticing the boundaries softening among the family stereo, the church, and the radio. The songs on *20 Years of Rock n' Roll* felt heavenly, too, and I secretly enjoyed hearing pop changes and lively melodies at Mass. I couldn't tell whether the Sunday music at St. Andrew's was infusing Casey Kasem's Saturday Top 40 countdown with sacredness, or whether it was the other way around.

I see now that over the years I internally grouped the songs on *20 Years of Rock n' Roll* into emotional clusters. Buddah sourced the songs across genres, eras, and publishers, pulling off a mammoth licensing ask in the process. There's great rock and roll on the album, songs that, grinning, drew me right into the party where I've stayed my whole life: Bill Haley's "(We're Gonna) Rock Around the Clock," Johnny Cash's "I Walk the Line," Fats Domino's "I'm Walkin'," Jerry Lee Lewis's "Whole Lotta Shakin' Goin' On," Duane Eddy's "Rebel Rouser," the Kingsmen's "Louie, Louie," Sam the Sham & the Pharaohs' "Wooly Bully," the McCoys' "Hang On Sloopy," and Young Rascals' "Good Lovin'." The joys of Fats and Duane and the thrill of the guitar break in the prechorus in "Good Lovin'" were immediate and eternal. Dion's "Runaround Sue" may have raised some issues I wasn't quite ready for, but then Joey Dee's "Peppermint Twist" would arrive, an early lesson in dancing away what you don't yet understand (or collapsing into giggles, the same thing when you're a kid). Bliss arrived with Otis Redding's "(Sittin' on) the Dock of the Bay," Tommy James's "Crimson and Clover," Lovin' Spoonful's "Do You Believe in Magic," the Everly Brothers' "All I Have to Do Is Dream," Van Morrison's "Brown-Eyed Girl." It's a wonder I didn't collapse in ecstasy on the rec room floor.

There was some corny stuff, for sure. I didn't connect with Gallery's "Nice to Be with You" or the Crew Cuts' "Sh-Boom (Life Could Be a Dream)," and though I loved the melody Paul Anka crooned in "Put Your Head on My Shoulder," the song was too easy to goof on, to deflect as silly, florid, as kinda gross. And Curtis Mayfield's "Superfly," as badass as it was (and is) was a bit beyond my ken at age ten or so. I'd have to catch up to that one (not to mention the way-out orgasmic middle of "Hang On Sloopy.")

Yet there were also songs the mystery and emotional complexities of which spoke to me in language different, and so much more vital, than everyday speech. Sometimes a melody would be so moving in its lilt and changes I felt as if I were on the outside peering in at the world of grown-ups, where loss mingled with joy, where I felt the pull toward something weighty, and not altogether welcome, that I couldn't yet name. The Orioles' transcendent "Crying in the Chapel" and Frankie Avalon's "Why" were, and in some ways remain, just out of my reach, stirring me so profoundly with their exquisite melodies and with vocals that feel as if in they're in touch with something beyond the men who are singing them. The Shirelles' "Soldier Boy" and the Shangri-Las' "Leader of the Pack" were theatrical and performative, stuffed with drama and melodrama, *camp* before I knew the word, and I fell hard for the songs' longings and griefs (and the women who were singing them).

These songs built dioramas, dimensional tableaus where kids like me collided, sure, but also where older people—my siblings and their appealing, and alluring, friends, my parents and their ancient parent-friends who'd sag with dejected sighs at the block party in the summer as the sun set, or, tipsy on gin, exchange meaningful glances that remained in code—enacted lives I could only imagine. Melanie's "Lay Down (Candles in the Rain)" and Edwin Hawkins' "Oh Happy Day" scored especially graphic terrain for me. I wouldn't know for years that the sublime Edwin Hawkins Singers performed on both cuts, but as a kid I dug the spirit-cousin grooves between them, the gospel-like fervor, the performances moving between control and release, the rapturous dynamics, the early lessons in the sublime power of a chord or a key change, of massed, wailed vocals or the command of one singing alone.

"Wherever anything lives, there is, open somewhere, a register in which time is being inscribed." —Henri Bergson. In recent centuries nostalgia has come to mean a sentimental craving for the past, for so-called innocent times, but further back nostalgia meant something more urgent: an intense, nearly feverish desire to return home, in all of the ways that we define that word. Nostalgia's Greek origins are *nostos*, homecoming, and *algos*, pain, grief, distress. Those suffering from this perceived condition were treated, if at all, as very sick patients. That version of home no longer exists, if it ever really did, and the ache of that paradox runs deep. If we've tamed the word "nostalgia," a consequence of a fuller understanding of human psychology, the anguish for the past is still present, faint, like a vocal that's been wiped off of a sound recording but is ghostly there.

Time is engraved on the four sides and thirty cuts of *20 Years of Rock n' Roll* yet, as in a magic trick, time is suspended, also. I'm nostalgic for those long afternoons listening to songs that were themselves packaged as nostalgia, signed, sealed, and delivered by Dick Clark. When I listen to this album what I feel isn't mired in the past, it's here still, in the present, further proof that great songs transcend their origins, the tiny kitchens or large studios where they were created, in time, and out of time.

A Genius Moment, or an Accident

In 1966, the 7-Eleven convenience store chain released "Do the Slurp," a promo novelty 45 that knocked me out as a kid and that I still can't shake. A brief history.

"Maybe I've lost too many brain cells from too many Slurpee-induced brain freezes."

That's my brother, Phil. I'd asked him and my other siblings if they can recall how "Dance the Slurp," a 1966 promotional 45 rpm single released by the 7-Eleven chain of convenience stores, ended up in our house in Wheaton, Maryland. "If I'm the one who first acquired it, I don't remember how or when," he admits. None of my other brothers or my sister can remember, either, but the journey wouldn't have been very far. There was a 7-Eleven less than half a mile from our house on Amherst Avenue, and over many years we ducked in to escape the sticky summer heat, and to load up on cherry or lemon lime and cola Slurpees, wads of gum, fistfuls of comics and magazines. The 7-Eleven was a regular stop on my solitary Saturday afternoon allowance walks, yet I too don't know how it ended up in the house. Yet for many years it was on high rotation on the Bonomo family turntable.

Tom Merriman was born in Chicago in 1924, graduated from Indiana University in Bloomington, and then studied music at Julliard. In the early 1950s, he moved to Dallas, Texas, the "Jingle Capital of the World," where he quickly earned a reputation as one of the most original, reliable, and productive jingle, radio advertisement, and station ID writers in the South. Merriman created jingles like you and I breathe air. In his long career he wrote and produced music for luminaries such as Louis Armstrong and Duke Ellington, won a Cannes Film Festival Award, toiled profitably as an independent producer at various production houses, founded and helmed the Commercial Recording Corporation, led the Liberty Network Band, and for many years was the music director at the elite Hockaday School—but he will chiefly be remembered as the Jingle King. Radio DJ Ron Chapman worked with Merriman at KVIL, a Dallas–Fort Worth FM station where Merriman was an early co-owner, and recalls that Merriman could compose arrangements "like Lincoln did the Gettysburg Address, on the back of an envelope." He added, "My first recollection of being with Tom was on a session for a jingle I had written for KVIL in its Glory Days. The song was called *Thank You for Making Us What We Are* and I wanted the finale to sound like the last chorus of 'Hello Dolly,' where the waiters come down the stairs carrying trays of champagne. Tom *nailed* it and even added a chorus of tap dancers, for a *radio* jingle!"

Such attention to arrangement and production details became Merriman's signature on the hundreds of compositions—not only jingles and commercials, but corporate musical events and theme park ride music—he produced over an impressive fifty-year career. "I learned music on my own," Merriman remarked in 2003. "I learned the technical side of transposition and all the things you have to know as a music writer. But it seems that there is something that has to be within you, native to your own abilities." At Indiana University, Merriman learned composition and counterpoint, "all the things you do as a serious composer," and at Julliard "a lot of legitimate techniques," yet, he added, "with serious music or pop, there are many common tenets that apply, natural basic laws and the things that are part of your experience."

At an industry tribute held in Dallas, Jon Wolfert, president of radio jingle facilities JAM Creative Productions and PAMS Productions Inc., lauded Merriman: "To use a horrible '60s term, we were the 'jingle freaks' and we were enamored, mesmerized by the work that was coming out of Dallas from all the different studios, but in no small part, the work you were doing," he said, adding, "and that's the reason why I'm still making these jingles, because I was attracted to it by listening to all this great stuff during all those years." That evening, Merriman was presented with a custom jukebox stocked with hundreds of his jingles and commercial spots, and was praised in video tributes from Patti Page and Pat Boone. "He wrote hundreds of spots, for Coca-Cola, Lone Star Beer, many of the jingles and themes for Marriott's Great Adventure," Tracy E. Carman, executive director of the Media Preservation Foundation, who was also at the tribute, told me. Consumed by the millions, lodged into the collective pop subconscious of America, these jingles remained anonymous to all but to industry insiders. "The list goes on and on, showing that he was very prolific in his abilities to adapt to the current music styles of the day," Carman said, adding that Merriman was scoring music "pretty much up until the time he died." (Merriman passed away in 2009.)

In 1965, the Dallas-based Southland Corporation, which owned a growing chain of 7-Eleven convenience stores, struck a licensing deal with the ICEE Company to sell the popular Icee drink, under the condition that it be renamed and its sales confined to 7-Elevens. Thus was born the Slurpee, an immediate, sugary hit named for the indelible sound made by inhaling, straw-wielding enthusiasts. Hopeful to branch out nationally, and eager for a clever and memorable promotional angle, Southland looked to Merriman Productions. (The company is now named TM Studios). In the previous decade, Merriman had written and voiced the wildly popular "Otto the Orkin Man" commercial spot; now, 7-Eleven charged him with composing a catchy song extolling the virtues of the frozen sweet drink, to be issued as a 45 single and given away with Slurpee purchases.

Merriman and his cowriter, Jim Long, went to work. "Not being a musician, the way I worked with Tom was to find tracks from records that we would use as a reference track to the basic style and the groove of the project," Long told me. "To the best of my recollection, the references I pulled for this project were from an album called *Bachelors in Space*." Alas, research reveals that no such record exists. Half a century later, Long admits to being stumped. ("Just spent a few minutes on Google looking for the ref track," he wrote me after our initial conversation. "There's too much stuff in the 'bachelors in space-lounge genre,' and finding it 35 years or so later would be finding a needle in haystack.") In any event, Merriman and Long had their ears tuned to the radio. "Tom could write in any style if you gave him the reference," Long says. The writing duo chose a Dance of the Week template, hoping to ride the (by then diminishing) wave of popular dances, such as the Stroll, the Pony, the Twist, the Mashed Potato, the Monkey, the Dog, the Frug, the Hully Gully, the Watusi, the Swim, and the rest. Merriman and Long swiftly banged out an instrumental arrangement, and set about finding the words to match: these lyrics had to be simple, easy to remember and to sing along with, and, most importantly, brand-specific. Merriman and Long soon realized that they only needed a single word.

"Dance the Slurp" was likely cut in or around May 1966 in downtown Dallas at Sellers Company, a recording studio located at 2102 Jackson Street, now a parking lot paving over a fascinating history. In 1935, James Earl "Pop" Sellers established a studio at his electronics store, at first producing high-quality recordings via an old phonograph. Over the years, he updated his equipment to state-of-the-art quality, recording countless obscure Dallas-area performers and singers who'd performed at the Big D Jamboree, the popular barn dance and radio program, but also early country and rock and roll musicians, including Gene Summers, Gene Vincent, Light Crust Doughboys, Trini Lopez, the Stamps Quartet gospel group, and Hank Thompson, who recorded his first session at Sellers. Sadly, no documentation exists of the "Dance the Slurp" session, or sessions. No log of takes, or of the personnel involved. Long can't recall the recording session down the years, let alone if he was in attendance. Over at TM Studios, Greg Clancy, the general manager and vice president of creative, assures me that any recording notes for "Dance the Slurp" are long gone, citing the tumult of multiple mergers and the moves from building to building over the years.

Hopeful for more information, I logged in to an online radio history forum. In response to my post, a helpful member responded, "Try looking up George Gimarc. If anyone knows about that or has a copy he would." He knows, and he does. In fact, Gimarc, a Dallas-area disc jockey, record and radio program producer, author, and music historian, sells a few copies of "Dance the Slurp" annually, mostly to buyers in northern Europe—Sweden, Norway, Denmark—willing to pay up to seventy-five dollars for the single. While Gimarc and I spoke on the phone, he posted and monitored his eBay record listings, scanned arcane online research, and moved among the more than sixty thousand records in his office. Providentially, he'd just been up to some Southland sleuthing himself. "I've been poking through the remnants of the Sellers Company archives, trying to buy all of it," he told me. "That's a hundred boxes of paper, and thousands and thousands of reels of tape. I've already purchased a small taste of it, and in it I found a lot of stuff from the Southland Company. I bought a lot of stuff that went all the way back to the midfifties through the midseventies. Commercials, jingles, what have you." Sensing my excitement, he added, carefully, "I haven't found the 'Slurp' master tape yet, but I'm sure it's in there. Everything *else* is in there."

On either end of the line, for nearly an hour, Gimarc and I held our copies of "Dance the Slurp" under bright light and squinted through magnifying glasses at the runout, the band of vinyl between the end of the song and the label, excavating among the mysterious acronyms and seemingly random letters and symbols emblazoned there clues to the song's production history. (A record's matrix stamped in the runout groove can indicate, in addition to the song's unique filing number, supplementary information such as take number, record pressing plant codes or logos, initials or signature of the disc cutting engineer, cutting or copyright dates, and so on.)

As we each scoured the record, Gimarc provided some background. "Starting around 1959, there were several products aimed at children, especially in Dallas, that were a record and merchandise pairing," he explained. "There was a coloring book called *Muley the one Eared Mule* which came with a free one-sided record of the song. *Mr. Peppermint*, a popular children's TV show, put out a coloring book that came with a little seven-inch record of songs, trucked inside the book." Well-known performers cut promotional tie-in records, as well, including Trini Lopez, for Fresca ("Presented by your local Coca-Cola Bottler") and Bobby Darrin, who, in the early 1960s inked a deal with Scripto Pens to issue a free record with purchase of a Wordmaster ball pen (and an ink refill, of course). "Putting a sound recording with a product was a thing in advertising culture to reach teenagers." Gimarc continued. "Since around 1961 or so, Coca-Cola had been doing commercials with rock and pop stars, like Roy Orbison, the Drifters. Over in England, even the Moody Blues did one. And you're in the era after the Twist—well, to be fair, ever since the Bop, in 1956—when there was a new dance coming along all the time for the teenagers. So tying what they thought was contemporary rock and roll music to a product was definitely in the wind."

Sometimes that wind kicked up a storm of concern. Scotty McKay, a rockabilly musician from Dallas, cut "Let's Do It," a 45 on the SS label that was issued with the purchase of a long pole (or the other way around). "A guy and girl were supposed to face each other and put this pole at basically belt-buckle level, and then dance while supporting the pole," Gimarc laughs. "So you couldn't get any closer. So the Lord could limbo between you, I'm supposing. I'm sure this was invented by some Southern Baptist who was appalled by the Twist." (The record label provides a helpful illustration of a decorously dancing, pole-separated teen couple.) Production and distribution of "Let's Do It"—the irony of that title slays me—were arranged by PAMS, or Production, Advertising, Merchandising Service, the major jingle company in Dallas. "I wouldn't be surprised if PAMS had some hand in the Southland 7-Eleven stuff, because it kind of has that sound," Gimarc remarked. At one point in his career, Tom Merriman worked at PAMS.

The trail had warmed a bit, yet the information in the matrix runout of "Dance the Slurp" was proving unhelpful, the string of letters and numbers failing to ring a bell for Gimarc. He *is* confident that the song was recorded at Sellers. In the archives he was able to track down the master recordings for other Slurpee "new flavor" jingles, as well as the masters for the "Dance the Slurp's" B-side—a mock interview conducted by Bob Stanford (a Southland advertising executive who'd coined the name Slurpee) with men and woman who experienced "strange things" while slurping—and definitively date those recordings to May 12, 1966. It's a safe bet that the A-side was recorded around that time. Gimarc and I were able to determine the acronym "SJW" on the runout, which may refer to Wakefield Manufacturing, a Phoenix, Arizona record plant, owned by Sidney J. Wakefield, where "Dance the Slurp" may have been pressed. Beyond these scant clues, we were stumped.

Gimarc might yet stumble upon the "Dance the Slurp" recording masters in the vast Sellers archives. (He's promised to keep me posted.) For many years I'd hoped to be able to put names and faces to the session musicians who played on "Dance the Slurp," and perhaps track down other recordings on which the musicians had played. Chop-rich, they were likely hired to bang out a tune in the morning, another in the afternoon, producing agreeable playing and singing that were ideal for the beguiling hooks of radio jingles and station IDs.

Their names are lost to history; still, I want to know: who played the spare and surprisingly funky drums, blared the bright, variety show–style horns, stabbed at the hokey, teen-a-go-go compact organ, sang the word "slurp" in its many cheery iterations? And who are the musicians, tethered to headphones, who created the most fun and identifiable sounds on the record—the slurps themselves that sent my brothers and I into hysterics? "Tom and I both would work the lyrics out, and in this case the in-house ad agency had the provided the basic theme," Long remembers, "but one of the things we added when we did the rough audition was the sound of the straw slurp." Slurp sounds used as percussion instruments—and in syncopation, no less!—was irresistible to me, as a fan of Slurpees and 1960s AM rock and roll and of-the-era go-go dancing. Yet, Long dashed my childish conviction that the slurps were produced with authentic Slurpees, cups wielded in the studio by session musicians with as much aplomb and style as Jerome Green wielded his maracas. Rather, the slurp sounds were created via studio effect, though having known this at the time wouldn't have stopped me from trying to re-create them, as I did, Slurpee in hand, in my suburban basement.

One thing is certain: "Dance the Slurp" was concocted with a singular objective, to move units. "7-Eleven were trying to hype themselves in creating, basically, the 1966 version of a viral video, something they hope becomes a massive hit," Gimarc says. "But look who's writing it and putting it together, a bunch of forty-year-olds, which in 1966 was doom." "Dance the Slurp" begins with a *Peter Gunn*–on-a-sugar-rush bass/guitar riff laid atop a danceable drumbeat. The musicians pause at the second bar and the sound of two noisy, reverb-laden *slurps* fills the space. Following a brief drum fill the groove resumes, only to pause again at the fourth bar, the space now filled by a man and woman merrily singing "Slurp! Slurp!," doubled by an exuberant horn line. The following four bars repeat the musical themes, as bass, drums, and then horns and *slurps* fill out the sound and set the groove in motion. After the first verse, an additional bar is added (another thirsty *slurp*) and then sixteen bars follow as an organ and the horns answer each other in half-bar phrases, merrily joined by the singing Slurpers. A four-bar bridge follows, leading to an extended fifteen-bar passage where—spotlight on!—an epic Slurp-Off commences, the slushy slurps thrown down on top of the drum beat in a syncopated, dance-floor whirl. The strutting horns and vocalists reenter for eight more bars, and then a sugar-crash *sluuuuurp* crescendo, and then the fade. It's over in two minutes and ten seconds. The song's as ridiculous as it sounds in translation, and as equally, and as ridiculously, fun and catchy.

The folks at Southland and 7-Eleven included an insert with the record, illustrated with a cheerful go-go-ing couple. The "How to do The Slurp" instructions explained, "Just follow the beat of the music naturally," before helpfully adding, "Do the Frug and the Jerk." The copywriters pedantically explain the steps:

> When the chorus sings "Slurp-Slurp!," the boy and girl look over each other's shoulder, first one side then the other, right in time with the "Slurp-Slurp" words . . .
>
> When the chorus sings the drawn-out "Sluuuurp," the boy and girl reach wide with one foot and then slide the other up to it, once again in time with the "Sluuuurp" word.
>
> A little after the middle of the music, actual slurping sounds come out loud and clear . . . the boy and girl now rock their bodies back-and-forth about as fast as they can!

By the middle of the 1960s, miniskirted girls and their dance partners were getting a little weary of grooving. Unluckily, "Dance the Slurp" was recorded and released at the tail end of a highly commercial era: *Shindig!* aired its final episode on January 8, 1966, and *Hullaballoo* closed things down three months later. The Top 40 chart in May 1966 was less hospitable to teen dance numbers: the Rolling Stones' "Paint It, Black," Bob Dylan's "Rainy Day Women #12 and 35," Cher's "Bang Bang," Simon & Garfunkel's "Homeward Bound," the Byrds' "Eight Miles High," and other iconic singles were vividly exploring interior states and sensual pleasures, pushing against and dissolving limits and boundaries in a way that made the Twist sound and look like your parents' dance. Indeed, I imagine that most kids who spun "Dance the Slurp" heard adults' overeager if well intentioned vocals exhorting them to slurp. This unhappy discovery vying with a major sugar letdown was a bad trip, indeed.

By the time my brothers and I were listening to "Dance the Slurp," over a decade had passed since Joey Dee and the Starliters tutored kids on the "Peppermint Twist," years since Freddy "Boom Boom" Cannon sang about his high school history teacher who dug red surfboards and doing the Monkey, and since Chris Montez whipped up "Some Kind of Fun" dancing the Stomp, the Wobble, and the Watusi. I was vaguely aware, in the long-haired Watergate and Patty Hearst era, that protest songs and FM radio and mind-altering drugs had long booted the Jerk out the back door, but we didn't care, as we just danced with adolescent joy, rocking our bodies back and forth about as fast as we could while laughing until irony caught up and lifted the needle.

A jingle is a song's little brother, the one who's forced to tag along at the game or the party and who ends up being a lot of fun to hang around with. He can do goofy imitations, make funny noises. Comes up with little sayings that people repeat the next morning. The girls think he's cute. At the next party, someone asks if little bro's coming again, too. He's a riot.

A few centuries ago, the word "jingle" referred simply to noise—pleasant enough noise, to be sure, small tinkling bells, a loosely linked chain, stray pieces of metal. Another usage developed earlier in history, and has run parallel: repetition of those sounds, or similar sounds, such as we hear in poetic language, and in any arrangement that results in a pleasing sound without having to make a whole lot of sense. In a word, *catchy*. This jingle is the basis for the irresistible nursery rhymes that live in us for a lifetime, of a memorable doorbell chime or vanity car horn, of your local auto parts radio commercial's earworm, and NSYNC (and hundreds of other band's Top 10 smash hits).

By the 1930s, our contemporary usage of "jingle" was at hand, as advertising began to dominate middle-class consumerism, and small, likeable musical passages were employed to get us to buy things, or to want to buy things, and to feel left out if we didn't. You can't help but hear the word "jingle" and think of the coins in your pocket or bag, clinking pleasingly, glinting in the jangly fluorescent light of the convenience store or supermarket after you've retrieved them. In Australian slang, "jingle" does indeed refer to pocket change.

In a sense, a jingle is the purest kind of music: notes arranged as a hook devoid of expression beyond itself. It gets in you as a featureless, transparent passage that might've been hummed a thousand years ago if not in the car on the way to work today. Paired with simple, easy to remember words, a jingle works because it works. Crass, a jingle's frowned on as purely commercial in intent, shallow in impulse; really, the pious songwriter is envious, wishing he could wield a hook as devastatingly memorable and enduring as the recognizable commercial jingles of the last seventy odd years. To those of a certain age group I apologize in advance for the earworms: *Buy Mennen . . . My baloney has a first name . . . Like a good neighbor, State Farm is there . . . I'd like to teach the world to sing . . . Plop, plop, fizz, fizz, oh what a relief it is . . . I don't want to grow up, I'm a Toys 'R' Us kid . . .* , not to mention countless regional examples. (Hey, Chicagoland: *O O O O'Reilly . . . Auto Parts!)*

At *Creative Ready*, a radio and production site, Jamie Aplin cites the work of Alan Baddely and Graham Hitch, who in 1974 "discovered what is now referred to as the phonological loop. This process consists of the phonological store (your 'inner ear') remembering sounds in chronological order and then the articulatory rehearsal system (your 'inner voice') repeating those sounds in order to retain them." He adds, "This incredible brain function is vital to children when developing speech and vocabulary as well as adults when learning new languages." At the jingle auditory level, the process is involuntary, and deeply pleasurable. If we judge a jingle because its primary function is to move units absent any complex artistic expression, do we betray our goofy smiles when we hear it, and sing along with it with our kids? Where's the line—and is it a precise one?—between music as commodity and music as art? That old story.

On a gray, chilly day in March 2006, Thomas Middleditch and Fernando Sosa, two Second City improv student-comics, stood on a sidewalk near a McDonald's in Chicago's Wrigleyville neighborhood and filmed a lo-fi, rudimentary rap about Chicken McNuggets, sending up a current commercial. "McDonalds was just starting its, like, urban campaign," Middleditch explained to Sean Evans on Evans's *First We Feast* YouTube series. "It's all, like, Hey, two guys playin' basketball, 'Let's go to McDonalds, like, whatever.' And I just thought it was so transparently pandering. It rubbed me the wrong way." Sosa beatboxed a hip hop rhythm as Middleditch nerdily rapped over it in an obvious satire of white teens' co-opting of Black street style—and the rap was so funny, catchy, and smartly scorning that tens of thousands of YouTube viewers watched, commented on, and, most importantly, shared the video in its first year or so. Executives at McDonald's noticed, bought the rights to the video (netting Middleditch and Sosa a nice chunk of change), and repurposed the rap into a consciously DIY ad extolling the virtues of McNuggets, in the process wringing out most of the duo's irony. What began as a jeering satire of corporate pandering became a viral video and a million-dollar boon—from goof-off parody to slick promotion. It wouldn't have happened if the jingle, however mocking, wasn't first an earworm.

"I love the backstory of songs that have these odd, unintended second lives," Gimarc told me. "There was a song by Susan Shirley called 'True Love and Apple Pie.' It came out in 1971. It's sung in English, and became a big hit in Denmark, Holland, and France. And then that song was purchased by an ad agency in America and had new lyrics put to it, and got turned into 'I'd Like to Teach the World to Sing.' And Coca-Cola probably used it for a decade. How'd you like to own the publishing on that?"

A couple of decades ago, my brothers Phil and Paul visited me in Illinois, a stop on their cross-country drive. While we were catching up, I pulled out my scratchy copy of "Dance the Slurp," which I'd spirited from the family house when I'd left home. None of us had listened to the record in years; fifteen seconds in we were collapsing in laughter, melting in nostalgia. Around the same time, in northern California, disc jockeys and music producers DJ Shadow and Cut Chemist were also listening.

"The first thing I think any child hears is commercial jingles and cartoon music and songs on *Sesame Street*. But I'm not going to pretend like that was a great, enormous influence because, at that time, you're soaking up anything and everything that's around you." That's Josh Davis, aka, DJ Shadow. Davis grew up outside San Francisco, and while a student at University of California–Davis in the early 1990s, began experimenting with making four-track mixes of obscure soul, funk, and R&B records, which he eventually distributed, building his reputation first locally, and then internationally, as a genius turntablist. His debut album, *Endtroducing*. . . , is a highly regarded, innovative masterpiece of trip hop. "And that is one thing I've always thought about, that music is just pervasive in our lives. But I also learned, at a certain point, that most people just don't even think about it. They're not affected by it either way, from the music that they hear in a department store or grocery store or on the radio." He adds, "Some people, it affects them, and other people, it doesn't."

"Dance the Slurp" clearly affected Davis, and Cut Chemist, the stage name of Lucas MacFadden, a Los Angeles–based DJ and producer who'd been a member of the hip hop groups Unity Collective and Jurassic 5. Davis and MacFadden sampled "Dance the Slurp" on their collaboration *Brainfreeze*, an astounding, fifty-two-minute live mix released in 1999 on Sixty7 Recordings, pressed in limited quantities of a thousand. (Due to high demand, the duo pressed another thousand, and then ceased production; *Brainfreeze* has since been bootlegged numerous times.) The CDs were sold during DJ Shadow's 1999 U.S. tour and during Cut Chemist's *Word of Mouth* tour with Jurassic 5 (as well as at two authorized record stores in California).

The cover is a grainy color photograph of Davis and MacFadden posing in front of a Slurpee machine, each holding a copy of a "Dance the Slurp" 45 and peering through the center hole; the CD label features a reproduction of the original single's label. Promoted on its insert as a "nonstop live mix of strictly 45's and exercise in vinyl destruction," the two-track CD is composed of fifty-six samples, ranging in length from several bars to several minutes, lifted from seven-inch singles in Davis and MacFadden's enormous, storied record collections. The sampled artists range from the recognizable (Grandmaster Flash and the Furious Five, Chuck Mangione, Albert King, the Mar-Keys), to the fairly well-known (Eddie Bo, Rufus Thomas, Original Soul Senders), to the obscure (the Mohawks, the Nu People, Wilbur Bascomb & the Zodiac, Singing

Principal, the Vibrettes, et al.). The samples range from chunks of antidrug PSAs and talky movie commercials to funky drum breaks, raw guitar solos, and blissy choruses from soul and R&B numbers.

If you're paying attention and aren't ecstatically zoned-out by the DJs' hypnotic spell, thirty-five and a half minutes in to *Brainfreeze* you'll hear a recognizable sound, a *slurp* deeply buried in the mix and then rising like a sonic bubble to the surface of Eddie Bo's 1966 single "From This Day On." The horns in Bo's tune sound familiar—and soon enough Davis and MacFadden mix in the horns and vocals from "Dance the Slurp" and allow the song to play, virtually uninterrupted, for two minutes, one of the longer samples in *Brainfreeze*. The DJs slow down the tempo of "Dance the Slurp" by a tone or two for a few bars, more graphically for longer stretches, add reverb to and scratch the slurp sounds, manipulate the horns, loop the drum break. Mixing, Davis and MacFadden subtly change the form of "Dance the Slurp," and so its sound, and so its meaning. And possibly its very purpose. They fundamentally alter the reasons the song might need to exist in the twenty-first century: less a commercial for a Slurpee than a context-free, pure sound groove, a smoothly moving piston in an engine of funk.

Merriman and Long, toiling in their jingle factory in Dallas, working with analog recording equipment, wouldn't have dared imagine (and, given the unprecedented race of technology at the end of the century, likely *couldn't* have imagined) what occurs in *Brainfreeze*: a spiked Slurp's at the center of a wild all-nighter with a guest list as unlikely, and possibly as dangerous, as it is preposterously fun. "When I sample something, it's because there's something ingenious about it," Davis says. "And if it isn't the group as a whole, it's that song. Or, even if it isn't the song as a whole, it's a genius moment, or an accident or something that makes it just utterly unique to the other trillions of hours of records that I've plowed through."

The effect in *Brainfreeze* is to elevate the obscurity of a generically performed, novelty merchandise tie-in song to the level of prime, righteous, if sometimes equally obscure soul and R&B. The nearly hour-long *Brainfreeze* invites Tom Merriman and Jim Long to the party, dynamically dramatizing, as the best sampling does, the egalitarian impulse behind music: mixing turns up the volume of the ongoing rhythm behind human expression, whether sampling a song that stiffed on the charts, was issued as a promotional record with no hope or interest in the charts, or sold in the millions.

Sometimes a sample leaps genres in startling ways. That's Eva Gabor—aka "Lisa Douglas" from the *Green Acres*'s theme song—in the chorus of Deee-Lite's impossibly fun 1990 dance floor jam "Groove Is in The Heart." The "I" in the line "*I* couldn't ask for another"? That's not the charming Lady Miss Kier but Mrs. Douglas, who's actually proclaiming, a quarter century earlier, "*I* get allergic smelling hay!" A catchy hook's a catchy hook. That Davis and MacFadden edit "Dance the Slurp" into Kraftwerk's "Numbers," from the band's 1981 album *Computerwelt*, shows how tuned their ears are to the absurd, surprising, body-moving pleasures of sonic, culture-spanning simultaneity: a dance-of-the-week number already hopelessly square when it was released grabs the glossy, cool hand of electronic avant-garde krautrock synth-pop and . . . well, the point is, don't think too much about it, just hit the dance floor.

Describing *Endtroducing* . . . , Davis says, "I was trying to find a sound different from everybody else's, so the source material had to be different from everybody else's. I was looking for records that I felt like were really obscure. Whether those were funk 45s, which nobody was up on yet, or kind of weird rock albums." Coconspirator MacFadden shares Davis's take on the possibilities opened up by sampling. "I really appreciate novelty records with drum breaks," he told me. "It's something I think beat diggers are attracted to probably because it's the least likely place to find one." MacFadden first heard about "Dance the Slurp" from Z Trip, a Phoenix-based DJ and producer. "He'd found out about it from an extended Beastie Boy member named AWOL, and I immediately was intrigued." He added, "I told Shadow and, of course, he found it fairly soon after. I think I got mine from a seller out here in Los Angeles a little bit after Shadow got his." Mixing and "playing old music for a new crowd" intrigues and moves MacFadden. "I doubt anyone had ever heard this jingle, and to blend it with Kraftwerk just seemed to be the right context to put it in. 'Slurp' became a household name with 45 collectors after that. We've since moved on to using Cola and milk jingle drum breaks for later projects."

My brother Paul carried "Dance the Slurp" inside of himself for decades as he dragged his record collection with him from suburban Washington, D.C., to San Francisco to Manhattan, where he worked for several years in a jingle factory, to Berlin, where he now lives and DJs and releases music under the name Snax. In 2002, he collaborated with the musician Kahn in the electro-disco duo Captain Comatose. In "Theme from Captain Comatose," the lead track on their album *Going Out*, those old drums and horns from "Dance the Slurp" pop up, repurposed as the jumpy foundation and funky, leap-from-the-turntable breaks in a dance floor jam. Some music just gets in and stays in.

Crate diving, beat digging, Shadow and Chemist recognized and celebrated one of Merriman and Long's prime goals: get up and dance, kids. The kinds of jingles that Merriman, Long, and so many others composed in a different context, in another life, now take on new values—rhythmic, cultural, sensual—in the hands of turntablists. But sometimes this new value comes at a cost. Witness the waves of lawsuits brought by copyright holders against DJs and artists in recent decades: once a record with samples begins to sell, the boundaries of permissions and uses can quickly tighten up. I broached the topic of such legal issues with Gimarc when we spoke. He searched the records of ASCAP (American Society of Composers, Authors and Publishers) and BMI (Broadcast Music), the two largest United Sates performance rights organizations committed to controlling and protecting artists' copyrights. After a minute of silence, he muttered, with a tone of mild disbelief in his voice, "Did they really *never* register this thing? I'm looking through ASCAP and BMI, and I don't see it under Merriman. He's an ASCAP guy. I'm just really shocked. I would've thought that once it started getting sampled that somebody would've registered it, just to makes sure. Southland *did* have something to defend after *Brainfreeze* was released, but they probably never had any intention of it going to a place where it would actually get used on the radio or in a movie or a TV commercial, or something outside of their control, which would be the only way you'd necessitate registering with ASCAP or BMI."

I asked MacFadden about a lawsuit that the Southland Corporation was rumored to have brought against him and Davis. "It never went beyond a cease-and-desist letter," he explained. "It was being bootlegged all over the world and making tons of money that didn't go to us. Although we didn't press more than two thousand copies, the project went on to gain so much traction that they saw us as the ones being responsible, so of course we complied even though we never planned on making anymore, and we explained to them that we weren't in control of the bootleggers so it may still be manufactured by someone other than us."

Meanwhile, MacFadden was struck by a bold marketing idea of his own. "I was trying to pitch them putting me and Shadow in a television commercial mixing doubles of 'Dance the Slurp.'"

Southland passed. "I think they really slept on a hip campaign idea," MacFadden sighed. "Oh, well."

Birds Sing to Breathe

Is *voice* a sound produced by vocal cords. or the way one lives one's life?

Lydia Loveless was born and raised on a farm an hour east of Columbus, Ohio, yet they sing as if they'd grown up hundreds of miles south. Their twang usually arrives snapping off the end of a line, as a kiss-off or a heartbreak, sassy or vulnerable depending on the mood. It's what I always hear first, before the words, before the story itself. Somehow every note that Loveless sings sounds as if it's set in a minor key. I first caught them and their band a decade ago, and the desperate sincerity in Loveless's voice plugged up my throat tight for most of the night. Richard Hell says, "Lydia is the only singer/songwriter the power of whose music and voice consistently makes me cry." I'm with Hell here. I'm glad there wasn't much close harmony that night. That would've put me over the edge. (Loveless is genderfluid and prefers they/she pronouns.)

Her band looked as if they'd been rounded up from a bar down the street, the beat-up gear as if it were collectively 150 years old. Jay Gasper played pedal steel and a very cool, bright-sounding twelve-string. Todd May got sounds out of his guitar that mocked weeping and howling, back-to-back. Bass player Ben Lamb (Loveless's then-husband) alternated from electric to stand-up, and Loveless moved between those ranges herself, as the band politely excused themselves from the stage near the end of the show and Loveless picked up an acoustic and sang solo, beautifully, heartbreakingly, for a few numbers. She wore heeled strap sandals, denim shorteralls, and a lace T-shirt— "I'm all about class," she drawled. She drained a forty-ounce New Belgium Fat Tire over the course of the show, and sang her songs with sobbing catches and with her eyes tightly shut, opening them occasionally to reorient herself in the landscape of loss and lust that they create.

We live in very personal times. Working musicians who post on social media invite us to share intimacies, offering tantalizing, curated glimpses into the studios where they're working, the touring vans into which they're piling, the homes (junky backyards, messy kitchens) where they live. They share embarrassing texts, go live on a whim, post heartfelt reels directed right at me. We respond with heartfelt affirmations, half sentences, and emojis.

The relationship feels oddly real. Loveless has been on Patreon for a while now. On it they post demos, the odd new song, poems, YouTube playlists, mental health updates, thoughts on what book they're reading, what views are blurring by their van window, or what they're eating on the road. Their posts can get very raw and confessional, 2 a.m. unburdening leavened with some very funny self-deprecation. (Their current Instagram description reads "Sometimes Comedian / Hopeless Romantic." They once tweeted, "I like my coffee like I like my men, troubled and Middle Aged." I once tweeted at them during the baseball playoffs that a couple of mustached-and-bearded Cleveland Indians players looked like I imagined the men they sing about look like. They were bemused.) Loveless is not shy about their tendencies toward depression and ennui, about exclaiming when they feel that they're at the emotional bottom. They'll sign off a letter with "Forever your over sharing pal, Lydia Loveless xo."

Cumulatively—especially if you're a fan of hers, as I am—the effect is of reading a close friend's journaling, or hanging out all night with them as they pour out their feelings. Her IG account is a blend of life-on-the-road, in-the-studio, self-promotion, and chill-at-home posts; she lets her followers into her kitchen, or her bathroom or bedroom, viewing her lounging around, makeup-free, glasses on, a cluttered counter or unmade bed in the background, her mild exasperation at her cat having killed an intruding lizard dovetailing with stacks of self-help books and evidence of over-drinking. Her friends and family members and everyone's texts are fair game. Loveless is honest, and available, and so is her voice. She sings about idealized romance bruised by clumsy hands; she sings about drinking, and fucking, and mornings waking up in dubious beds. She sometimes sings about her own career ("Paid") and about singing. (And singers. Cue up "Steve Earle.")

I'm wondering how much of a story a voice, alone, can tell. Loveless's quivers at its top range, and they use this effectively, capturing a kind of vulnerability or falling-apartness that their songs, the quieter or more reflective ones especially, narrate. They do as much with that voice as they do with the tales they spin and the images they present, often sounding like they're about to burst into tears, and be really pissed off at themselves when they do. They can sing with a hard edge and soften outward in the same line via a sudden insight or swoop of an octave, shaking with indignation and then defenselessness; their voice at its most casual sounds untutored, and so conversational, a barroom or basement voice that's authentic and powerful in its confident looseness. I wish Lydia all kinds of fame and success, but they'll always sound to me like someone who feels most comfortable in a dimly lit dive bar, where hard-won truths and the voice strong enough to sing them are that much more intimate.

At *The Naked Scientists* the zoologist Max Gray reports that birds, rather than possessing a chest that swells when they breathe, have

> a lung that doesn't really expand and contract very much. But they have, coming off from that lung, nine air sacs which then fill up and have muscular development around them that allows them to be pushed in, basically like bellows, so they will then force air through these different air sacs to breathe. And what that allows them to do is to kind of have loads of little different pockets of air that they can push out when they're singing which allows them to sing for a long time.

Imagine that: multiple sacs of air surrounding a lung, working in tandem—I like to believe that one is exhaling in one mood, one in another, joy issuing from this sac, grief from that sac. The very act of breathing creates music. Existence as song.

"I like to sing. I don't know how to sing and I sing completely out of tune; but I sing all the same—occasionally, very quietly, when I am alone. I know that I sing out of tune because others have told me so; my voice must be like the yowling of a cat. But I am not—in myself—aware of this, and singing gives me real pleasure. If he hears me he mimics me; he says that my singing is something quite separate from music, something invented by me."

This is Natalia Ginzburg in "He and I," an essay from *Le piccole virtù* (*The Little Virtues*) published in Italy in 1962. (Dick Davis translated the book into English in 1985.) In the piece, Ginzburg moves back and forth between her husband and herself, blithely drawing minor and sometime profound distinctions between the two of them. The end result is a dimensional portrait of a long-term relationship; that is, it gets complicated. Any attempt by a lover to explore boundaries between herself and another is usually revealing and, when writing about her own singing, Ginzburg—though modest, deferring, and reserved—reveals herself as a passionate fan.

"When I was a child," she continues, "I used to yowl tunes I had made up. It was a long wailing kind of melody that brought tears to my eyes." Etymologists say that we put the name to that noise sometime in the twelfth century; the noun "yowl" was recorded starting in the middle of the fifteenth century. Interestingly the word derives distantly, as if in a fading echo, from the Old Norse "*yla*," related to the idea of jubilance, "to let out whoops." Ginzburg's singing may be an embarrassment to herself, and a public embarrassment to anyone unfortunate to be within earshot of her, but it's really a kind of jubilation, a triumph of sorts. Look: she brings herself to tears.

Though she allows herself pleasure, she twists herself in knots trying to undo her love for her own voice, to diminish the interior life that it sings. "It doesn't matter to me that I don't understand painting or the figurative arts, but it hurts me that I don't love music," she writes, adding, "But there is nothing I can do about it, and I will never understand or love music." For Ginzburg, the intellect trumps the wail, emotional authenticity—even pure enjoyment—no kind of argument for itself. "If I occasionally hear a piece of music that I like I don't know how to remember it; and how can I love something I can't remember?" I'll offer my own rhetorical question here: what's more important, the knowledge or the song, the context or the tears?

In a Loveless song, romance is often undercut by a turn toward confusion, ruefulness, or liberation that always feels honest. On *Real* (2016), coproducer Joe Viers smoothed the group's sound a bit; gone is the cowpunk bar-band noise of the earlier records, replaced with studio finesse and laid-back pop grooves, but Loveless's yearning twang is intact, and is as affecting and powerful as ever. As before, Loveless is singing about sex and love, about the ideal and the bitterly real, and the cynical humor to be found in it all.

That show a decade back was one of the best I'd seen in years. Happily, onstage Loveless and her band play with raw edges and humorous abandon; their songs benefit from that kind of loose-limbed, barreling sound. Several cuts on *Real* suffer from studio claustrophobia and, though Loveless maintains a sure grip on their subjects, a bit of a sonic identity crisis. On the strongest songs—"Longer," "Heaven," "Out on Love," the title track—Loveless's voices cuts through the gray studio weather to add pulse and personality. She's especially effective solo and acoustic, as in "Clumps," where she gives the impression of having rushed to the studio with the song, anxious to track its emotional interior before she'd had much time to flesh out a band arrangement or talk herself into fancier chord changes or distracting instrumental textures. She's singing but somehow talking to us at the same time. Often, especially in intimate settings in the studio or onstage, Loveless sounds like an adolescent wise enough to be singing about a grown-up's problems, and an adult who feels youthful and alive still to the energy of a reckless, often childish world, finding strength she might've surrendered when she was younger and stupider. These are things that are best left unadorned, I guess. Loveless's guitar and her melancholy voice—in a bedroom, kitchen, car, or in a bar—is all she really needs.

Tinuviel Sampson, writing in a press release for the Olympia- and Portland-based record label Kill Rock Stars, in 1993:

> I've noticed that this is a pattern in my life to how I live. When something is kinda fucked around me, I withdraw and make something and only later (sometimes years later) I realize that it was directly related to inhumanization of art. It's so constant. It's why I quit art school. I never fit in cuz I didn't care about galleries and I didn't understand why I didn't care about galleries and thought that maybe I wasn't really a painter or artist and then later I realized that galleries were a way of killing art.

Sampson goes on to admit that she hardly ever gets to museums, that they depress her.

> I thought that museums were full of dead art. I thought that they were like graveyards and all the statues were screaming to be let outside and see the world and see the people walk down the street and see the sun and feel the wind but they were stuck indoors in temperature climate control environments. and the paintings wanted to go to dinner parties and eavesdrop on some gossip and instead they get a hush hush, look at the contrast in the tones and the brushstrokes of pure feeling and how lovely and oh the poor man was crazy but he sure was talented, too much absynthe, you know AND YOURE GODDAMNED RIGHT THERE WAS TOO MUCH ABSINTHE AROUND AND MAYBE THERE WAS A REASON AND MAYBE THERE ISN'T ENOUGH NOW!!!! oh fuck it all cuz it keeps happening over and over so now i put out records and haven't had much time to paint since august (what with all the other turmoil in my life).

She adds, "I find noisemakers more easily, it's a more social art and I'm not the best at being a complete recluse (though I am very reclusive). Music keeps me less lonely."

The same year that Sampson composed her lo-fi manifesto, Kill Rock Stars released a three-song seven-inch from the band Bikini

Kill, Kathleen Hanna (on vocals), Billy Karren (guitar), Kathi Wilcox (bass), and Tobi Vail (drums). The band had already self-released their debut cassette *Revolution Girl Style Now!*, a self-titled EP, and a split album with the U.K. band Huggy Bear when they ducked into a studio in Seattle, with Joan Jett recording, and swiftly cut "New Radio," "Demirep," and a new version of "Rebel Girl" (an earlier version had appeared on the Huggy Bear album). Noisemakers making social art: "New Radio" and "Rebel Girl's" four-on-the-floor drive and unstoppableness are frighteningly exhilarating, crystalizing Bikini Kill and songwriter Kathleen Hanna's intense sonic demands, new yellsinging and new sex.

"Rebel Girl" is in many ways the band's signature tune, an anthem for all time, and one of the great rock and roll songs of the postpunk era, paying homage to the past and offering something fiercely new and necessary. Many adjectives have been used to describe Hanna's screams—from cathartic to gut-churning to sexy to scary; I'll add hair-raising and otherworldly, clichés all but what can you do when faced with the untranslatable?—and those screams are, without a doubt, clarion calls. She rises to—surrenders to? falls victim to?—an astonishing scream in each of those two lines, detonating girlishness, brattiness, adolescence, grown-up frustrations, and sensual bliss in a single, ascending screech. A defining sound not only of Riot Grrrl but of the late twentieth century.

In addition to recording the tracks, Joan Jett played second guitar on "Rebel Girl," and the muscular sheen in the sound she discovers in the band only underscores Hanna's primal shrieks: politeness is gone, gender decorum is meaningless, binaries collapse under the weight of the ear-ringing decibels. Hanna's the little girl who can't stop pulling up her dress in "New Radio." In "Rebel Girl" she's the one who wants to be that girl's best friend, to take her home, try on her clothes, kiss the revolution on her lips and in her mouth and tumble down her endless dark screaming throat. Hanna's two-second yowl in the line "I taste the revolution" is as powerful as rock and roll gets, a *fuck-outta-my-way* force of nature impossible to contain or ignore or believe never existed, rounding up in pure sound the rebellion and sexiness and gender-transcending bliss of the best and most important rock and roll. Want, scream, grab, possesses. Melody as squall, or is it the other way around.

I was born and raised in suburban Washington, D.C. Though I've lived in Ohio and Illinois for most of my adult life, I'll always feel like an East Coast guy, and I'm charmed as an outsider by Loveless's take on the men who they grew up with in the Midwest. They discussed the origins of their song "Midwestern Guys" with David Anthony at *A.V. Club*: "I was thinking about it when I was writing that one, the fact that most of my friends are middle-aged men," they said. "I was laughing at myself and thinking about how those are my girlfriends—older dudes—and how they all sort of have the same story and the same upbringing. A few of the guys in my band went to school together or grew up near each other, and I love sitting in the van listening to their weird rural Ohio school stories."

A story that her bassist Ben Lamb told her triggered the song.

> He had a half-brother who was doing some drug up in a tree and fell out and died. That inspired one of the verses, which ended up getting cut from the song. Maybe it was too depressing. But I don't know, just the boredom of the '80s and how everyone was driving around drunk, and the guys always talk about how at least two times a year people would drive into a tree. I listen to their stories and wonder how they survived. It's a tribute to all my sensitive guy friends that are weird.

Wry, yearning, haunted, and packed with narrative detail that ignite moments, "Midwestern Guys" is prime Loveless. She addresses a figure pretty common in her songs, someone to whom she's maybe attracted but of whom she's wary, also, burned by a type even as she finds it hard to resist the flame, someone she studies because a story's told even though neither one can articulate what that that story is. He's romantic with her, but he has a dirty past. It's hard to know, behind the song's careful pace and the lilting melody, what the singer makes of this person: still hot, or a loser? Easy to mock or hard to fathom, and, so, more attractive because of that? It's great stuff, and "Midwestern Guys," in its humor, sexiness, and longing, is one of Loveless's finest songs. At its best, *Real* confirms that Loveless's wise, honest, and skeptical take on men and women and the lives they enrich and fuck up is always worth hearing, always worth singing about.

Songs so often begin in utter mystery. R.E.M.'s "Perfect Circle," from their 1983 debut album *Murmur*, arrived after a tour-exhausted Peter Buck watched some kids playing pickup football at dusk in a park in Trenton, New Jersey. The poignancy and beauty of the scene devastated him; the weary music he wrote with Mike Mills and Bill Berry scored and evoked that vulnerability. Later, Michael Stipe put lyrics to his own gently descending melody—to my ear they are, as much of Stipe's early lyrics were, essentially nonsense, but they don't distract from the music, which, vibing off the deep image tableau of end-of-day, end-of-innocence, boys-playing Americana that Buck witnessed, puts music to impression, converts sensation, abstractions, even. I've long believed that R.E.M.'s early albums, up through *Fables of the Reconstruction*, before the band adopted more graphically articulated political stances, are some of the best instrumental music of the era. Stipe's vocals and surreal wordplay are musical instruments, really, no more, no less.

It's tempting to call Loveless's *Daughter*, released at the end of the pandemic summer of 2020, their "divorce album," the latest attempt in an unhappily long tradition of an artist working out marital woes in song and lyric, but that would be limiting. Loveless sings about loss and disappointments, gains and setbacks, in eternal ways, moving from their own private travails to sketch out a persona that morphs into a silhouette of rueful longing, cut with cynicism and humor. As all great artists do, Loveless moves from experience that begins in the dark to a shared understanding of what makes all of us get up in the mornings, uncertain that today's going to be any better than yesterday. One song, "Dead Writer," seems interested in art and legacy, and signals one of *Daughter*'s chief concerns: work, the value it brings against the lofty promises it makes. A trio of songs—"Wringer," "Can't Think," and "Don't Bother Mountain"—addresses the dilemmas of a singer who's never shied away from singing about their vocation. The arrangement of "Can't Think" plods and moves sideways, frustrated, the phrase *work is the reward* repeated like a hopeful mantra.

Over a few months on Instagram I watched Loveless and her band piece together their latest album, *Nothing's Gonna Stand in My Way Again* (2023), catching stray nascent tracks in the background as Loveless and her fellow musicians played, recorded, and goofed around. Such a fly-on-the-wall perspective on a band pulling together an album is no longer new, yet pull wide and, in the era of updates and ever newer platforms, you realize that that such 24/7 "insider" access is still a relatively recent phenomenon. Loveless had included a manually typed, parchment-y lyric sheet in *Daughter*, and you felt special holding it in your hands. When I caught her in Chicago in December 2022, I walked past her at the bar before she played, and for an instant the feeling was, *Oh an old friend, let's catch up*. I resisted.

"Ghost" is the strongest and most affecting song on the album, and the most beguilingly weird. A midpaced threnody to death, the song captures the in-betweenness of a ghost that's haunting a house—spying, putting fingers on a windowpane, turning the TV off and on, switching on all of the lights—and that has achieved a kind of ideal space to inhabit, where risks no longer leave burn marks. In wonderful Lovelessian irony, this somber, downcast song provides the album's seemingly cheery, optimistic title, here in service of an eerie, hovering life. And it's droll as hell.

It's easy, I think, to misread Loveless's penchant for darkness (and minor chords): they're a vivid lyricist for whom metaphors are a native tongue: death here, and in "Runaway," is less a rejection of the world the way the world's offered than a perversely imagined safe space, free of heartbreak, self-damage, and damage done to others. "Ghost" is a self-help manual about dying and becoming a shadow, if that strikes a chord with you. ("Ghost" also provides the album's funniest line, about owing one of its images to AI.) Such resolve lifts “Do the Right Thing.” Against a rolling Buddy Holly rhythm and cheery, midsixties AM-radio backing vocals, Loveless sings about keeping a secret, their unrequited crush on someone who’s taken, and of their determination to keep their distance. Here the singer chooses the safe, healthy choice—maintaining a friendship at the expense of destructive drama—even if it hurts when the crush says goodbye. (As Loveless has it, the song ends unresolved musically.)

There’s some mentally healthy willpower on display in “Poor Boy,” too, a tune played with power pop crispness by Loveless and her core band—Jay Gasper and Todd May on guitars, Mark Connor on bass, and George Hondroulis on drums—aided here and there by Jay Gonzalez’s evocative keyboards and Michelle Sullivan’s sunny backing vocals. Loveless has been making music and banging around with this crowd for some time now, and her playing is tasteful, complementary, and warm. (Loveless recorded and coproduced the album with Sean Sullivan in Tennessee.) The album’s stuffed full of durable, memorable melodies, most of the choruses hook-filled.

On November 8, 1974, singer Connie Francis performed at the Westbury Music Fair, in Long Island, New York. Francis returned to her second-floor room at a Howard Johnson’s Lodge with friends, and went to bed around 2:30 in the morning. She was awakened a few hours later by a young man, who raped her at knifepoint. (A *New York Times* article published the following day reports, “The police said they did not know how the man got into the room”; Francis later sued the Howard Johnson motel chain for damages and was awarded over two and a half million dollars. The highly publicized trial, devastating for Francis, is credited with spurring industry-wide reforms in motel room security.) Following the attack, the assailant—who was never found—tied Francis to a chair, bound her hands behind her, pushed her over, and then covered her with two mattresses and pillows, nearly suffocating her.

After more than an hour, during which she quietly sang lyrics to cheerful songs in an effort to calm herself, Francis was able to crawl to the telephone in her room and dial the number of a secretary who was sleeping in the next room. The police were summoned. The experience shattered Francis. After a decade and a half of recording, concerts, television and film work, and international traveling, limiting herself to the occasional performance or guest appearance on television shows, she'd been living in semiretirement. After the assault she tumbled into years of depression and abuse of prescription drugs. Seven years after the incident, she remarked to UPI reporter Vernon Scott that she still was physically and emotionally unable to move forward with her career. "I suffered from a morbid fear of audiences. Every time I looked into a crowd I saw the face of the man who raped me. And I hated the feeling that when people thought of me it was in terms of the girl who was raped." She added, "All of my life before the rape, the fun and enjoyment was negated. The rape became an obsession. I couldn't think of anything else."

She was speaking to Scott on the occasion of her tentative return to performing. Following nasal surgery (and the subsequent, though temporary, loss of her voice) in 1977, she'd released an album, the gamely titled *Who's Happy Now?* featuring a disco version of her signature song "Where the Boys Are," and had carefully worked her way back to the stage. "Three and a half years after the rape I tried to get my career going again," she related. "I went to England and did an awful live show. I didn't sound like myself. And I cut a couple of albums. It took me twenty takes per song whereas I used to click them right off. The albums were just fair." Francis's world collapsed. "The only thing I'd been sure of all my life was my voice. And now I'd lost that." She continued, "I was in complete depression. And I had to live with the memory of the trial which became a carnival. It was a terrible ordeal. They asked horrible questions about my marital sex life. It contributed to the breakup of our marriage. My husband—we are friends now—just couldn't handle all of that invasion of privacy."

I was thinking about all of this while driving through rural DeKalb County last summer on the way to a tiny farm stand at the sprawling Lamb of God Farm in Big Rock, Illinois. Amy and I were listening to Lydia Loveless on shuffle, and after a while Amy, inspired, suggested that we play some Connie Francis, who neither of us had listened to in years. She pulled up a YouTube playlist, and we played the hits, the iconic career-making numbers that have sold in the millions worldwide—"Who's Sorry Now?," "Where the Boys Are," "My Happiness," "Lipstick on Your Collar," "My Heart Has a Mind of Its Own," "Don't Break the Heart That Loves You," and the rest—and as Francis's gorgeous, controlled yet sexy, smooth yet emotionally complex voice filled the car, the decorum in the music quarreled in my head with memories of hearing about her rape when I was young. Sadly—and this is, of course, partly generational—when summoning Francis I recall the trauma first, then the songs. (Just as she feared might happen.) I vaguely associated her with a story I'd replayed many times in my youth, of a female singer who'd been assaulted—I think that there was some drug abuse, also—and who was so debilitated by the attack that she could no longer sing. In the studio, while trying to record, she found herself unable to complete verses, simple phrases even, and the producer was obligated to piece together the song, surgeon-like, using whatever bits and pieces of singing he was able to get on tape.

The story scared me, less for the attack than for the result: a powerful voice in pieces on the ground, able to be reassembled but at what cost? Like F. Scott Fitzgerald's cracked dinner plate—his brutally powerful metaphor for his own nervous collapse—the singer was unalterably damaged, could never perform again as she used to. A voice that once embodied personality, sensibility, communion with the outside world and with others, now suppressed. My story may be apocryphal, or I may have revised it over the years in my lurid imagination, beginning with Francis's assault and creating a general narrative of collapse, a voice, then a scream denied, and then silence.

On October 30, 1981, Francis appeared on Dick Clark's *American Bandstand 30th Anniversary Special* lip-syncing to a medley of her hits. Clark was a longtime and close friend of Francis's, yet the comeback was bittersweet: by that point she'd spent thousands of dollars on doctors, most of whom told her she would never sing again because of the damage incurred during the nasal operation. She felt that her career was over. "I didn't know what I was going to do," she said to Scott. "Then eight days ago I was talking to a man I date about the whole ordeal of the rape and operation and I began to cry. I just broke down and the floodgates opened." Francis acknowledged that this was the first time she'd wept about the rape, and then, released, she wept also about the trial, the operation, and the murder of her brother George, in May of that year. (George Franconero Jr. was a former district attorney and government informant who was murdered by Mafia hit men.)

The following day, Francis was walking on a Manhattan street with the same man. She was startled to see that she was singing to herself "What I Did for Love," from *A Chorus Line*, surprised because after her operation she hadn't had the range to even consider attempting such a song. She abruptly stopped walking and in the middle of the block, amid the din of the city, turned to her companion and told him,

> "I can sing!"
>
> Then I got into my car and turned on the stereo tape of an album I'd recorded 10 years ago. And I sang along with it. My voice was as good or better than when I'd done the recording.

Francis claimed that the improvement wasn't a gradual thing but was, remarkably, instantaneous. "Magical," she said. "I swear it was a miracle. All of a sudden my voice was back. I'm not a religious girl, but I believe in God now. I stopped the car and telephoned my father and my manager. I told my manager to book me back in the Westbury Music Fair. And he did . . . It's my way of overcoming the fear of the rape. I know it's paranoid, but I'll have two bodyguards with me. And I'll drive home two hours every night rather than stay in a motel.

"But I'm really happy and elated. I can sing again. And I can work again!"

The press releases that Francis's agent issued at the time ran with this story—it appeared in *Billboard* and other media outlets—in the hopes that this redemptive account of a voice regained would be the triumphant narrative carrying Francis forward.

A voice can be both fragile and resilient, and the songs it might sing take many shapes, some full-throated, some in a minor key searching for a way to resolve. The man who assaulted Francis ordered her not to scream for at least half an hour after he left the room, or he'd come back to kill her. Kathleen Hanna didn't need permission to scream; by the patriarchal generation into which Francis was born, and by her assailant, Francis was denied Hanna's roiling outrage. Francis's father considered her damaged, dismissed her; her attacker vanished along with the opportunity for justice.

Francis pressed on with her career, though the going was rough. In the late 1970s she was diagnosed with manic depression, and would ultimately stay in seventeen different hospitals for treatment, a fraught period during which she became suicidal. In 1984 she reemerged in the public eye with her autobiography *Who's Sorry Now?*, a bestseller. The remainder of her career has seen Francis record sporadically, score the odd hit in Europe, release archival recordings on her own label, Concetta Records, devote her time to various social causes, and write and publish another memoir. She lives in Florida, and has retired from performing. "I no longer do concerts because I just can't sing as well as I used to," she said recently. "I would never want to disappoint the fans who have been so good to me throughout my life."

Some fans let Francis's rich mezzo-soprano take them back to their past, dazed with nostalgia for those years, for a more innocent time; others hear in her voice a soundtrack to an era so far away as to feel stiffly unreal. Still others hear survival. By enduring, by living each day in the past and the present, Francis gives voice to other victims of sexual assault, countless other silenced and fearful women who might read her books, watch her interviews, listen to her songs and sturdy performances—urbane, wistful, immaculate, aching in her early years, bruised and hesitant but still strong, and now knowing, in her later years—and hear what it means to be alive.

Margo Price Macro Doses

I'll follow Margo on whatever trip she's taking . . .

> "I equate it with a snake shedding skin: Every time that I took [an acid trip], I got rid of some luggage that I really didn't need and I got rid of some things that weren't me anymore, that didn't fit. I cleaned my closet a lot and got rid of clothes that weren't me anymore, and I learned a lot."
> —CARLOS SANTANA

I was reading Margo Price's memoir *Maybe We'll Make It* recently, startled to learn that in the early aughts, before Price split for Nashville, she was a student at Northern Illinois University, where I teach. (She was born and raised in Aledo, a small farm town in western Illinois.) She briefly studied communications, right down the hall from the English Department. I don't remember if I had her as a student. Judging from her candid memories about her time in DeKalb she probably wouldn't have made it to class all that often.

"At the beginning of my sophomore year of college, I took psilocybin mushrooms for the first time. It turned my world inside out in the best possible way. I bought a couple of ounces of mushrooms from my ex-boyfriend Billy to sell for some extra cash. We were on good terms again and decided to take them together platonically. Per Billy's instructions, I consumed an entire eighth myself and downed some orange juice to intensify things. We walked around outside and the world came alive, visually and sonically. Colors flew at me and my whole being was tapped into a deep vibration I had never felt before. I experienced a great sense of peace and a connection to all living things."

Price is a difficult artist to box up, for those so inclined. She's lived in Nashville, Tennessee, for decades, and has both courted and shied away from Music City's trappings. A dynamic study in contrasts, she grew up in rural Illinois but sings with a Southern accent; her debut album was released on maverick Jack White's Third Man Records, hardly a Nashville industry staple (though it may be on its way); she cut a live album at historic and revered Ryman Auditorium, waltzing (and rocking) within a storied tradition.

In January 2023 she released her fourth studio album, *Strays*, recorded and coproduced with Jonathan Wilson at his Topanga Studio in Los Angeles, a different beast from her previous records *Midwest Farmer's Daughter* (2016), *All American Made* (2017), and *That's How Rumors Get Started* (2020), and a major artistic achievement. Her sweetly evocative, tender-but-tough Tammy Wynette/Stevie Nicks vocals are still there, as are the duets and collabs with celebrated musicians (among them Mike Campbell, from Tom Petty's Heartbreakers band), the commercial sheen, and the muscular, nuanced playing of her band, which features her husband Jeremy Ivey on guitar. (Ivey also cowrites many songs with Price; in addition to Ivey on guitars and bass, her band's currently comprised of Alex Munoz on acoustic and electric guitars and pedal steel, Jamie Davis on acoustic and electric guitars, Kevin Black on bass, Dillon Napier on drums, and Micah Hulscher on keyboards. Price adds acoustic guitar and percussion.)

Yet *Strays* arrived bearing news beyond its ten songs: before recording sessions began, Price and Ives rented an Airbnb in South Carolina and over the course of six intense days ingested magic mushrooms. "We ate a lot of them," Price acknowledges in *Consequence*, "and then, through osmosis, decided to listen to a ton of music and talk about sonically where we wanted [*Strays*] to go." Price and Ives woke up the next day ("when we were not high") and swiftly roughed out "Been to the Mountain," "Change of Heart," and "Light Me Up"—"and the list just kept growing from there." Price wrote twenty songs that week and has since remarked that she worked longer and harder on *Strays* than she's worked on anything. Her hope is that "people would have something to listen to when they are going down into the rabbit hole, going to the mountains, going inward. I have also listened to it while on shrooms later on, so it worked."

She adds, "It came out exactly as the recipe said."

> "The hallmark feature of the mystical experience, that we can now occasion with high probability, is the sense of the interconnectedness of all things—a sense of unity, a sense of openheartedness or love, and a noetic quality suggesting that this experience is more real than everyday waking consciousness. I believe that the experience of unity is of key importance to understanding the potential existential shifts that people can undergo after having these kinds of experiences."
>
> —ROLAND GRIFFITHS

"Music had never felt more symbolic," Price writes in *Maybe We'll Make It* of that first mushroom trip of hers, at the age of twenty. "We listened to the Jimi Hendrix Experience, and I watched the patterns of the curtains mutating before my eyes. It's really hard to describe what that first intense trip was like, but it felt like a conversation with God. It stripped away parts of my ego and revealed to me what I already knew in my heart. We are not our bodies, we are souls, temporarily imprisoned inside of this human experience. My value was not in my beauty or the lack thereof." The trip "shined a light" on Price's insecurities, also, and required that she "face my fears about the future. We are all going to grow old and die one day, so why sacrifice your life to do something that doesn't thrill you? There was renewed hope in my dreams. In that moment, I had found the secret to understanding the universe and what my role was in it: I would drop out of school and become a musician."

Price is unsparingly honest in her memoir, which was published by Texas on the eve of *Strays*. She writes about her fitful adolescence, alcohol abuse, a three-day prison stint, years of brutal hangovers, and the tragedy of losing an infant son (she also has a son and a young daughter). Her courtship with and marriage to Ivey are narrated in all of its glory, and the seams show: there are doubts; infidelities; some meanness; epic money problems; long, shitty nights given to menial jobs; drinking and drugging; and graphic career disappointments. Price and Ivey separated briefly; she carried on an affair. She ultimately quit her corrosive drinking. Now "California sober," Price smokes and trips with the zeal of an evangelist.

It's all in the memoir, which is heavily narrative—she's got a van full of great stories to tell—complemented by the occasional insightful moment of self-reflection. There aren't too many. Price keeps her lens focused on her story, a carefully crafted if reckless trajectory from small-town Midwestern farm girl and struggling, alcoholic Nashville-transplant to a married, road-touring mother of two and Jack White–blessed Next Big Thing singing and performing at the Grand Ole Opry.

In October 2023, Price and her band released *Strays II*, not quite a sequel but an extension of *Strays*. An album as an evolving, organic thing. Partially written during that six-day shroom trip in South Carolina, and recorded during the *Strays* sessions, the new material conceived by Price is shaped as a trio of three-song acts: *Topanga Canyon*, *Mind Travel*, and *Burn Whatever's Left*. I ordered the album bundled with a box of Mind Travel Mushroom Tea; a "Mind Melt Marble" colored vinyl edition will also be made available. "When you thought it was just a micro dose," Price teased on social media.

Those expecting Price's psychedelic excursions to have yielded conventional psychedelic music might be thrown off. Only a few songs on *Strays* and *Strays II* evoke what one might think of as typical hallucinogenic experiences. There are no guitars or organs holding trance-like drones, no backward tapes, phasing guitars, or corny panning across the stereo spectrum. No studio attempts at re-creating temporal dislocation, or the feeling of being high. Price's journeys have clearly and profoundly touched, even changed, her—she's rawly honest and forthcoming in interviews—but her music, with its modest twang, straightforwardness, and formal attention, remains rooted in traditional music.

Psychedelics seem to have brought Price closer to her true, reckoning self, where her professional ambitions and personal struggles are cast in sharper relief and, in their paradoxical urgency and pettiness, pale in the light of eternity and are rendered humbling against the vast scale of the universe. Tucked into the sleeve of the vinyl edition of *Strays* is a facsimile of a handwritten note from Price. In it she quotes Chief Seattle, the indigenous Suquamish and Duwamish chief famed for championing ecological obligations, who wrote, "All things are connected like the blood that unites us all. Man did not weave the web of life. He is merely a strand in it. Whatever he does to the web, he does to himself." Price, moved, adds below this, in her own words,

I belong to no one
I am cosmic dust
I am a speck on a speck
I am air, I am a shadow
I am a leaf in the forest
I am a star in the darkness
I am a red tailed hawk
I belong to no one

Such earnest epiphanies, glanced at an angle, can strike one as facile, yet that's the nature of a deep, sudden insight: what feels startlingly true and unique to you has been revealed to countless others before, each person reverberating in the overwhelming newness and clarity of their exclusive experience, each feeling as if they've been gifted something fresh. There's a reason we have clichés (and a reason why we've evolved, over millennia, in perfecting the eye roll), and clichés must be transcended in art if they're going to feel authentic and not hackneyed. Price manages to do this by burrowing deeper inside, trusting that her psilocybin days brought her to genuinely valuable, enlightening places that were inaccessible otherwise. In "Time Machine" (written by Napier and Christopher

Houston Denny, but of a piece with Price's own songs), she sings about wanting to feel reality.

Strays opens with the charging "Been to the Mountain," with its strutting, "Gloria"-like riff and stirring rock and roll dynamics that build and crest. (A rousing track, it killed when I saw Price and her band play in Chicago.) The driving performance pushes against a carefully calibrated arrangement, and indicates just how transformed Price is, confident enough in her newly cleansed point of view to let it rip with her band. The lyrics cycle through personalities and personae as if the singer's shedding skins, evolving toward something urgently felt yet hard to name.

In the first verse, she makes a key self-discovery, yet the larger insights arrive at the end of the song as Price plays mischievously with time itself, losing and finding herself, then murmuring, and then belting out lines about the end not being the end as the words collide against each other in reverb, in a bit of studio trippiness. "I always saw ["Been to the Mountain"] as being the peak of a trip because I wanted this album to be a whole psychedelic experience in itself," Price remarks in *Stereogum*, going a bit further in a comment on Apple Music:

> This was one of the very first songs that flowed out the next day after we came down from our mushroom trip. I just really wanted to incorporate poetry. I wanted it to be really psychedelic, and I wanted this album to be able to serve as a record that people could put on if they were going to maybe dabble in psychedelics. I think it can be a companion piece in that regard. I feel like whenever I have taken a psilocybin trip, there's always that moment right before everything starts happening in your brain and your body, and you feel like you're about to go on a roller coaster. That's what I wanted—to capture that feeling.

"Do you want to be different? Do you want to do something that's not the chosen path?" Price asked rhetorically in an article in *Billboard* on the occasion of *Stray*'s release. "You can absolutely do that. That's really what mushrooms have taught me." Such revelations don't come without their more complicated flip side. "Sometimes I feel so 'different,'" she confessed in a tweet, virtually shrugging. "My musical style can be hard to describe these days. We play country music for people who like psychedelics."

The tyranny of taxonomy: Price pops up in music database searches under "Americana," "neotraditionalist country," and "contemporary country," but never in searches of further-reaching genres such as "cosmic American music," "cosmic country," "stoner country," or even the broader "alt-country." As an artist she seems fated to drift between and among polarities, a stimulating if frustrating journey.

> "Psychedelics are not a substance for faith. They are a door to authentic faith, born of encountering directly the sacred dimension of everyday experience. This is not the only gate to that discovery, but it is the most ancient and universal, and potentially the most accessible to the majority of the human race."
>
> —RICK DOBLIN

With "Where Did We Go Wrong," on *Strays II*, Price seems to have written a genuine UFO song. (And meanwhile her head's in the Milky Way. Metaphors? Maybe.) And she dabbles in psychedelic imagery in the closer "Burn Whatever's Left," with its tea-brewing mystic and church bells tolling in ancient hills. Yet in "Closer I Get" she reckons with the harder moments before and after illumination. Originally written as *Stray*'s opener, the song was "conjured from the ashes of our initial psychedelic trip," Price comments on her website, adding, "Sometimes your perception and depth of field changes depending on where you're at in life." With its gentle, Fleetwood Mac roll, affecting melody, and irresistibly catchy chorus, "Closer I Get" mines the poignant place between getting and losing.

"Mind Travel" explicitly explores a psychedelic state. Written in response to an out-of-body experience Price had while tripping, the song is "pretty much beat poetry on drugs with a back beat," she explains, noting the she and Ivey had "some pretty incredible breakthroughs about accepting death and just reckoning with how fast it's all going," before adding, "It's okay to be reflective and remember the past as long as you don't get stuck back there." Price feels that the song and the album's "second act" are about learning to be content in the present. The smoothly undulating arrangement, anchored by an assertively searching, inviting piano lick, *feels* satisfied, at home and rooted, but the song can't help but evolve in its final minute into the closest thing to a "freak out" that a Price song reaches, that piano riff smilingly leading the listener through a brightly lit door in front of which the song had been otherwise pleasantly loitering. The final twenty seconds offer—what, the sound of crashing waves? Radio static? A distant thunderstorm? My wife hears whirring chopper blades. Anyway, the attempt in noise to aurally pin down where Price went, now that she's returned.

Price seems to have always considered herself in vivid ways. In an arresting passage in *Maybe We'll Make It* she describes a job she took working at the fabled Belcourt Theater during her mean, early years in Nashville. When she wasn't selling tickets or beers, she'd catch whatever flick was playing there; one was Albert and David Maysles and Charlotte Zwerin's 1970 documentary *Gimme Shelter*, about the Rolling Stones' ill-fated concert at Altamont Speedway outside Tracy, California. "One of my coworkers, Manda, convinced me the best seat in the house was sitting on the stage behind the screen," Price writes. "We both quickly shotgunned a beer and then walked up the small wooden staircase to the stage." The screen was transparent (Price: "translucent"), and, by turning her head, Price could regard the audience through the film's projection. "Mick Jagger was up there shaking it like a Vegas showgirl. I gazed through his image to see the crowd's reaction. It was exhilarating and terrifying." Unseen by the theater crowd, she and her friend shared a joint as Price looked up at Jagger and rock and roll spectacle, reveling in their shared-screen moment, their hallucinogenic transparencies.

> GEORGE HARRISON: That's the thing about LSD. You don't need it twice.
> INTERVIEWER: You've only taken it once?

HARRISON: Oh no, I took it lots of times. (*laughing*) But I only needed it once.

My experience with cannabis runs from the ridiculous (the time I was so high I nearly passed out at the top my living room stairs and then, alarmingly, "forgot" how to breathe) to the sublime (hearing the Beatles' harmonies in "Here, There, and Everywhere" one evening in a way so startlingly beautiful and new that, the next morning, sober, hearing only traces of that miracle, I was both enraptured and kind of heartbroken). More recently, I listened to the Who's *Quadrophenia* in its entirety on good, strong edibles. Jimmy's fraught journey from crowded London streets to a lonely rock off the coast of the English Channel, and Pete Townshend's songs singing that journey, felt thrillingly dimensional and cinematic. And those new neural pathways have stuck with me.

I listened to *Strays* and *Strays II* recently on edibles, and the experience was unedifying. In *Turn On Your Mind* Jim DeRogatis references a remark made by the Grateful Dead's Phil Lesh, that "psychedelic music is any music that's heard while tripping." Price herself imagines her new album as the soundtrack to a psilocybin journey. Maybe I haven't taken the right drugs. But I'm not complaining, nor feeling defensive or left out: the music on *Strays* and *Strays II* is striking, thoughtful, and deeply felt, and more profound than listening to it while tripping (perhaps) is the sober knowledge that shrooms have changed Price and Ivey, and thus have altered their songwriting. What matters are the songs, whatever they're filtered through on arrival.

In a suburban Chicago record store a year or so ago, I was struck by an album that the clerk had put on, a loud, trance-like jam that sounded through the small store like a sonic edict from somewhere else, and yet here I was standing in the middle of it. The album was *11:11* by the Glasgow-based collective Kundalini Genie. Moved—I was *sent*—I bought the record on the spot and have jammed to it countless times since, the top of my head prying open a bit more with each listen.

Three decades ago in Athens, Ohio, I was strolling to my house on the west side of town when I caught wind of an enormous and ecstatic sound coming from my neighbor's front porch. "What's that?" I cried out.

"It's Nirvana," she answered, her face blissy and complicated, her eyes alive. I hadn't heard *Nevermind* yet. What I heard was my neighbor saying the word that meant paradisical, joyous—and the language fit. Something happened inside of me in that moment that I can only describe as mood-altering—and perhaps mind-altering—a vivid connection to something that I most certainly could not have accessed a block away, or a minute before. Talk about contact highs.

"I think that we have been psychedelic in our live performance for a really long time," Price remarks in *Consequence*. "I'm not trying to compare my band to the Grateful Dead in any way, but there is a lot of improvisation that comes along with us getting on stage. You know, stretching songs out, changing tempos, changing things up, we've been doing that for a really long time." She adds, "I am trying to get more psychedelic lights. I would love to have more of a budget, a production. But we're not quite where I wanna be yet. I would love to have projections and really trippy things going on."

In the Chicago show at The Vic, Price's choice of cover songs was striking. After "Radio," the rousing statement of purpose from *Strays*, she leapt behind a second drum kit as her band strutted through Elvis Costello and the Attractions' "Pump It Up" (Black's grin while grooving the bass line was indelible), and ended the night with an elated take on Paul McCartney and Wings' "Let Me Roll It," a tune tailor-made for Price to find inside some winking, playful joy. (Her band also played Lesley Gore's "You Don't Own Me"—Price has a variation of the title tattooed on her arm—and Sleater-Kinney's "Turn It On" during that year-long tour dubbed "'Till the Wheels Fall Off.")

Early in the set, led by Napier's striking, expressive snare march, the band worked their way through Jefferson Airplane's "White Rabbit," a choice that might surprise an onlooker who would assume that Price's only debt is to Nashville. In the band's hands the song, a half century old now, built menacingly in its still-startling way, moving the show into something more dimensional and fuller of edgier possibilities than it had been. (I can bet Price was imagining those trippy projections.) Clearly grooving with the vibe and the crowd's knowing participation, she chose to have fun with the song, the flip side to her darker and more complex stuff—providing an answer song to the preshow Willie Nelson piped over the PA and theme music of sorts to the *Women in Weed* informational booths positioned at the front of the venue.

I regularly teach Walter Benjamin's essay "Hashish in Marseilles" in my "Writing Creative Nonfiction" workshop. Part of a series of "protocols" that Benjamin hoped to gather for a book he was writing about the philosophical and psychological consequences of drug use, the piece can be read both as "drug lit" and as a stroller in the "walking essay" tradition. The conversations about the essay are nearly always interesting, as students are eager talk about recreational drug use (and are definitely more comfortable doing so relative to a decade or so back). Invariably we get around to the "stoner's epiphany" and the eye rolls it generates—my students are familiar with 3 a.m. dorm room epiphanies gifted by edibles—but also the genuine enlightenment that can come from smoking weed or taking hallucinogens.

When we zoom in on the handful of insights that Benjamin reached as he walked, very stoned, the streets of his French port city, some of the more skeptical students come around to recognizing the value in Benjamin's experiment: his unexpected discovery that "ugliness could appear as the true reservoir of beauty"; the uncanny thrill "of recognizing someone I knew in every face"; the startling and profoundly moving recognition, while in "the deepest trance," that a couple of men whom Benjamin strolled past ("citizens, vagrants, what do I know?") could reveal to him the truth that "All men are brothers." ("When I meet a stranger there's nothing stranger / feeling that I'm meeting them all over again," Price sings in "Black Wolf Blues.") These gifts of illumination, shivers of intuition bordering on empathy and universal love, were revealed to Benjamin because he was high. But were such insights already in him? Do we need drugs to experience such intense things?

One student, who's never smoked weed nor taken hash, said to the class, "I don't have to now." She gestured at Benjamin's essay. "I've read this."

I drive on the long, straight roads of DeKalb County, past enormous farmlands and rural buildings, toward an endlessly flat horizon, listening to *Strays* and *Strays II*. The landscape I gaze at is keenly familiar to Price, who evokes it in her memoir, sings about it both nostalgically and ruefully in her songs, and who's never fully shaken off its dirt. Her grandparents lost their farm in the 1980s during the agriculture crisis; in May of this year Price was invited to be a member of the Board of Directors for Farm Aid, an honor "beyond my wildest dreams," she said. If Price carries western Illinois eternally in her mind, she's also made room in there for Nashville, and for the cities and countries she visits on tour, and she keeps carving out space there for wherever her travels, psychedelic or otherwise, may take her. Wherever she goes, when she returns, she'll pick up her guitar and she'll tell us.

All These Things Engulfing Me

Melancholy often flows through pop songs, tugging them toward complications and darkness, or setting them free from those conditions. The late Tommy Keene exquisitely balanced sorrow and brightness in his best songs.

I resisted melancholy when I was in my twenties, and I also courted it. The paradox of youth. In bars and clubs, certain songs sent me to the back or, if I was feeling extravagantly melodramatic, out the door, leaving behind me groups of people colliding urgently to music that was too despondent for me. I wanted to drink and grin.

I'd tell a joke in the mid-1980s, unfunny to most, that the only bands that could drive me out of a bar were the Cure and the Smiths, two groups I didn't like at the time and yet whose fans—among them a few of my best friends—I'd eye enviously as they lost themselves on the dance floor. I have clearer purchase now on what I was rebelling against. It wasn't that I couldn't identify with what I heard as the moodiness, affected doom, and sighing melancholy in these and other like bands; the problem was that I related too much. I had the voices of Robert Smith and Morrissey running in my head all day long; not their words, but the edgy, disconsolate tone, a claustrophobic ennui that I struggled with in my worst moments. I didn't want to hear that on the dance floor. I wanted to get away, leave my head and my body, exchange my blues, self-doubt, and self-consciousness for rock and roll.

Beers and barre chords! Riffs and hooks! Echo and the Bunnymen's "Bring on the Dancing Horses" might've sounded great at Cagney's or Back Alley Cafe, but it was the Flamin' Groovies, Hoodoo Gurus, the Godfathers, and others, in whom I found an urgent sense of purpose. There was a reason why I was teased at my college radio station as the Guy Who Played the Knack more often than, say, New Order. Even when I did spin songs that soundtracked my dejection, they were usually by R.E.M., Rain Parade, Pop Art—sadness never too far from the jangle.

I sought out moodiness in books and art, in Joyce and Eliot and Franz Kline and Joan Mitchell, and during long walks in the then-deteriorating Old Downtown in Washington, D.C. My morose reflection was cast back at me most graphically in my art history, literature, and philosophy courses, where in the quiet of reading, or in the endless stacks at the campus library, I could stoke my melancholy and self-pity across the centuries. I'd indulgently lose myself in dramatic sadness during dusk hours.

Though I've never fully warmed to the metronomic "Blue Monday," my distaste for the song in my twenties blocked a rightful appreciation I ought to have felt for Joy Division, another band I resisted at the threshold, fearful of how swiftly they might invade. Of course, back then I hadn't really *listened* to the Cure or the Smiths, to Bauhaus, Cocteau Twins, or Siouxsie and the Banshees, or for matter much of what I'd overheard or read was Gothic—childishly, I wouldn't let myself. (And I missed a lot of the humor, too.) I forgive a lot for youth and yet as it turns out, hey, the Smiths were a great guitar band all along! Johnny Marr's trippy vibe in support of Morrissey's emotional nakedness was beyond my ken when I was twenty, putting me at odds not only with my friends but with pop culture, and history.

If I'd only looked more closely at the dance floor I'd have seen guys and girls rejoicing and identifying in a language I was too petulant or cowardly to try to learn. But the release on their sweaty faces and in their limbs transcended language, as great music does. These are minor regrets, yet I wished I'd opened up some neural pathways earlier than I did. Anyway, life is pretty much about catching up. File all of this under Too Bad I Didn't See It at the Time, a bulging, still-growing folder.

Tommy Keene was a local guy. He grew up in Bethesda, near me, and, as I had, he'd studied at the University of Maryland. He was handsome, and he had a great rock and roll name. The songs of his I'd hear on WHFS, the area progressive music station, would send me into waves of complicated happiness. He'd always resisted (though he eventually grudgingly accepted) the Power Pop label with which fans and critics identified him, yet there was no denying the power behind his pop songs, energy that both darkened and sought release. I aped his modish, golf-jacket, flat-collar-shirt, and narrow-jeans sartorial style when I could. I caught a lot of his area shows. His was the kind of melancholy to which I could surrender.

Keene was born in Evanston, Illinois, in 1958. His parents moved to Bethesda, Maryland, when he was an infant. His native love of pop and rock and roll stoked by his like-spirited older brother Bobby, Keene first fooled around on drums and piano, later moving to guitar as the Beatles, the Who, the Rolling Stones, Bruce Springsteen, Roxy Music, and the hooks, melodies, and life force of AM radio soundtracked his heady teen years. While at Walter Johnson High School he played in a band (Blue Steel), but wouldn't join a serious group until he formed Rage with Richard X. Heyman while both were students at the University of Maryland.

He then stepped in as guitarist and nascent songwriter in Razz, a high-profile D.C.-area band that would release three singles and tour to well-received shows up and down the East Coast. After Razz imploded in 1979, Keene dropped out of college and moved to New York City, where he worked with a pickup band backing singer Suzzanne Fellini, whose Blondie-styled new wave music never caught fire but who, for a brief time, enjoyed major label support. Wide-eyed in his early twenties, Keene dug staying at the Gramercy Park Hotel in Manhattan and playing shows on the East Coast, in the Midwest, and in Europe, but he couldn't really connect with Fellini's songs, and was growing homesick. After that gig ended he banged around in New York City for a little while longer, couch surfing, auditioning for bands. He formed a group called Pieces, but they split up when a four-song demo failed to land them a record deal.

Keene moved back to Bethesda, licked his wounds, vowed to avoid toxic band politics where he could, and wrote and wrote, inspired by his first major creative rush of marrying sense to sound. Growing confident as a guitarist, committed to being a solo artist yet curious about the appeal of his self-described "quirky" voice, Keene recruited bassist Ted Niceley and drummer Doug Tull, with whom he'd played in Razz, and got down to business. After placing two songs on a local compilation album (*Connected*) and releasing a mini-album of promising demos (*Strange Alliance*), he recorded the terrific EP *Places That Are Gone* in 1984 with a core band of Niceley, Tull, and Billy Connelly on guitar.

The record kicked up a lot of interest—the title track was a hit on college radio, remaining Keene's signature song to this day. Buzzing, gigging around, aloft on the mid-Atlantic music scene, Keene swiftly signed with Geffen Records. To us locals, it felt as if he'd ascended to royalty. He released the highly anticipated *Songs from the Film* in early 1986. Glossy, heavily produced, the album felt at the time like a misstep; there were rumors, correct as it turned out, that the band had cut a better-sounding record with producers T-Bone Burnett and Don Dixon but that Geffen had refused to release it. (The label also forced Keene to fire his manager.) Regretfully, Keene rerecorded the album down in the West Indies at George Martin's AIR Studio with producer Geoff Emerick. The results were mixed. Keene loved the songs, and lamented their sound. *Songs from the Film* didn't sell particularly well, the commercial backlash and local resentments stung Keene, and in 1987 his band broke up. He moved to Los Angeles the following year.

For a variety of tiresome industry-related reasons, his follow-up, *Based on Happy Times*, wouldn't arrive until 1989, an eternity in pop music wilderness. I picked up the album in a record store in Athens, Ohio, gazed at Keene's gauzy, movie-star headshots on the front and back covers, and felt that he was far away. It took several years for me to catch up with the pensive, richly downbeat mood of the album, and now, though the production's a bit dated, it's one of my favorites. One song in particular embodies the melancholy that I'll forever associate with Keene's music. "Light of Love" is mid-paced, yet driven hard, typical of Keene in that it navigates wistfulness and loss with churning guitars. The musicians—Keene singing and on guitar, Jack Holder on guitar, Joe Hardy on bass, and John Hampton on drums—take a stand against the minor key in which the song's written, bravely strutting in the verses, playing their guitars as if they're sharpening blades even as the lyrics evoke sadness: there's lightning, a dozen roses in the rain, love that's waned. As often happens with Keene's songs, with great pop music, the chorus complicates things further. Shifting to the major, Keene paradoxically shadows the mood, sketching out a complicated relationship of desire and loss.

Vintage Keene: the swift, brutal replacing of having with losing. The melody rises expectantly, falls at the title phrase, extends higher at "dreaming of"—a phrase that might accurately subtitle Keene's catalogue—then again falls. The despondency I hear in many of Keene's songs arrives via those gently, often subtly descending melodies that score gains and losses—listen to "Nothing Happened Yesterday" from *Places That Are Gone*—in this case a figure longing for another while recognizing that all he'll get is purchase from afar, dreams of the thing rather than the thing itself, yesterday and tomorrow pulling him from his, from their, present. Add a characteristic guitar solo that, riding changes, tries to burst the song's very seams but is fated to land back, always, at those dejected verses.

"I can barely conceive of a type of beauty in which there is no Melancholy." That's Charles Baudelaire, writing about Tommy Keene. Not really. But, also, yeah. I've been inside of Baudelaire's observation for a long time. It feels truer every day, and comes to mind when I listen to "I Don't Feel Right at All" from the *Run Now* EP, released at the end of 1986. Cut with T-Bone Burnett and Don Dixon for the shelved *Songs from the Film* sessions, the song positively shimmers, especially in its jewel-like opening bars, where

Keene's guitar sends sparkles in the air. Gorgeous, the phrases are soon joined by Tull's muscular drumming and a typically thoughtful bass line from Niceley. (In his best playing on Keene's records, Niceley gives the impression of ruminating along with the singer.)

Many of Keene's lyrics are obscure—there are first-name references to people from his past, more than one shadowy hallway at the end of which something ambiguous happens, abstract narratives, truths that feel private to Keene and so are at times tough for a listener to enter, or even comprehend. Bruce Springsteen has described his own songwriting as being "emotionally autobiographical," a phrase that I love. Rather than load them with details that will resonate for a few listeners, he'll open his songs outward. The music begins, as all art does, inside the dark, then moves toward a wide, well-lit emotional landscape that only the writer could imagine yet in which friends and strangers collide, nodding at each other in shared understanding. Keene's greatest songs work this way, too. Unless they're decoded by a loved one, dear friend, or colleague, they remain private, yet somehow relatable.

"I Don't Feel Right at All" is among the most forthright songs that Keene wrote. The stakes laid out in that title phrase couldn't be clearer, the lyrics less disguised in figurative finery. The melody is typically forlorn, and thoughtful, if a melody can be said to think. Mining a storied songwriting tradition, Keene tries to, if not right things in the bridge, then to nudge everything down a slightly different path in the hopes that there might be sunlight at the end of it. I can see the singer looking hopefully at the person with whom he's speaking, seeing the kindness in their shining eyes, understanding the words they offer about suffering and acceptance, yet singing, in that eternal melancholia of melody, the real truth. That's the sorry fate of a bridge in any song, especially for a traditionalist like Keene, who's happily bound to song conventions, to the forms that told a million stories over AM radio: a bridge, no matter how cheery or optimistic or caring, must end, and then it's back to the verses of the chorus and whatever powerful story they're telling.

In my early and midtwenties those two lines were on high rotation on my interior jukebox, a sweetly terrifying ode to the truth of my unhappiness, strangeness, my misfit-ness, whatever the term: You can say I'm okay but you're not living it, I am.

Late in 1967, Pete Townshend was noodling around in his home studio on Ebury Street in London, working on a song titled "Melancholia" about depression, "around the time [the Who] were facing a void in their career," he'd write in the liner notes to his demos collection *Scoop*, in 1982. "It's a tremendously haunting song," he remarked, adding, "I suppose I was really melancholic when I wrote it." He incorrectly surmised that the Who had never heard the demo. In fact they recorded a version of "Melancholia" but it remained unreleased for decades. Nearly half a century after writing the song, Townshend revisited it on the occasion of the release of the box set of the Who's 1967 album *The Who Sell Out*. "This was one of my first attempts to write about depression and anxiety," he told Rob Hughes in *Uncut* in 2021. "Interestingly, in light of Covid, the working title was 'The Virus'. Once depression sets in, it's so difficult to escape it. It's like drowning, in a sense."

"Melancholia" is vintage Townshend: lamenting, inward-gazing, risking self-indulgence, and gorgeously forlorn. The melody's stately, simple even, moving among five notes in the verses as the singer dryly yet achingly names the problems: his coffee's cold, his paper's old, his clothes are torn, his shoes are worn. The dust is thick, the dog's sick, outside the kids have picked most of the flowers. Unsurprisingly, a broken heart's the source of the downheartedness, the departed leaving behind a world of sad and meager grays. Famous for the care he lavished on his demos, Townshend produced a one-man full-band performance on Ebury Street. He sings against the ennui, his multitracks and overdubs crest and fall, yet plainly "the virus" has driven him mad. No song can fully deliver him.

It's amazing that this poignant thing never made it onto a Who album; it was allegedly earmarked for a 1968 collection that never materialized, and I guess it blew out the window in the gust of the ambition and majesty of *Tommy*. The full band version of "Melancholia," recorded in May 1968 after a run-though the previous December, is unsurprisingly aggressive. Keith Moon's drums tumble and roll, and John Entwhistle's/Townshend's bass-and-guitar interlock with punchy, slashing force. Townshend's backing vocals are predictably lovely and rich, sweetening things a bit, and Roger Daltrey is able to check his laddish tendencies and find himself in the vulnerable, confessional lyrics, soaring by the end in a remarkable performance that looks ahead to his robust singing at the end of the decade and into the next. Yet to my ears the theatrical arrangement overall is a bit melodramatic.

I bet that Keene adored "Melancholia," both its intimacies and its grandeurs. He was a lifelong fan of Townshend's songwriting and guitar playing, making it clear in interviews throughout his career the debt he owed the founder of the Who, one of his favorite bands. He covered several of Townshend's songs, and recorded a few, including a sublime version of "Tattoo" in the mid-1980s, eventually issued on *The Real Underground* compilation in 1994, "Much Too Much" on his wonderful 2013 covers album *Excitement at Your Feet* (the title, of course, a quote from *Tommy*'s "See Me, Feel Me"), and a ragged, half-serious dash through the first verse of "It's Not True," an unlisted track closing out 1996's guitar-heavy *Ten Years After*.

I wish he'd recorded "Melancholia." The song feels tailor-made for him, from its evocative opening arpeggio to the revealing interiority of the lyrics. I don't know if he ever played it live, or ever recorded it in private, but anymore it's difficult for me to not hear Townshend singing Keene, and the other way around.

Keene was gay. He lived in an era when it was still difficult to navigate a career with an open and public queerness. We'd heard the rumors. "In the '80s, Tommy was more asexual than gay," his brother Bobby told me. "I never talked to him about this, so it's still a brother speculating, but I think he moved to Los Angeles so he could be gay. It wasn't the music [in L.A.]. To the extent that people will say, 'Tommy always held back and never embraced fame or celebrity,' it was being gay that held him back. Because when he signed with Geffen, they wanted to make him a teen idol, and he resisted it. Totally. And there were a lot of women that threw themselves at Tommy. I know. And that made him uncomfortable. He didn't want to come out and say, 'I'm not interested' because of this. He just kind of was asexual about it."

In 2006, Keene was asked by Bob Mehr in *Magnet* magazine if being gay had been problematic for him in his professional career. "It really hasn't caused a problem," he replied, effectively outing himself. (He'd open up again that same year for the *Advocate.*) "Occasionally, I get a little tired of tit jokes in the van. But hey, I like tits, too. Seriously, though," he added, "it probably hasn't been a big deal because I haven't sold a lot of records. If I sold a bunch of records, maybe people would care. If I were someone like Michael Stipe or Tom Cruise, it might be an issue. I don't mean to be flippant, but it's never been any kind of thing for me."

The great obsession in Keene's songs is the passing of time. It's hard not be rueful, at the very least contemplative, about the inevitable and accruing losses that we experience over time. Since that first rush of creativity in the early 1980s, Keene writes about days and places gone by, yesterdays regretted, opportunities missed, memories fading, his despondency in the face of it all—perhaps even his bravery about it all—soundtracked with his trademark bittersweet tones. A sample of song titles: "Twilight's in Town," "Places That Are Gone," "Nothing Happened Yesterday," "Tomorrow's Gone Tonight," "You Can't Wait for Time," "As Life Goes By," "Waiting without You," "My Mother Looked Like Marilyn Monroe," "Alone in These Modern Times." In "Away from It All" he sings about never feeling connected with anything, belying the cheery melody and sprightly arrangement. He titled one of his albums *Into the Late Bright*—the brightness will end sooner rather than later. In the title track he sings, "I cannot feel anymore."

It's possible that any personal issues with his queerness were seen through this lens of loss and regret, yet the strongest and most powerful effect on Keene's lyrics was the undertow of grief. In August 1977 his mother Jeane was struck and killed by a drunk driver in Ocean City, Maryland. Bobby was with his parents, Tommy was at school, in College Park. He had turned nineteen two months earlier. "All of that emotion that you can wrap up in melancholy forced its way out in his songs," Bobby shared with me. "Otherwise he had this thick wall of defense, so you never saw it in his everyday life. His songs are the only place that really came out. And I have to say that it's hard to find a song of his where it *didn't* come out. A lot of his songs have of some sort of reference to our mother being killed, our lost loves, or things like that. But if you knew Tommy, that never came out in real life."

He continued,

> We all know people like comedians. They seem like the happiest, funniest people in the world, but we all know that most comedians are very broken inside, and that there's this insecurity and this, "I'm never good enough." And that's why so many of them self-destruct. It's like a romantic novel author that writes about these huge, flowery, affectionate relationships, and they're a loner. So I think, yes, all of Tommy's songs have that melancholy sort of bittersweet good-and-bad touch to them. I'm sure that's real, given what we went through growing up.

Shortly after Keene died, Bobby wrote a touching tribute to his younger brother. In it he described a powerful and revealing episode. "As if it was yesterday, I can remember after our mother's funeral, Tommy sitting at the family piano in the next room and playing for the first time as if he was possessed," he wrote. "He played with a tone of sadness and soul that few musicians can and which Tommy had not displayed to this point in time. He played with that passion and soul as if the tragedy had at once transformed his latent talent through some supernatural fission process into the very same gamer passion he played with through this last tour with Matthew Sweet." He continued, "It was a lightbulb moment for the older brother in the next room. The emotion you can feel from his songs, lyrics and guitar was Tommy's signature. . . . That guitar tone and the bittersweet melancholy themes described by all the critics, that are so associated with Tommy, were born on that day on my mother's piano."

Bobby revealed to me that what Tommy played on that sad afternoon of their mother's burial was the moving coda of Derek and the Dominos' "Layla." "And he hates Eric Clapton, always hated Eric Clapton," Bobby said, laughing. "But he played that. And I don't think he had ever played it before. He hadn't played a lot of piano at that point. And so I think he had a lot of that walled up inside of him, and he found an outlet for it after my mother died." He added, "That brought it out. And it also really, really built up the wall more."

Most anyone who knew Keene professionally or personally describes him as a fun, and funny, guy. ("Hey, I like tits, too.") "He made any room he was in a much happier place with his smile and quick wit," Guided by Voices' Robert Pollard remarked on the occasion of Keene's death. "Nobody loved the party more than Tommy," his brother acknowledged. Fiercely energetic onstage, he was often loose and witty up there, too, and in interviews, where the "tales of woe" of his own up-and-down career and his incisive and hilarious stories about fellow musicians are legion. (There are many conversations online, of course, and I recommend Jim Lenahan and Patrick Foster's lively and warm *Rockin' the Suburbs* podcast from 2017, one of Keen's final interviews.) He covered the Beach Boys' goofily innocent "Our Car Club" for *Based on Happy Times*; during the song's opening bars one of the guitarists—it might've been Keene's studio guest, Peter Buck—mimics a car engine struggling to turn over, and Keene busts out laughing while singing. It's a fun and hilarious moment, and Keene wisely kept it on the album. (My smile lasted for days after hearing it.) When I caught Keene and his band at George Washington University in the fall of 1986, I approached the stage between songs with a request. I'd heard somewhere along the grapevine that he'd covered the Beatles' "And Your Bird Can Sing," long a favorite of mine. I got Keene's attention, he leaned over the edge of the stage, I asked. And he laughed. Not in a dismissive way, but in a pleased and very amused way. They couldn't play the song, but his bright-eyed guffaw remains with me to this day, as indelible a Keene memory as any.

Recently, I asked a few of the musicians with whom Keene played down the years if they felt that he was a melancholy person. "Not particularly, not for the time I knew and played music with him," Ted Niceley replied. "I think one has to consider that Tommy had a, quote, unquote, outside persona and a private one. He didn't wear his emotions on his sleeve, was very private about his mother's death, and him being a closeted gay man during the time I was in his day-to-day life, I would think, had a lot to with his putting it into his songs. He was kind of cynical but he was never what I would term a gloomy person." He added, "I think L.A. made him a bit more melancholy."

Matty McLaughlin was a close friend of Keene's for two decades, and he now runs Keene's website. He, too, recognized something essentially despondent in many of Keene's tunes, "but usually when he cranked out that kind of material I think it was to get it out and make something better of the emotion," he told me. "There were ups and down in his life that I witnessed, mainly over the second ten years, but even during difficult times he never really wallowed in despair. He was pretty happy-go-lucky if he had the essentials in his life." He described Keene as charming and dashing, "never looking to grab the spotlight at the party but just enjoy himself and dig the scene." He fondly recalls Keene hosting dinner parties, enjoying late night Tecates while deejaying from his enormous record collection.

McLaughlin noted that Keene often quoted his own songs in an arch, self-deprecating manner, making fun of them and, by extension, himself. "As I started doing his website and helping him do things like burning CDs via iTunes and we'd be on the horn while I tried to walk him through the process and he'd groan 'alone in these modern times.' There were the times when he'd be sure he was sick or had finally contracted lung cancer from years of smoking—I think many of us thought he was a hypochondriac—and you'd hear him quote the title 'I Don't Feel Well at All', always delivered in a decided iambic pentameter, stressing the key words." More than once Keene would groan his own song titles in a deadpan manner, "but never without a chuckle."

"I don't really think of him as a melancholy person, but obviously I see where the question's coming from." That's Brad Quinn, who played bass on Keene's records and toured with him for a decade and a half starting in the early 1990s following Keene's release from Geffen, the start of many years hopping from indie label to indie label. "Tommy had his moods like anyone, though it's possible that he luxuriated in them more than your average person." He, too, feels that the death of Keene's mother informed his songwriting

> in its themes of loss and ephemerality, I'd say. It wouldn't be too hard to pull that out of a number of his better-known songs. However, Tommy was a really fun person, overall. He loved to party and have a good time. He was very social and pretty much made friends with every single person that came to one of his shows. He also really loved what he did. He basically made records for himself, and he made the music that he made because that was the music that he dug. Tommy perhaps had a melancholy streak—and a number of other streaks, as well—but it was not his overriding essence. He was a generous, levelheaded, and well-balanced person.

He added, "And, of course, the opposite is also true."

"I have a kind of different, distinctive voice," Keene once said. Many days I wonder if that difference, that distinction, was the source of the bittersweetness in his songs. His voice was certainly imperfect, was often described by critics as "nasally" or "reedy." He wasn't a crooner, a smooth balladeer. When he pushed against the top of his range, as he often did, in his rockers as well as his midpaced songs and ballads, his vocals sounded slightly labored, strained, with a hint of struggle; the impression was that they were in conflict with something in the words, in the mood that they and the melodies create. In his greatest vocal performances—in "Back to Zero Now," say, or "Nothing Happened Yesterday" or "Silent Town," to name but a few—this inelegancy added to the emotional richness of the music. Even Keene's sweetly sung tunes like "Baby Face" and "Safe in the Light" benefitted from the rawness, the limitations, of his vocals.

"When Tommy was young, his enlarged tonsils and adenoids were removed, yet several years later they grew back. They were removed again, and the trauma left its mark. And I'm not so sure they didn't grow back *again*," Bobby said. "If you think of yourself as sort of having a sore throat and then singing? That's exactly what it sounded like and felt like." Bobby feels that these nasal surgeries ultimately took his brother's life, contributing to the sleep apnea from which Keene suffered for decades, and which grew more severe in his final years. "And I kicked myself," Bobby said. "If you now read about sleep apnea, it's a debilitating condition that ultimately will get your heart." Tommy Keene died of cardiac arrest in his sleep on November 22, 2017. He was fifty-nine years old, and otherwise in good health. "If you'd ever heard him sleep, or anybody with sleep apnea from that matter, there's a point in time, a millisecond, when they stop breathing. Those milliseconds over sixty years add up to break your heart. To literally cause you to have cardiac arrest. That's what's on his birth certificate."

Sometimes I fantasize about swallowing a pill or taking a shot that would allow me to hear a song again for the first time. Imagine! Sam and Dave's "When Something Is Wrong with My Baby," Howlin' Wolf's "The Red Rooster," the Everly Brothers' "Like Strangers," the Beatles' "Please Please Me," Dusty Springfield's "I Only Want to Be with You," Pharoah Sanders's "Upper Egypt and Lower Egypt," Nirvana's "Smells Like Teen Spirit," Blondie's "Dreaming," the Stooges' "T.V. Eye," an overplayed radio hit, a hammed Christmas song, a child's lullaby, that tune that scored the summer I turned thirteen. So many more. Stripped of nostalgia, of intensely emotional context, what would I hear in these songs? The same notes, the same performances. More intriguingly, what *wouldn't* I hear? When a song passes through the weather front that is a listener's life, it's affected, it morphs from something private to something personal, exponentially, is no longer only the singer's or the band's but the listener's also.

I grew up with a moody father who, when the mood struck him, would play his cherished Frank Sinatra albums on the family stereo, his eyes moistening as the songs brought him to places his children couldn't see. If I could hear Sinatra and Antonio Carlos

Jobim's "Change Partners" for the first time again, I know that I'd be struck dumb by its devastating beauty (that bridge!), but missing would be the overlay of my dad in the rocking chair in the rec room after dinner. I'm not so sure being allowed to hear a favorite, well-worn song for the first time would be the blessing that I imagine. The beauty, fun, and hooks or the anger, ennui, and punk recklessness would be there, fresh, but the song would feel less personal. Until it felt personal again.

I believe I'd hear the same poignancy in a Tommy Keene song if I could hear it new again—the ragged exquisiteness in his best, most affecting songs, in any great song, transcends a listener's private attachments. The descending melodies, the voice straining to sing them, the disconsolate lyrics written in a bid to translate what's untranslatable yet must be voiced—it's all there before I hear it, as it was in the songs that so moved Keene in his lifetime. He titled what ended up being his final studio album *Laugh in the Dark*, a cheery stay against confusion. (He released a live album, his second, in 2016, the year before he died.) His last several studio albums—*Crashing the Ether* (2006), *In the Late Bright* (2009), *Behind the Parade* (2011), and *Laugh in the Dark*—are richer and warmer sounding than the records he made in the 1990s, partly a consequence of shifting tastes and trends in production, partly of Keene's continued maturation as a songwriter and singer.

"I make records for myself," he said to the *L.A. Record* on the occasion of the *Laugh in the Dark*'s release. "And this is what I want to hear. I'm my biggest fan and I'm my worst fan. I'm the most critical person of what I do. But it's got to be a record that makes me wanna put it on on a Saturday night and jump around the room." He added, "And it'll have some thoughtful and some melancholy songs. But that's what I wanna hear."

"All Gone Away," the final song on Keene's final studio album, is difficult to listen to. An epic six and a half minutes, paced luxuriously, the song's a natural album closer, and it plays now also as a heartbreaking theme song of sorts: as you listen, end credits of a film about Keene's life virtually scroll in the air. The Beatles' "Dear Prudence" and Electric Light Orchestra's "10538 Overture" are clearly the song's musical touchstones, and Keene was also clear about another key ingredient, "a funky '70's Baldwin organ called a Fun Machine that I found at a consignment shop out in the Desert some time ago." The ironically named organ contributes a solemn, churchy majesty to the proceedings, and an air of resigned bittersweetness pervades. How much of this mournful tone I hear retroactively, I'm not sure; I bought the album soon after Keene's death, and everything's colored. If you need a song to listen to while imagining Keene exiting a stage in slow motion, waving back to the crowd before he vanishes through a side door, this is it.

His humor's intact here: the opening line, "Plant you now, dig you later" cracks an adolescent half grin, and Carmen Electra, of all people, makes an unreasonable appearance in the second verse. But I write this on the cusp of the five-year anniversary of Keene's death, and the poignancy of the rest of the sorrowful lyric, married to the inevitably downward pull of the melody, is nearly overwhelming.

The final two minutes are devoted to Keene's splendid guitar playing into the fade, giving a frustrated but finally a freeing voice to all that's left unsaid in the song, the last of his, and characteristic of his best in every way. "I've never ventured off into any other genres or experimentations because I thought, well, that's what people do when they've made it at what they do," Keene said a couple of years before he died. "They say, 'Let me try this because I've already proven myself with that.' But I've never proven myself. So I'm still struggling to make that perfect record."

Brief Histories

A worldwide titan in pop music and an obscure local indie rocker offer me early lessons in grief.

When Stevie Nicks's "Edge of Seventeen" was soaring across the radio in 1982 I was paying little attention, poised as I was for a lifelong deep dive into indie, alt, and punk rock. But I heard the song, plenty; it was impossible not to hear it. As many hit songs do, "Edge of Seventeen" entered my consciousness, then settled in my subconsciousness, and has stayed there for decades, lifted to the surface bidden by a stray memory or a snatch of melody overheard in a bar, its chorus a reminder of earlier places and people. A few months back I was half-watching the Super Bowl halftime show and heard the song again, this time performed by Miley Cyrus, who'd recently released a mashup mix of Nicks's song with her own tune, "Midnight Sky." There it was again.

The song that heralded Nicks's solo career originated in random moments. She was on a plane flying home to Phoenix, Arizona, in 1980 when she read about the white-winged dove, native to the Sonora desert and its saguaro cacti, whose song gives the impression that it's singing: *ooh, ooh, ooh*. "As you well know, I was very taken with that whole picture," Nicks wrote to her Instagram followers in April 2020. That post included a video Nicks had taken of what she'd assumed was an owl—perched atop a high, bare tree branch, starkly grey-white against a brilliant blue sky—but which was, rather, a friend told her, the infamous white-winged dove.

"Over the last 40 years I can honestly say, I have never heard a dove sing—until now," she wrote, adding, "I started to cry. This dove had come here to watch over me." That this moment occurred for Nicks as she and the rest of the world were on lockdown during the pandemic, that she could share it with her eight hundred thousand–plus followers worldwide, added a touch of poignancy.

Birdsong aside, there had been other influences on the song. Nicks had at some point in the 1970s met Tom Petty's wife, Jane Benyo, and in conversation with Nicks, Benyo said that she'd met Petty when he was at the "age of seventeen." Fooled by Benyo's Floridian accent, Nicks heard *the edge* of seventeen. The evocative phrase lodged in Nicks's mind, and she set about to use it.

Darker currents were also at play. Nicks's uncle Jonathan died as she was writing material for her album. The evening she completed work on a song responding to her grief, another major figure in her life died. She was in Australia in December 1980 when John Lennon was shot and killed. "Everybody was devastated," she said. "I didn't know John Lennon, but I knew [producer] Jimmy Iovine, who worked with John quite a bit in the '70s, and heard all the loving stories that Jimmy told about him. When I came back to Phoenix I started to write this song."

Elsewhere, she remarked, "The line 'And the days go by like a strand in the wind,' that's how fast those days were going by during my uncle's illness, and it was so upsetting to me. The part that says 'I went today . . . maybe I will go again . . . tomorrow' refers to seeing him the day before he died. He was home and my aunt had some music softly playing, and it was a perfect place for the spirit to go away." She added, "The white-winged dove in the song is a spirit that is leaving a body, and I felt a great loss at how both Johns were taken." (In later interviews, Nicks implicitly linked the white dove in her song to Lennon's peace campaigns.) Quite a confluence: the image of a cooing bird nestled in the spiny shelter of a cactus foregrounded against loss, discovery and defeat at odds.

My maternal grandmother died in December 1980, and her death was the first loss—other than a childhood friend having moved away six years earlier—that I felt keenly, that is, which moved me to speechlessness. I tried to cry when Karl's family left the cul-de-sac behind my house for faraway suburban Chicago, as I felt that that's what I was supposed to do, yet at that early age I intuited, and years later recognized, that insincere weeping was a cheap substitute for that which I deeply felt but couldn't yet name. When my grandmother died and I gazed from the door at my mom lying prostrate on her bed dissolved in tears, the word *loss* became something more dimensional, though it was no easier to speak.

One week earlier, I was in my bed listening to *Monday Night Football* on the radio when Jack Buck and Hank Stram interrupted their call with news of Lennon's death. My family had visited my mom's parents in the small town of Coldwater, in western Ohio, for a week each summer, and I'd cherished those days with my grandparents, yet I felt as if I knew Lennon better, or was somehow closer to him. I obsessively played the family copies of the "Red" and "Blue" albums, and the songs affected me as profoundly as any expression or gesture of family love. My mom's weeping was among the first displays of unbridled emotion I'd seen her surrender to; after Lennon was murdered, I gathered in my sister's bedroom with one of my brothers, the three of us stunned into silent disbelief.

These images commingle now in memory as my first headlong descent into the strangeness of grief. Neither loss was as personal as losses would come for me later, of course. I knew my mom's mother well, and loved her, but from the cooly reserved and guarded distance that most children choose to love distant, aged family members they see once a year. I didn't know Lennon personally, but knew and possibly loved him as deeply as I knew and loved anyone. The man who sang "There's a Place," "No Reply," "Help," "Strawberry Fields Forever," "Imagine," the still-new "Watching the Wheels" was now bizarrely, absurdly, gone.

In the following weeks, I wordlessly pieced together how I was supposed to feel. One thing clear to me was that my response to Lennon's death was as sharp as my response to my grandmother's—one person I knew directly, one I didn't. What should have been a wide gap between those reactions was in fact uncomfortably narrow, and if you'd asked me, in the months that followed, which death was harder for me, I'd have answered you honestly only after I was sure that my mom was out of earshot. In retrospect, this is unsurprising: as a freshly minted, inward-looking teenager I didn't know how to deal with intimate family loss, a rawly grieving parent, the profound breadth of generations, but I knew how to deal with the loss of a beloved if starrily distant pop music figure, one who gave me countless hours of pleasure. I now forgive my fourteen-year-old self's unspoken allegiance to the memory of John Lennon over the memory of Frances Mueller.

By 1980 Lennon was an enormous figure in my life, looming as large as any friend or family member. The year before, I'd clipped an article in the "Style" section of the *Washington Post* about rumors that the Beatles were going to reunite for a concert for the Vietnamese Boat People. This pseudo news filled me with excitement, and my friends and I buzzed about it that morning on the blacktop at St. Andrew the Apostle as we gathered to file in to classes. By this time I knew most Beatles songs, and many Lennon solo songs, by heart, their news as potent and valuable as any I'd learn in school, in church, in books, in the mirror, or around the family dinner table. After Lennon's death, as we all remember, his songs were everywhere, what my older brother's friend cynically (and accurately) dubbed the Dead Lennon Factor sending *Double Fantasy* up the *Billboard* charts and into the hearts of Grammy voters. The tinkling of the bell at the start of the now-ubiquitous "(Just Like) Starting Over"—the irony of the title obvious to me, though I didn't know that word yet—now tolled at the onset of something other than a pop song: the arrival of death and loss, personal and cultural, and the start of adulthood, or anyway my fumbling attempts at describing it all, at the edge of fifteen.

In the summer of 1988 I worked for Telesec, a temporary agency that staffed libraries in suburban Maryland, Virginia, and the District of Columbia. I'd be off to graduate school in Ohio in a couple of months, and, biding my time, I more or less enjoyed the menial work that the agency put me to. In June, I was sent to the

National Library of Medicine in Bethesda, Maryland, to report for a weeks-long job, the details of which now elude me—I remember sitting in the immense stacks of the library's bound periodicals, hauling a truck of medical journals behind me, filing and refiling, and taking endless statistics. It blurs. What helped pull me through the tediousness, often compounded by a hangover or the vagaries of a late night, was the Walkman I was allowed to carry, and my coworkers, who, because they were also temps, toiled with varying and amusing levels of seriousness. I stoked crushes on and flirted with a couple of my coworkers, who I'd never see again come September, and when I was in the mood for some company during lunch, I looked forward to hanging out.

Early that summer I occasionally worked with a tall, gangly kid named Lou, who with his gentle eyes and bushy 'fro looked like Art Garfunkel's little brother. He charmed me with his quiet humor, yet there was also something edgy about him that I couldn't place; he seemed cool in a way that I couldn't define. He was kind to me, which was nice, and we'd talk or goof around within the endless rows of multicolored medical journals. He was a guitarist in a local band, Braille Party, whose lone album, *Welcome to Maryland*, had come out a few years earlier. I remembered seeing the album, and cautiously spinning a track or two on my show at WMUC, the student-run radio station at the University of Maryland. But I resisted the record. In my mind Braille Party was a hardcore band, which I had little interest in, in part because the music and the local scene scared me a bit, in part because I was turned off by the earnest seriousness and full-throated fury of many of the bands. I went for grins in rock and roll, was shy in embracing anarchy and nihilistic void in those days, or anyway preferred to study it in a Goya painting or an Eliot poem in class rather than as noise in my chest cavity and sweaty fists and boots at my head. I'd never seen Braille Party live, as they weren't in the circle of bands I regularly saw during those heady years of endless weekends stuffed with rock and roll shows. None of this mattered. Lou and I didn't talk much during work. As I think of it now, we might've worked together only once or twice.

On a Friday morning in June, I arrived at the library, and in the stairwell encountered my manager, who was ashen-faced. She told me that the night before Lou had been killed in a car accident. A few hours later, I sat in that same stairwell and tried to name what I was feeling. I didn't know Lou well, and yet the proximity to a sudden, senseless death struck me with great force, and the mild conversations we'd shared in the stacks were instantly recast with a pall. I worked that day in a fog. A day or so later, in a downcast mood I couldn't name, I searched the *Washington Post* for an article about his death, found it, cut it out, and saved it. I learned that we were born a couple of months apart—he'd seemed older than me, it must've been because he'd played and toured in a band—and that he had grown up only five miles from me.

Within two months I was living in Athens, Ohio, far away geographically and culturally from the Eastern Seaboard punk scene, but I carried Lou's death with me when I moved. It had mattered to me that he was in a band. Beyond the unspeakable grief that his family and friends felt, which I couldn't share, I'd dimly feel the wake of his loss on stages when I went to shows, as if a kind of transparency had been lifted. Over the decades, I'd forget about him, as I wasn't nursing a wound where a close friendship had been, but sporadically the memory of his death rises to the surface, sometimes as an impulsive response to the news of like heartbreak, as when the band Exploding Hearts, whose album *Guitar Romantic* I love, lost control of their van in Oregon driving home after a gig in July 2003, killing three of its members (one member and the band's manager survived). Such loss is incalculable, to family, loved ones, and fans, and forever affects how you listen to the music—the notes and chords and melodies remain the same, but the weather they pass through has changed, and the atmosphere the songs live in forever altered, and so their sound and the stories they tell change also.

I wish I'd listened more generously to *Welcome to Maryland* the first time around. Friends tell me that they recall Braille Party as the artsy outsiders on the D.C./Maryland scene, and the album's knowing eclecticism and varied textures support that. The record came out on Fountain of Youth, a local post-punk label (its tagline was "Where sincere kids make real noise"; I only really loved one record on the label, Abbreviated Ceiling's fun, rocking self-titled EP). And it's a hard album to categorize, which is likely what turned me off at the time—I've spent decades half-ashamedly catching up to musicians and artists whom I was too bashful or cowardly to embrace when I was younger. *Welcome to Maryland*'s an ambitious and curious blend of hardcore thrash and dreamy psych pop, witty and ironic, and listening gives the impression of being inside of the head of a thoughtful, preoccupied kid tripping balls at an all-ages Minor Threat show.

The 4/4 hardcore stuff—minute-long blasts of superfast anti-government, antiestablishment, anticomplacency roar—dates the album a bit, but that might be my own biases, the noise conjuring the mosh pits and straight-edge crowd I wasn't a part of. More transcendent, to my ears, is the pop stuff, "Evil" in particular, a lovely, nervy song with blissy melodies that belie the cynicism and meanness of the lyrics. There's a bit of funk on the album, one reggae song, some aggressive Hüsker Dü–styled power pop, an atmospheric instrumental, jagged time signatures popping up in surprising places keeping everything and everyone alert. Throughout, Lou Gigger's supremely confident guitar playing is nothing short of superb: he moves from distorted, overdriven power chords to brittle, intense thrashing to ethereal, Andy Summers–like washes and spiky yet melodic leads, often in witty counterpoint to bassist Matt Riedl's winsome vocals. Gigger's playing does what the best guitar playing in a trio does, adds characterful touches that move noise and textures from the background to the foreground and back again, fluidly.

Welcome to Maryland ought to be considered a standard-bearer of highly original, evocative, independent art from a particularly fertile era in D.C./Maryland musicmaking history; instead, it rates as a footnote at best, a melancholy *whatmighthavebeen* at worst. I find it impossible to listen to the record nearly forty years later and not conjure stray images I have of Lou in the library, only now he holds a guitar, playing songs that add dimension and tenderness to the fading images. My memories of him mean little compared with the future he never had.

I wrote my first poem in December 1980. I titled it "The Year," and it was an earnest response to the deaths of John Lennon and Francis Meuller. I think about that poem, or my impulse to write the poem, to write anything. The sorrow that I felt during that month pulled me in two directions, one toward the intimacies of family love and loss, an at-times claustrophobic and overheated place where I could barely speak the language, or lacked the maturity and bravery to attempt to learn it; the other toward pop culture, celebrity, the kind of baffling defeat we feel when a stranger we would never meet, who's given us deeper pleasures than our closest friends and family, cruelly vanishes.

I attempted to honor both Lennon and my grandmother in the poem, and, if the result was laughingly Early Bonomo, a parched weed next to Stevie Nicks's verdant pop forest, the impulse to express myself was as genuine as anything I'd felt to that point in my life. I've come very late to Braille Party and their smart, witty, evocative *Welcome to Maryland*. The ghost of Lou Gigger has led me here. Later today I'll take a walk with my cat in the woods, under the songs of the birds, and listen to the album again, and honor a young man I never really knew yet whose loss lingers in me as a song that never quite fades out.

Acknowledgments

These essays, in earlier versions, first appeared at the following places:

"Touch Me, Baby," "Home," "Is It Me? . . . ," "Much Too Real to Ever Disappear," "You Don't Own Me," "On *Exhibitionism*," "A Groovy Way to Grab a Musical Bag That Turns On the Sounds of Today," "Dispatches from the Past Present, or Dick Clark's Face," "A Genius Moment, or an Accident," "Birds Sing to Breathe," "Margo Price Macro Doses," "All These Things Engulfing Me," and "Brief Histories" in *The Normal School*

"'I'll Get Her!'" (as "Van Halen's 'Panama'") at *March Shredness*

"Thirteen Ways of Thinking about the Cramps" (as "The Cramps' 'Human Fly'") at *March Vladness*

"Nowhere" (as "Green Day's 'Brain Stew/Jaded'") at *March Plaidness*

"It'll All Be Over Soon" (as "The Stooges' 'Louie Louie'") at *March Faxness*

"Amplified," "Let's Have a Big Fuckin Party" (as "Big Fuckin Party"), and "No Heroes" appeared, in earlier versions, at *No Such Thing as Was*

Thanks to Nicole Walker, Jon Davies, Elizabeth Adams, Bethany Snead, Ivo Fravashi, and everyone at University of Georgia Press. Thanks also to Steven Church, Sophie Beck, Petra Meyer-Frazier, Jer Xiong, Sydney Hinton, William Freeney, Jefferson Beavers, Cristina Sandoval, Mialise Carney, James Morrison, and the whole gang at *The Normal School*, and to Ander Monson, Megan Campbell, Will Stockton, D. Gilson, and every behind-the-scenes editor whose name I never learned but whose hard work made these essays better.

Thanks to Joseph Perry, Dan Epstein, and Steve Coleman for early hands-on help. Cheers to Dan Libman for coming up with the title of this book at the bar one night and for letting me keep it!

Above all, thanks and love to Amy Newman, who was with me through lots of loud rock and roll, all-day ear worms, and each dark night of my soul as I wrote these essays. Her eyes and ears shaped the writing in countless ways.

The book's epigraph is by Lester Bangs.

ALSO BY JOE BONOMO

No Place I Would Rather Be: Roger Angell and a Life in Baseball Writing

Field Recordings from the Inside, essays

This Must Be Where My Obsession with Infinity Began, essays

Conversations with Greil Marcus (editor)

AC/DC's Highway to Hell (33⅓ Series)

Jerry Lee Lewis: Lost and Found

Installations

Sweat: The Story of The Fleshtones, America's Garage Band

CRUX, THE GEORGIA SERIES IN LITERARY NONFICTION

Debra Monroe, *My Unsentimental Education*
Sonja Livingston, *Ladies Night at the Dreamland*
Jericho Parms, *Lost Wax: Essays*
Priscilla Long, *Fire and Stone: Where Do We Come From? What Are We? Where Are We Going?*
Sarah Gorham, *Alpine Apprentice*
Tracy Daugherty, *Let Us Build Us a City*
Brian Doyle, *Hoop: A Basketball Life in Ninety-Five Essays*
Michael Martone, *Brooding: Arias, Choruses, Lullabies, Follies, Dirges, and a Duet*
Andrew Menard, *Learning from Thoreau*
Dustin Parsons, *Exploded View: Essays on Fatherhood, with Diagrams*
Clinton Crockett Peters, *Pandora's Garden: Kudzu, Cockroaches, and Other Misfits of Ecology*
André Joseph Gallant, *A High Low Tide: The Revival of a Southern Oyster*
Justin Gardiner, *Beneath the Shadow: Legacy and Longing in the Antarctic*
Emily Arnason Casey, *Made Holy: Essays*
Sejal Shah, *This Is One Way to Dance: Essays*
Lee Gutkind, *My Last Eight Thousand Days: An American Male in His Seventies*
Cecile Pineda, *Entry without Inspection: A Writer's Life in El Norte*
Anjali Enjeti, *Southbound: Essays on Identity, Inheritance, and Social Change*
Clinton Crockett Peters, *Mountain Madness: Found and Lost in the Peaks of America and Japan*
Steve Majors, *High Yella: A Modern Family Memoir*
Julia Ridley Smith, *The Sum of Trifles*

Siân Griffiths, *The Sum of Her Parts: Essays*
Ned Stuckey-French, *One by One, the Stars: Essays*
John Griswold, *The Age of Clear Profit: Collected Essays on Home and the Narrow Road*
Debra Monroe, *It Takes a Worried Woman: Essays*
Joseph Geha, *Kitchen Arabic: How My Family Came to America and the Recipes We Brought with Us*
Lawrence Lenhart, *Backvalley Ferrets: A Rewilding of the Colorado Plateau*
Sarah Beth Childers, *Prodigals: A Sister's Memoir of Appalachia*
Jodi Varon, *Your Eyes Will Be My Window: Essays*
Sandra Gail Lambert, *My Withered Legs and Other Essays*
Brooke Champagne, *Nola Face: Memoirs of a Truth-Telling Latina in the Big Easy*
Maddie Norris, *The Wet Wound: An Elegy in Essays*
Cris Mazza, *The Decade of Letting Things Go: A Postmenopause Memoir*
Lydia Paar, *The Exit Is the Entrance: Essays on Escape*
Joe Bonomo, *Play This Book Loud: Noisy Essays*